TIJERINA AND THE COURTHOUSE RAID

TIJERINA
AND THE
COURTHOUSE RAID

Peter Nabokov

Albuquerque
University of New Mexico Press

The opinions expressed by the author do not necessarily reflect the views of the University of New Mexico or its Press.

For my fellow writers and editors
on the Santa Fe *New Mexican* newspaper,
May 1967 to April 1968

CONTENTS

CONTENTS

MAP

ILLUSTRATIONS

CHRONOLOGY
OF
MAJOR EVENTS

1966

July 2-4   Alianza protest march from Albuquerque to Santa Fe

July 11   Audience with Governor Jack M. Campbell to discuss Alianza's land claims

October 15   Occupation of Echo Amphitheater in attempt to "revive" land-grant community of San Joaquin

October 22   "Trial" of two forest rangers at Echo Amphitheater

1967

April 21   Meeting between Governor David F. Cargo and Tijerina

Early May   Arson and vandalism in northern New Mexico

May 14   Alianza rally in Tierra Amarilla to discuss recovery of three land grants

May 19	Federal court order demanding list of Alianza members
May 24	Tijerina's "resignation" and "disbanding" of Alianza
June 3	"Showdown day" at Coyote
June 5	Raid on the courthouse at Tierra Amarilla
June 6	The hunt for Alianza leaders "Cattle pen" incident at Canjilon
June 15	Hearing for raid defendants: Jailer Eulogio Salazar fingers Tijerina
July 4	Surrender of Baltazar Martinez
August 3	Surrender of Cristobal Tijerina
October 21-22	Alianza's annual convention in Albuquerque
November 6-11	Echo Amphitheater trial at Las Cruces and Tijerina's conviction
December	Release of state attorney general's investigation of Alianza

1968

January 2	Slaying of Eulogio Salazar
January 29- February 8	Preliminary hearing for raid defendants in Santa Fe
May 31-June 24	Poor People's Campaign in Washington, D.C.
November 12	Start of first trial for courthouse raid, in Albuquerque
December 13	Tijerina's acquittal on three charges stemming from raid

PRINCIPAL DRAMATIS PERSONAE

NEW MEXICO OFFICIALS

David F. Cargo, governor
E. Lee Francis, lieutenant governor
Joseph Black, state police chief
Pete Jaramillo, Naranjo's deputy
John P. Jolly, adjutant general, New Mexico National Guard
Benny Naranjo, Rio Arriba County sheriff
Lawrence Prentice, governor's aide
Daniel Rivera, Naranjo's undersheriff
Nick Saiz, state policeman wounded at Tierra Amarilla
Eulogio Salazar, jailer at Tierra Amarilla
Alfonso Sanchez, district attorney
Boston E. Witt, attorney general

ALIANZA LEADERS AND MEMBERS

Reies Lopez Tijerina, founder and president
Santiago Anaya, vice-president

PRINCIPAL DRAMATIS PERSONAE

Eduardo Chavez, secretary-treasurer

Baltazar Apodaca, First World War veteran, abductor of Larry Calloway

Tobias Leyba, host at Canjilon "picnic" after the raid

Jose Madril, Korean War veteran, alleged participant in the raid

Baltazar Martinez, abductor of Deputy Sheriff Jaramillo

Felix Martinez, young bondsman, resident of Tierra Amarilla

Jerry Noll, "King of the Indies"

Tijerina's brothers: Anselmo, Cristobal, Margarito, Ramon

Mary Escobar Tijerina, Reies's first wife

Patsy Tijerina, Reies's second wife

Reies H. Tijerina Jr., Reies's oldest son

Rosa Tijerina, Reies's oldest daughter

Juan Valdez, Canjilon resident, alleged participant in the raid

OTHERS

Joseph M. Montoya, U.S. Senator from New Mexico

Thomas Morris, U.S. Representative from New Mexico

Doyle Akers, Espanola correspondent for the *New Mexican*

Joseph Angel, district judge

Robert Aragon ⎫
Hector Burgos ⎭ consulting team from California

Joe Benitez, field representative for VISTA program

Larry Calloway, UPI reporter

Don Devereux, poverty program consultant active in negotiations

Robert Garcia, state OEO director

Rudolph "Corky" Gonzales, Denver militant

Clark Knowlton, Texas professor of sociology

Paul Larrazolo, district judge

Alex Mercure, director of HELP program

Bill Mundy, rancher

Emilio Naranjo, U.S. marshal in Albuquerque (father of Benny Naranjo)

John Quinn, U.S. attorney in Albuquerque

James M. Scarborough, district judge

TIJERINA AND THE COURTHOUSE RAID

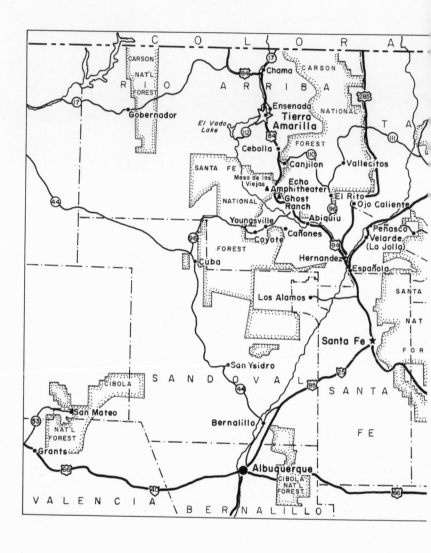

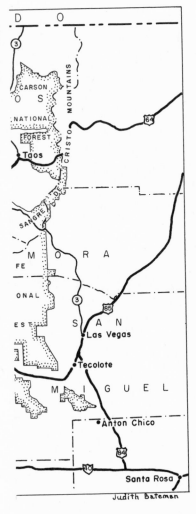

North Central New Mexico

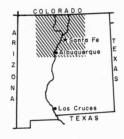

National Forest Boundaries

U. S. Highway

Interstate Highway

State Highway

▲ Point of Interest

0 5 10   20   30   40

Scale in miles

Judith Bateman

INTRODUCTION

This is a chronicle of a violent afternoon in northern New Mexico and of the man whose dramatic personality made that afternoon memorable.

It is no definitive reconstruction. It is a recording of events immediately prior to, during, and stemming from a textbook peasant community insurrection, a "rising against a civil authority" under the influence of an archetypal primitive rebel. My narrative is an attempt to set straight the sequence of actions which reached their peak on June 5, 1967, in the village of Tierra Amarilla.

But the story is a contemporary fragment of a much older epic. Deepest into America's history runs the discovery and settling of the terrain itself, the drainage basin of the Rio Grande. That first gunshot in Tierra Amarilla two years ago had its origin in the last decade of the sixteenth century when Don Juan de Oñate led settlers into the wilderness of northern New Mexico.

In 1821 Mexican jurisdiction over the New Mexico Territory briefly followed Spanish "ownership"—a controversial concept throughout these pages. Then in 1848 a foreign culture and alien judicial mentality began to enter northern New Mexico. The United States won its two-year war with Mexico and signed the Treaty of Guadalupe Hidalgo. The American presence was first an occupational force rather than a homesteading invasion. This changed in the 1880's, however, as the coming of the railroads opened up the lush valley range lands. Simultaneously the price of beef, mutton, and wool skyrocketed. As the neglected land became economically attractive, the inevitable occurred.

The villagers' loss of land was often imperceptible and usually "legally" justifiable. Today their ancestral land-grant holdings are in the hands of the federal government or form parts of extensive cattle ranches. But the tier of central northern counties of the state still exist culturally on the margin of today's American pace. Their remnant hamlets still exhibit the manifestations of their unique racial mixture—the tribal native and the colonizing Latin.

This saga of centuries is told in appropriately sweeping fashion in Paul Horgan's Pulitzer Prize winning *Great River*. But it remains an essential background for the acts related here. It will occasionally intrude as the past demands to be reevaluated.

A more direct cause of the Tierra Amarilla insurrection is traceable to another corner of the southwest. Reies Lopez Tijerina, son of a timid sharecropper, was born in 1926 amid the poverty and discrimination visited upon Texas's Mexican-Americans. He began a character growth unlike that of his New Mexican brothers—an existence which was to take him out of the traditional Catholic religious context, a life minus sedentary pastoral economy, extended and landed community responsibilities, and the protective insularity of wilderness. Tijerina approached manhood within that national crisis which threw an entire generation onto the roads and the rails of the 1930's. Along with most of his Texas-born kinsmen, he experienced the added weight of everyday racial prejudice. That goad assured the eventual focus of his innate talents—his vision of cultural renewal for his people in the old land-grant communities of mountainous northern New Mexico.

His road there was sinuous. His arrival brought to a climax a century of smoldering conflict. His presence was instrumental in creating the Tierra Amarilla incident.

As a journalist I observed the Tijerina story from the Coyote crackdown by police officials to the Tijerina trial a year and a half later. But my first awareness of the land-grant campaign began earlier.

I had finished a southwestern vacation and was being driven from Santa Fe to Albuquerque for a flight to New York. It was a hot, dry, glaring morning on July 2, 1966. I noticed a line of people heading in the other direction along the scorching shoulder of the highway. Despite the heat they walked with a determined gaiety, staring defiantly at gawking motorists.

"That's the land-grant people," the driver explained. "Look at those kids. They're going to see the governor." Then she betrayed the magnetism of the anachronistic, the attraction of people who force reality to fit their dreams. "They want the land back, that country given to their great-grandfathers years ago. Look at them, there's something, I don't know, moving. . . ."

Before the straggling column an elderly man with shoulder-length tresses rode a plodding burro and carried a large banner. Behind him strode a fellow of medium height, his face shadowed by a black cowboy hat. There was nothing unusual about him.

In the early months of 1968 I was speaking on the telephone with the man in the black hat. By then I was well acquainted with him and the organization he had launched five years earlier, the "Alianza." Still basking in the reputation of the courthouse raid, Reies Tijerina had just returned—via a California stopover with Labor Organizer Cesar Chavez—from a meeting with Dr. Martin Luther King Jr. at the Paschals Motor Inn in Atlanta, Georgia. They had discussed a massive Washington demonstration to pressure government recognition of "poor people's" human rights. Tijerina was in characteristic form as he described the encounter.

"It was terrific, fantastic, everybody was drugged with happiness. We all knew we were experiencing the most historical event."

During their all-day conferring Tijerina had exchanged backgrounds and dreams with spokesmen from white Appalachia and American Indian reservations, fellow Spanish-American militants, and a wide range of black militants. The plan was for a

Washington march between April 22 and 27. Tijerina proudly disclosed that King had agreed to merge the Alianza's land claims with the demonstration's demands that the blacks finally get their long-promised "forty acres and a mule." Tijerina had clearly been affected by the heady potential of pooled protest. Over the phone he talked as if to a packed auditorium:

"Everyone felt like I feel," he said, "that this is the testimony, that they were witnessing one of the greatest events and the greatest foundation for interracial pursuit of justice."

Between the Alianza's march to Santa Fe and the Poor People's March in Washington, Reies Tijerina and his faithful created an historical event in southwestern life. In the nearly two-year interval between the Alianza's first tactic of public pressure and its participation in the first coalition of the nation's deprived minorities, dramatic events happened to make that progression possible. The most far-reaching of these was the armed assault on a courthouse in the seat of Rio Arriba County.

A history is a relative severance of time. This narrative is such a cut-out chunk, isolated because the principal actions which boosted the Alianza into prominence took place within the span between march and march.

As the story began unfolding with new urgency in the months just before the raid, it was partly the scanty or erroneous information of the moment that accelerated the breakdown in communication between official and militant camps. Negotiation was prevented by suspicion on the part of both lawmen and Alianzans. That process of polarization is what I have tried to describe, as it developed, in the first six chapters of the book.

The second part of the book treats the raid and the following tension-loaded days until Tijerina's capture. Here again I have attempted no definitive repiecing from the miles of often contradictory courtroom testimony. I have concentrated upon the reports of witnesses shortly after they experienced the drama. Later recollection, coerced by reflection, lacked the spark and perhaps the veracity of those impressions from the heat of involvement.

INTRODUCTION

In the final six chapters I have tried to trace the raid's immediate ramifications, the new arena into which it plunged the Alianza, the surfacing reactions of congressmen, police, and social reformers. Also here I have taken the opportunity to incorporate the new data which came forth at this time concerning Tijerina's personal history and the infant years of his New Mexican movement. The book ends with an epilogue on the five-week trial of Tijerina for charges resulting from the raid, surely as dramatic a closing as any storyteller would wish.

Of course the story continues today. Its situations, tensions, and effects still have to unravel themselves or become tied into more complex knots. This "instant history" has been pulled together from the often intimate perspective afforded an on-the-scene reporter and abetted by after-the-fact research. It is a tale of dreams and frustrations colliding with realities and misunderstandings, of the past looming to plague the present, threaten the future, and imperil fortunes. It may also be an account of mistakes which need not be repeated, or which remain to be repaired. It touches the Old World Spanish colonial years of New Mexico, the rough, land-lusting frontier territorial era, and the ongoing political and multiracial growth of the state.

As a fledgling general assignment reporter for the Santa Fe *New Mexican* newspaper I enjoyed many strokes of luck and excellent contacts that gave me a ringside seat throughout this story. On a few occasions I was propelled into the ring. When I left the *New Mexican* eleven months later I kept an eye on the ensuing developments in the hope of fulfilling an obligation to what I had witnessed. I wanted to bring continuity to the confusing succession of preliminary acts and postures, recapture the week when the Alianza and the United States were antagonists, and pursue the event's immediate results.

I was an unprofessional note-taker. But I did hoard every scribbled-over envelope, shred of copy off the wire service machines, and xeroxed official documents in a bin, which I later collated into workable files. From that lode, memories, and subsequent interviewing I have written this narrative. I doubt if it contains any revelations of spectacular nature. Unfortunately limited funds and the modest scope of the project prevented intensive probing into the Salazar murder, the multitude of contradictions in courtroom testimony concerning what actually occurred during the hours the courthouse was invaded and occupied, and other unanswered questions. Nor have I made a thorough delving into the state's archives and private sources to ascertain the legitimacy of the Alianza's claims and the detailed record of a century of land transferal. That, I fervently hope, will be the job of a state or federal commission.

Racial terminology is always a touchy reflection of the times, and few decades have been more conscious of this than ours. A vice-presidential candidate endangers his partner's shot at the White House because of incautious remarks on an airplane. From "Spanish-speaking peoples" to *chicano*—an affectionate derivative of *Mexicano*—the titles are many for southwesterners of mixed Spanish and native American ancestry. With "blacks" now an acceptable term for peoples classified as Negroes, one is tempted to employ Tijerina's name for his people: "Indo-Hispano." But to date it remains only his, so I have reluctantly stayed with the bland "Spanish-American" since most of northern New Mexico's Spanish-speaking are not truly "Mexican-Americans." By reverse token, "Anglo" is customarily used in the southwestern United States for those of Western European ancestry. I have employed it when necessary to avoid the color stress of "white" or the inaccuracy of "Anglo-American."

I feel deep gratitude to Don Devereux, without whose immediate trust and comradely conniving I could never have seen so much so intimately. Individuals from both camps in the conflict almost always made themselves available. I understood the exceptions, and I thank the rest.

Steve Bunker's hurried but perceptive survey of the northern militants and local feeling just after the raid was most helpful. I am thankful for the notes, friendship, or guidance of Carrol W. Cagle, Richard Gardner, Diana Gould, Larry Hamm, Nigel Hey,

INTRODUCTION

Michael Jenkinson, Bill Olson, and Facundo Valdez. Dr. Clark Knowlton led me to sociohistorical writings on northern New Mexico, crucial for a comprehension of what was taking place before one's eyes. Once again Mr. and Mrs. Laidlaw Williams of Carmel, California, sheltered and fed a writer during his fight through a first draft. St. John's College in Santa Fe kindly provided a temporary office. Finally, I hope some of the integrity of my *New Mexican* editor, Bill Feather, has rubbed off onto these pages.

In a piece for the *New Mexico Quarterly*, winter 1968, I speculated on Tijerina's unconscious drives and the raid's root factors. Later I updated these "Reflections on the Alianza" in a talk at Colorado College in Colorado Springs. I have tried to prevent that kind of analytical approach from infecting this text. Here is a record of attitudes, decisions, and actions for others now to ponder.

Pacific Grove, California   Peter Nabokov

1

WARNING
SIGNALS

For most Americans the drowsy little village of Tierra Amarilla in northern New Mexico was first placed on the map June 6, 1967. On the second morning of the Arab-Israeli six-day war, newspaper readers all over the United States turned from the Sinai struggle to a national item that made them hastily recheck the dateline to be sure they were still in the twentieth century.

The previous afternoon some twenty Spanish-Americans bearing pistols and rifles had descended upon a dilapidated county courthouse in Rio Arriba County in northern New Mexico just south of the Colorado border. After two hours of shooting and threatening, the band had fled into the mountains. In setting, characters, and action the item was straight out of the gun-law Old West—a familiar television episode, but wildly incongruous in modern times.

The "shootout" ended with one policeman on the edge of death, state police cars shot apart, a UPI reporter and a sheriff's deputy taken hostage in a getaway caravan, and a town paralyzed with fright. Explanations in the media also read like a cinema script. The attack was apparently tied up with the protest efforts of a militant rural Spanish-American organization in the southwest. Known

13

as the Alianza, this group had for four years been demanding the return of millions of acres of federal and privately owned land. They insisted it was their legal inheritance through old Spanish and Mexican land grants given to their ancestors.

Leading the group was an equally fictional-sounding individual, a Spanish-American ex-evangelist named Reies Lopez Tijerina. One of ten children born to an impoverished Texas sharecropper, Tijerina possessed all the qualities for charismatic leadership of backwoods folk. He was a man of immense nervous energy and raw acumen. His youthful experiences had given him an underdog's knowledge of "Anglo" prejudice. His later years as a penniless cross-country evangelist had sharpened his natural rhetorical gifts. By the time he had arrived in New Mexico in the late 1950's he had the checkered past of a fugitive from the law and a Bible Belt fundamentalist turned political insurgent.

It was unclear whether the forty-year-old Tijerina had personally commanded the Tierra Amarilla raiding party. First accounts identified him at the scene, however. Immediately he and a small band of followers became targets of the largest manhunt in New Mexico history. National Guard convoys, state police from all northern counties, local sheriffs and unofficial posses, Jicarilla Apache police and cattle inspectors, all joined the search. Equipped with two ammunitionless tanks, clattering helicopters, droning spotter planes, a hospital van, and patrolling jeeps, these forces combed every hamlet, gully, and pasture for the insurrectionists who had staged the "bold daylight raid."

The events unfolded with such dramatic predictability that Americans outside the five southwestern states were suspicious of the basic seriousness of the story. But New Mexicans, with a long history of racial friction, did not need to be told that the raid had brought to a head a century of unresolved cultural conflicts. In one afternoon, the social fabric of the state had been irrevocably altered.

Light was shed on the motives of the raid during the ensuing weeks. It became clear that the desperate move had been not so much a long-planned maneuver as a frustrated, flailing-out reaction to the deafness of state and federal officialdom towards rural Spanish-American grievances. The immediate cause, however, was the felt persecution of the Alianza by a local district attorney, Alfonso Sanchez. Also, in the dust-settling days after the shootout everyone began to remember that Tijerina had been circulating in New Mexico for a number of years already.

Reies Tijerina has a mobile face and sturdy physique which jump into motion whenever his torrential speech needs illustration. His wide mouth stretches into his cheeks as if actually giving birth to the rushing words. When mentally translating his convoluted rhetoric for the English listener he reveals irritation with the imprecise syllables which have not done his Spanish logic justice. His teeth bare as he tries to enunciate. His eyes half-shut when his tongue knots over a word. He will sometimes interject with emphasis a Spanish word which simply has no English equivalent.

Above Tijerina's large, angular nose his dark eyebrows charge into a point when he is caught in the middle of animated explanation. Beneath them his hazel green eyes literally flash fire. Then he looks positively ferocious, although he is an uncommonly good-humored revolutionary. His hands fly out, clap with loud retort, clasp and crack knuckles, or are nervously imprisoned beneath his thighs as he tries to keep his seat and listen. Most people who have come to know Tijerina over a period note something saddening and fatalistic about the man.

This was the bundle of nerves and dreams which entered the adobe shacks of northern New Mexico in the late 1950's, preaching of land grants and the final attainment of *la justicia*. This was the catalyst who would fuse the *bandido* image of Joaquin Murieta and Vicente Silva, the violent nightrider tradition of the Mano Negra (Black Hand) and the Gorras Blancas (White Hats), with his own vision of the cultural renewal of the historic Spanish-American world.

In the early 1960's Tijerina's following seemed to be only the

15

latest in a string of land-grant-heir clubs. They had consolidated around memories of ancestral acreage and the common experience of economic and cultural alienation. Some of them controlled remnants of old grants, but they had never been effective politically. In urban pockets of the state Tijerina himself was dismissed, often sympathetically, as a quixotic anachronism with little knowledge of New Mexico's special history and problems. There was truth to this. But Tijerina was intuitively aware that in the hearts of rural villagers property rights and civil rights were wedded in a fundamental, mystical union. In October 1963 he incorporated the Alianza Federal de Mercedes (Federal Alliance of Land Grants), thereafter called simply the Alianza. Then people watched with greater attention.

Tijerina had finally been able to organize a grass-roots protest group in the north of the state because he had not been reared within the traditional political structure which hamstrings progressive young villagers. He had never belonged to the social system that has made the peasant populations of the area fodder for local *patrones* and politicos. Through his utopian message he was able to transform the backwardness of the northern New Mexico villagers into an organizational asset. He spoke of a golden era before the U.S. Forest Service "occupied" *their* land, he harped on blood ties of Spanish language and Spanish-American folkways. He thrilled their hearts with his religio-political pictures of *their* Promised Land, the revived and unified free city states of the southwest.

Tijerina's flamboyant harangues about the notoriously questionable legal maneuverings of the state's nineteenth-century land barons and territorial governors caused mild embarrassment. But the Alianza's sweeping claim that its members were the heirs to millions of acres once granted to southwestern colonizers by local representatives of the Spanish crown and the Mexican Government were generally regarded as legally groundless and potentially dangerous. The common opinion admitted there had been shady justice in the long-ago struggle for northern New Mexico's rich high-country forests and pastures. But most people felt that the only constructive hope for the rural villagers of Spanish-speaking ancestry lay in more roads, jobs, and education. Nostalgic fantasies dreamed up by a self-styled messiah were no answer.

During the Fourth of July weekend in 1966, however, the state learned of the contagious attraction of Tijerina's vision. By this time fervent organizing had built latent rural resentment into a full-fledged *causa*. A grueling hot two-day, sixty-two-mile protest march from Albuquerque, the Alianza's base, to Santa Fe, the state capital, signaled the organization's entry into the by then familiar arena of nonviolent protest. The march was climaxed by a respectful conference between Tijerina and the governor at the time, Jack Campbell. The governor went so far as to agree to forward the Alianza's argument to the White House. A Denver newspaper commented prophetically on this meeting:

"It is reopening a fascinating and little known chapter of western history. And it will be interesting to see what comes of it."

The first event that came of it took place three months later. Members of the Alianza, 350 strong, took armed possession of a national campground known as Echo Amphitheater. A mammoth natural hollow in pastel-toned sandstone cliffs, the amphitheater with its picnic tables and hiking trails can be seen from Highway 84 in Rio Arriba County. Living in tents, Tijerina's followers proclaimed their revival of the nineteenth-century land-grant community of San Joaquin del Rio de Chama.

San Joaquin had been a Spanish grant, actually awarded by an acting governor of Mexico in 1806 to a group of settlers led by Francisco Salazar. About 1,400 acres, it now lies mostly within the confines of the Kit Carson National Forest. Echo Amphitheater borders the old grant's perimeter, and during their camp-in Tijerina's followers elected a governing body headed by a "mayor" in beaten sheepherder's hat, a direct descendant of the original Salazar. "Marshals" were given badges and assigned to patrol the campground with loaded rifles. The standoff ended as police and sheriffs disbanded the Alianzans.

TIJERINA and the COURTHOUSE RAID

Memories of this episode and its threatening new flavor were kept alive through the winter of 1966-67 by criminal charges resulting from it and by further challenges. It was difficult to determine the strength of the Alianza's membership accurately. In January 1966 *Newsweek* had estimated it at 3,000 families, or about 14,000 individuals. Tijerina boasted from 30,000 to 50,000 members. The local district attorney suggested 5,000. But hardcore support was probably about half this. A welfare official gave perhaps the most accurate reading of the Alianza's strength:

"While about 90 per cent of those northern people think that the land was really stolen from them, only about 20 per cent think Reies can get it back."

During the cold winter months Tijerina vaguely threatened other stands in Albuquerque and La Joya, communities which also lay within historical land-grant borders. When the snow melted in the Sangre de Cristo Mountains of northern New Mexico that spring, however, more pressing problems aggravated the unresolved antagonisms over land use and legal concepts. First, serious friction between the U.S. Forest Service and the subsistence ranchers and farmers had grown critical. Second, state officials had become extremely edgy about the Alianza's escalated defiance. In the spring of 1967 these tensions gave new urgency to a situation that had been only bothersome through the winter.

A few months remained before Tierra Amarilla exploded on a cloudy afternoon. But the first indication of the unsettled mood came in April 1967 when the Alianza staged demonstrations in Albuquerque and Santa Fe. In the scatter-gun rhetoric to which New Mexicans had grown accustomed, Tijerina proclaimed "a march with our bodies to issue to the public and the federal government and the world the last human legal notice exposing the truth."

About 500 men, women, and children, some on horseback, others swinging banners reading "USA is Trespassing in New Mexico," herded down Albuquerque's streets after Tijerina. The slogan of the July 1966 march—"We want justice, not welfare powdered milk"—was heard again. Red and blue flags were carried by some. Tijerina explained, "The red was a warning to the government and the blue to symbolize our legal position and our human rights."

Speaking from a Mexican-style bandstand in the center of Albuquerque's historical Old Town Plaza, Tijerina awakened memories.

"The government is being warned and advised," he shook his finger for emphasis, "if anybody is found trespassing on these land grants they will be arrested and punished."

Some of his listeners had tried this tactic three years before. As members of the Abiquiu Corporation, a forerunner of the Alianza, they had moved to regain the Tierra Amarilla land grant by posting the area.

The "TA" grant was one of the southwest's 1,715 land grants awarded during Mexican jurisdiction over the area. In 1832 its 594,500 acres were given to one Jose Manuel Martinez, eight male children and followers, "for cultivation and pasturage." Afterward its ownership became a matter of bitter controversy. In 1964 the Abiquiu Corporation continued the long agitation by assigning armed border guards and sending homemade eviction notices to current Anglo landowners. Albuquerque Judge Paul Tackett ordered the organization immediately dissolved and its inflammatory activities halted.

Two other points stood out in Tijerina's Albuquerque exhortation. One quickly became a hot issue, the other revealed the widening scope of the Alianza's crusade. First Tijerina charged that "the land grants include the national forests in New Mexico and those lands being illegally occupied by the Bureau of Land Management." Then he said, "The people generally feel that our sons are being sent to Vietnam illegally, because many of these land grants are free city states and are independent."

Following their morning turn-out in Albuquerque, about 200 of the demonstrators entered cars for an afternoon rally around the circular arcade of the new state house in Santa Fe. A chattering group of all ages, they exuded the spirit of a Sunday afternoon

19

picnic. Their appearance prompted the newly elected young governor, David F. Cargo, to arrange a meeting with Tijerina the following Friday.

"He wanted to know if I had any objections to him taking over New Mexico," explained the unruffled governor. "I told him to come up and talk about it."

The surprising victory of Republican dark horse David Cargo the previous fall had been largely attributed to rural Spanish-American support. Aided by an attractive, dark-haired, Spanish-American wife, the thirty-seven-year-old lawyer had courted what is delicately known as the "ethnic vote." Cargo's forays over dirt roads into the isolated strongholds of the Democratic machine in the northern counties undercut the traditional political status quo.

In line with this back-country emphasis, Cargo also addressed the Alianza's "fourth national convention" late in 1966. Its village participants were the most alienated of the northern voter bloc. The earnest, blond young candidate vowed willingness to hear all complaints. His appearance was regarded as a gamble by some analysts and as decidedly ill-advised by others. Many politicians, noted Spanish-Americans among them, were violently opposed to the Alianza. "Communist" accusations had been made against Tijerina for years.

Alfonso Sanchez was the thirty-nine-year-old district attorney whose jurisdiction —Santa Fe, Rio Arriba, and Los Alamos counties—included the Alianza's battleground. He typified the Spanish-American official whose patriotic sensibilities and professional code were deeply offended by a man of Tijerina's messianic obsession and outlandish strategies. Like Tijerina, Sanchez was one of ten children. He had been born in a four-room adobe home on the outskirts of Albuquerque, where his father was a machinist. After his years at Albuquerque High School he passed two stretches in the U.S. Army. In 1962 he was appointed First Judicial District Attorney. In the spring months of 1967 he was principally responsible for the nature of police response to the Alianza's new activities.

Cargo's campaign strategy had paid off. Some observers suggested, however, that he probably wished he had given the Alianza a wider berth. Now he had been cornered into scheduling a meeting with the Alianza contingent. This session promised to be less conciliatory than his predecessor's encounter with Tijerina the previous year.

When Cargo finally greeted his northern visitors on April 21, 1967, about 100 Alianza members had been milling about the capitol corridors for five hours. Although their conference had been scheduled for the afternoon, the protesting men, women, and children had been trickling into Santa Fe since the working day began. The long wait without lunch had not eased their tempers.

Overflowing from the small executive dining room where the meeting was held, Tijerina's crowd spilled into the hallways of the state capitol's fourth floor. Cargo was guarded by three stony-faced armed policemen; they knew that a few Alianzans bore concealed weapons.

"These people won't hurt anyone," Cargo reassured a guard.

In suit and tie, Tijerina stood at one end of a conference table, talking and whirling his expressive arms. As the governor calmly took notes, Tijerina described a futile visit he had made a few months before to the U.S. State Department in Washington. He had been solemnly informed that the federal government had no jurisdiction here.

Then Cargo stood up.

"I can't adjudicate this thing," he said. "I can only judge whether your petition has been properly handled."

Some press reports described the meeting as "orderly" and its outcome as "constructive." Other observers said the atmosphere had been "extremely tense." Attempting to soothe his agitated visitors, the governor tried to encourage the folksy rapport which had earned him rural trust during his campaigning. He recalled

21

his vow to listen to all problems. A crashing sound came from the back of the crowded room.

"We want action!" yelled a young man.

"Put that guy on a committee," quipped the governor.

The outburst had come from twenty-two-year-old Baltazar Martinez, the last man to be disarmed during the Echo Amphitheater incident.

The hour-long meeting ended with Cargo requesting Alianza documents and correspondence to forward to Washington. He mentioned taking them personally to the State Department during a projected June visit.

"I will be happy to examine the records," he told his audience, "and to assist you in any way I can. . . . I don't think you can ask me to do any more." He warned the Alianzans to avoid violence, and invited them to an "open house" at the governor's mansion the following week.

"You better take me up on it," he laughed. "The next administration may go high society on you!"

Finally Cargo conferred behind closed doors with seven selected Alianza leaders. As the crowd trailed down the stairs of the capitol their mood was "bitter, hostile, frustrated, and impatient of more talking." Vague threats to "burn and raise hell" were muttered.

Tijerina was ambivalent in evaluating the session. "This is the first time we've been given satisfactory attention," he said. But in the same breath he referred to the San Joaquin land grant: "There are already two hundred people up there and only three rangers. We could just take over and arrest them."

Threats of "house-burning" were also overheard after the meeting. This was a traditional form of protest. After New Mexico gained statehood in 1912 greater chunks of the Tierra Amarilla grant were fenced off from local grazing, watering, and wood-gathering. The Spanish-American vigilante group known as the Mano Negra resorted to arson and fence-cutting in response. Tijerina was questioned about a recurrence of this.

"The Alliance is flexible," he answered. "We're human. We can't stop these people from burning down houses."

Earlier in the week Cargo had been visited by Don Seaman, the supervisor of Carson National Forest. The chief forester was worried that spring would bring another "occupation" attempt. Then during the night following the inconclusive Alianza meeting with Cargo, the Echo Amphitheater campground was vandalized. Its wooden signs were hacked apart, restrooms were chopped up, concrete picnic tables were chipped—an estimated $3,000 worth of damage.

Eight days later a blaze mysteriously broke out near Yeso Tank, a reservoir in Carson Forest. Winds were blowing at forty miles an hour. Locally recruited emergency crews snuffed out the flames within a ten-acre area. The Forest Service bolstered its night patrols.

While suspicious fires began to spread in the north, preparations were being secretly made for the next date on the Alianza's calendar. No word reached the press, but Tijerina was planning a meeting in the little hamlet of Coyote, also in southern Rio Arriba County. He had already invited a militant colleague from Denver, Rudolph "Corky" Gonzales.

Gonzales had risen from barrio poverty to become a Golden Gloves champion, bail bondsman, and finally director of Denver's Neighborhood Youth Corps. Differences with the city's mayor, in whose election he had played a vital part, made him turn against the power structure. The Crusade for Justice was his creation. Its efforts to protect the civil rights and cultural integrity of Denver's *chicano* population had come to the Alianza's notice as early as May 1966, when the Crusade staged a 160-mile protest motorcade from Walsenburg, Colorado, to Denver.

In his letter of March 25 to Gonzales, in Spanish, Tijerina asked the *valientes* (brave ones) of Denver to "see personally the valor of the sons of San Joaquin." He promised the *toma* (taking) of San Joaquin about June 3.

23

TIJERINA and the COURTHOUSE RAID

Tijerina asked for a delegation from Gonzales's Crusade for Justice organization "so that thus they can see the details at first hand. Answer and let me know. Because it could be that this will happen suddenly and take place before the 3rd of June. In this way we can give you immediate communication by telephone. . . . I hope some of you can be present in this cause, which I think will last many days."

The move from polarization to confrontation had begun.

2

RANGE WAR,
1967 STYLE

The gravity of forest fire outbreaks in federal woodlands increased in northern New Mexico during the early weeks of May 1967. Rumors that they were the work of land-grant arsonists kept fire spotters, forest rangers, and lawmen on their guard.

Three small fires flared into a large blaze on May 7 near the tiny mountain community of Vallecitos. Flames swept up narrow pine-covered canyons thirty-five miles from Tierra Amarilla. All of the timber stood within the boundaries of Carson National Forest, and the FBI was soon asking questions. The Forest Service offered a $500 reward for information about the origin of the fires. No arrests were made. The Vallecitos blaze smoldered for a week, destroying 600 acres of wooded slope.

Further east, in Taos Canyon, three similarly suspicious fires burned 450 acres of woods. These also came under FBI investigation. Carson Forest Supervisor Don Seaman considered them "definitely man-caused."

A week later a large forest fire on Barranca Mesa near the once "secret atomic city" of Los Alamos, within view of Santa Fe, brought out local fire experts. They discovered two other blazes

25

nearby. "They just had to be set by somebody," was the conclusion. It seemed unlikely that these fires were linked to those on Forest Service land, but they heightened local anxiety.

The burning of federal woodlands was felt by many to result from the deterioration of communication between the Forest Service and neighboring ranching communities of Spanish-speaking families. The poverty-level husbandman, trying to support his family on fifteen acres, found the Forest Service's tightening restrictions on the use of federal lands incomprehensible and degrading. He remembered hearing of a time when those lands belonged to his great-grandfather. He looked on the Forest Service as "an army of occupation." That problem might have been alleviated if certain attempts at negotiation that spring had been pursued with greater sensitivity. A March meeting between Forest Service officials and struggling ranchers with meager holdings had been arranged with the cooperation of the governor's staff, HELP (Home Education Livelihood Program, an Office of Economic Opportunity project focusing on New Mexico's 25,000 migrant worker families), and the Catholic Church. About twenty-five wind-hardened Spanish-American grazers, elected spokesmen from their mountain communities, got specific complaints off their chests about pasture use, water, and firewood rights in national forests. This helpful session gave rise to a series of hearings planned for May 1-2. A principal drawing card was to be the presence of Assistant Secretary of Agriculture John Baker.

But the villagers were to wait a full year for Baker's visit. The assistant secretary sent a disappointing message: Regional Forester William D. Hurst could handle the testimony expected from the attending grazers.

Then at the last minute the Forest Service shortened the hearings to one day, effectively eliminating men driving the slow roads south from their adobe homes for the second day's sessions. Cattle tagging for stock going into summer grazing had been scheduled by the Forest Service on the same day as the hearings, a coincidence which kept other delegates from appearing. Conflicting

26

directions on the site of the hearings caused some northern ranchers to wander for hours around the state office complex in Santa Fe.

Only fifteen men finally showed up, most of them Spanish-speaking. The Forest Service spokesmen used most of the time explaining, in English, the service's responsibilities under its "multiple use" policy. National forests and parks were for the enjoyment and use of the entire country. The local ranchers' need for cattle pasturage had to be balanced against the recreational desires of tourists and the conservational health of the land itself. The men described the service's hopes for economic development through forest resources and ticked off its expenditures to improve range, forest, and recreational prospects. The villagers listened patiently.

The hearings closed on a note of unhappy stalemate. One observer summarized:

"Their [Forest Service] rational-legal approach to the problem of grazing unfortunately makes no more sense to the villagers than does the traditional village view make sense to the Forest Service."

That traditional outlook dates back to before the Treaty of Guadalupe Hidalgo between Mexico and the United States in 1848. Since that time Spanish-Americans in the United States have lost over 4,000,000 acres of land-grant territory. These ancestral holdings had originally been awarded to single people or to communities of at least ten village families. A man had his private home and a narrow rectangular plot which usually gave him access to river water. But the community's grazing and wood-gathering acreage, called *ejido*, was understood to be held commonly, and forever, a perpetual trust. A large percentage of the New Mexico *ejido* lands had been put in the public domain by the surveyors general of the period 1854-1880 because they recognized only claims made on behalf of individuals, not communities.

Since the beginning of this century federal encroachment on these lands in northern New Mexico has been a source of conflict. Anger over dwindling pastures for feeding cattle was aggravated by legislation originally designed to assist small ranchers. In 1934 the

TIJERINA and the COURTHOUSE RAID

Taylor Grazing Act provided for individual permits to graze prescribed numbers of cattle, horses, and sheep for limited periods on federal property. Village resentment rose against the paternalistic overtones of these alien procedures. Occasional increases in grazing fees, reductions in the number of available permits, the seemingly arbitrary shortening of the grazing season, and federal inability to explain these decisions in cultural and linguistic terms intelligible to the villagers—these had reduced relations between the Forest Service and the village grazer to a new low early in 1967.

Dr. Clark Knowlton, a sociologist familiar with the historical land loss and cultural patterns of the villages, warned in March that "Spanish-American feelings about the Forest Service are becoming so bitter that undoubtedly there will be demonstrations and protest activities directed against the Forest Service in the future."

By May about three-fourths of a mile of fence had already been systematically snipped along the boundary of Carson National Forest and the Ghost Ranch conference center, a neighboring church educational facility. Now private northern landowners too began suffering from the traditional symptoms of unrest—selective cattle rustling, irrigation ditch and fence wreckage, shot-up water tanks, and arson.

During the early weeks of May Saul Luna lost a haystack in a nighttime blaze and Joe Branch saw an old house filled with grain and hay go up in flames. Tony Casados woke to find the charred remains of two sheds loaded with hay bales. Bill Barton watched the smoke of 2,000 bales lift into the sky. A $4,000 barn was burned on Bill Mundy's ranch; it was the third he had lost to suspected arson. In all, an estimated $30,000 worth of buildings and high-quality alfalfa went up in flames. The Rio Arriba County sheriff's office wryly commented that the worst was over because there was so little left to burn.

During the 1964 threats the Abiquiu Corporation had made against private ranchers with large holdings, Mundy had been

28

plagued with eviction notices for spreading his 25,000-acre ranch on part of the old Tierra Amarilla land grant. Already he had found his favorite studhorse shot, his fences cut, and his $40,000 home burned to the ground. Mundy left the charred brick chimney of the old house standing beside the new one he built. When his third barn was fired he visited with other victims of noctural burnings and fence-cutting. The lean, hard-working rancher estimated that "two or possibly three teams of these arsonists were working here, with two or three men to a team." In his view they attacked "from cars and close to the highway—even the fence cuts—but they don't show any particular bravery. They don't seem to get very far from their vehicle or their wine bottle."

State police agreed. "The evidence has been that most were set on purpose," said District Captain Martin Vigil. "I think they've used kerosene or gasoline." Rio Arriba Undersheriff Dan Rivera had been assigned to Mundy's ranch. He suggested plastic explosives, which allowed time for flight. The burnings occurred when there was either a local school board meeting or a bingo game that evening. Footprints discovered near the blackened remains of one haystack led to a roadside where investigators believed a car had waited.

"If necessary," said Rio Arriba County Sheriff Benny Naranjo, "I will mobilize the sheriff's posse and assign a man to every haystack in the area."

Governor Cargo, in Illinois drumming up tourist interest in New Mexico, began receiving pointed letters at his state office. "We are wondering," asked an irate northern Anglo, "why he is junketing to pleasure spots afield instead of to the hot spots in his own state where rampant vandalism is at the point of lighting the fuse to outright warfare." Newspapers began suggesting that a "range war, 1967 style" was in the offing.

Cargo hurried home for a personal survey of the arson-struck Chama area. He called an emergency meeting May 23 to deal with "the inflammatory situation" and told law enforcement officers around his desk that he would stand for no more burnings. Refusing to detail his plans, Cargo would say only that six state police were on full-time investigation of the fires. Then he added candidly:

"I'm a bit reluctant to discuss it, because we're going to have more trouble up there."

Two days later, a Forest Service advisory board anxiously endorsed "all actions of the U.S. Forest Service in meeting the Alianza thrust."

With this exception, all concerned had displayed unusual restraint in publicly connecting the Alianza and the arson. Even District Attorney Sanchez, who had handled the 1964 Abiquiu Corporation case for the state and who made no secret of his antipathy for the Tijerina cause and methods, was wary in his attribution of the burnings.

"Just the fact that it's arson," he said, "doesn't make it possible to prove who did it. . . . I don't like to speculate. . . . There are so many ramifications in this thing. . . . Once we get the facts we can decide."

Tijerina had not been lying low during these weeks. Of the fire rash he said that the only burnings he had heard about were forest rangers destroying herdsmen's shacks in the Taos area. (This was a dig at the ending of open grazing in certain grasslands in Taos County the previous year.) Then he announced a Sunday rally, May 14, in Tierra Amarilla. Means to recover three grants—Tierra Amarilla, San Mateo (near Grants, New Mexico), and San Joaquin —would be discussed.

"The title of the state is no good, as far as we have been able to ascertain through the documents," announced Tijerina.

Another point of irritation was on Sunday's agenda: the thirteen-mile tunnel being drilled for the San Juan-Chama Transmountain Diversion Project. This $86,000,000 scheme to channel the Rio Grande's tributaries had worried local people. They resented imported laborers when Rio Arriba County unemployment was over 20 per cent; they were afraid their irrigation supply would be drastically reduced.

"This summer," Tijerina vowed, "the Tierra Amarilla land-grant heirs will raise very strong protest against the federal government for the drilling."

About 500 followers attended the Sunday rally. The sixty-seven direct heirs of the Tierra Amarilla grant voted in a "governing council" for the grant which had been the bone of contention for so many years. The duties of the Tierra Amarilla council would, Tijerina explained afterwards, "include such things as taxing residents and establishing a port of entry." The council's officers could "go into roads, streets, private property and private buildings" in performance of their duty. "We don't have to step on so-called U.S. Government property." Tijerina promised that "the Spanish pueblos will be enforcing their rights this summer."

It was the night after the rally that the haystacks of Bill Barton and another rancher went up in flames. A few days later a federal judge in Albuquerque ordered Tijerina to surrender a complete list of the Alianza's membership.

Various reasons were given for the timing of this order: It was encouraged by the Internal Revenue Service, which suspected financial irregularities in dues-soliciting procedures; it was an effort to see whether the Alianza's new activities could be curbed under the 1964 court injunction against the Abiquiu Corporation; it grew out of an order, previously ignored, forbidding Alianza members to harass Forest Service employees. Tijerina was given five days to deliver the files.

On the expiration day no one had appeared before Judge H. Vearle Payne. Immediately issuing a show-cause order, Judge Payne demanded that Tijerina explain why he shouldn't be held in contempt of court. It took another five days for this document to reach Tijerina. During an afternoon when a national television network was doing a filmed report on the Alianza's claim near the Tierra Amarilla courthouse, U.S. Marshal Emilio Naranjo finally found him.

Naranjo's father had been sheriff of Rio Arriba County and a leading northern political figure. Emilio had in turn become the county's sheriff and Democratic Party boss. It is said that in northern New Mexico "Politics is a religion above the family; it streams into the *niño* from his mother's breasts." The Naranjo machine had become one of two principal Rio Arriba political factions warring in the old style. Now, as U.S. marshal, Emilio operated out of an Albuquerque office. His twenty-nine-year-old son, Benny, had inherited both important county jobs.

It was a little after 3 p.m. when Marshal Naranjo handed Tijerina the show-cause order near the pink and blue courthouse. Tijerina had anticipated the move. He produced a copy of his letter of resignation as Alianza president. A few days later the Alianza membership in Albuquerque sanctioned these evasive measures by voting to disband under its old incorporated name. At this point the federal government asked that the Alianza be placed in receivership until a suit resulting from the Echo Amphitheater "occupation" damages could be decided.

During these cat-and-mouse moves there had been no public leak about the proposed meeting at Coyote to which Tijerina had invited his militant colleague Corky Gonzales. But Tijerina was at the point of announcing it and giving all sides a definite test to prepare for.

As the legal maneuverings picked up in mid-May against the disturbing backdrop of arson, District Attorney Alfonso Sanchez pulled out for ready reference the patchwork files his office had assembled on the Alianza.

Sanchez is a small, trim man who glides around an office or a courtroom with a boxer's clipped grace. He often speaks to a visitor in an unusually low voice. This does not seem to be from shyness but to emphasize the seriousness of the matters at hand. He remembers the first time Tijerina walked into his office in the early 1960's.

"You could tell he was dangerous," Sanchez says, "because he really believed in what he said." As soon as Tijerina raised the land-grant question, the district attorney "fingered him for a Communist right then. I told him that if he wanted to take over any country to go to Cuba. I told him to get out of here. There are courts to decide that. I took an oath to uphold the law. He'd have to go past me." According to Sanchez, he threw Tijerina out of his office.

In a still disputed incident in 1958, Sanchez had privately consulted heirs of the Tierra Amarilla land grant at the request of the Spanish-American veterans organization, the GI Forum. In this civil action to "quiet title" to the controversial grant acreage Sanchez became convinced, he says, that the hundred or so heirs had no case against the Payne Land and Cattle Company. He says he withdrew before taking any fee. Northerners have a different memory of the event, however, recalling that Sanchez advised them to cut fences and drive their cattle onto the land. They relate Sanchez's role at this time as proof of the local saying that the "TA grant is a stepping-stone to the district attorney's office."

In Sanchez's bursting file folders there was no reference to the sophisticated and knowledgeable coverage of Tijerina's movements in the Mexican press since 1959. Of Tijerina's research trips to Mexico, the state's U.S. Attorney John Quinn said vaguely, "It is our understanding that he had the same type of organization going in Mexico that he has here." Nowhere in the files were there any copies of the close coverage given the Alianza during its early years by a tiny Albuquerque paper called the *News Chieftain*. Instead, Sanchez's material included the Tijerina brothers' arrest records, press clippings, and "undercover" reports from the 1964 Abiquiu Corporation trouble. One such secret document illustrates the caliber of information in official hands. It read in part as follows:

"It appears that there are one or two ring leaders and in particular one Reyes Lopez Tijarina (*sic*). Various inforamtion (*sic*) has been learned about him but a great many people in the Tierra Amarilla region seem to be afraid of him. Rumor has it that he was born in Las Vegas, New Mexico, and was educated in Mexico. Rumor has it that he is a cult leader and school teacher and has been on the scene for a good many years, he is considered as a crackpot by many who have come into contact with him. The original rumor that I heard was that he and another man were here at the insistence of the Communist Party . . . a far left radical.

"The State Police files indicate that, although he was supposed to have lived at Ensenada for some time prior to moving to Tierra Amarilla, the people there have heard of him but have not seen him. He may be from Nuevo Lorado (*sic*). . . . However the inhabitants on both sides say that Reyes is always there when the trouble starts and continues."

During the troublesome summer of 1964, when the Abiquiu Corporation had been active, Sanchez had sent queries to the FBI and Emilio Naranjo, then Rio Arriba County sheriff. In his request for factual background Sanchez described Tijerina as "allegedly involved in communistic activities."

From the FBI the district attorney received a "rap sheet"— arrest and conviction record—on Anselmo Tijerina, the eldest brother. He had been arrested seven times beginning in 1943. The most serious charge was assault with a deadly weapon, and it concerned an incident on May 26, 1958, in Tierra Amarilla. Reies had been clubbed from behind while talking to a rally and Anselmo had entered the fray.

For Reies himself the FBI listed three arrests. Two were for grand larceny in Casa Grande and Florence, Arizona. A third was for aiding a prisoner to escape. Following up, Sanchez wrote to Arizona officials. He shortly learned of a utopian commune called Valle de Paz (Valley of Peace) which Tijerina had apparently led. The charge of aiding an escaping prisoner referred to a hacksaw jailbreak attempt to free another Tijerina brother, Margarito. A grand larceny charge stemmed from the stealing of some hardware belonging to the Forest Service. It was dismissed for lack of evidence.

The Arizona statute of limitations had run out after Tijerina dropped out of sight before coming to trial for the attempted jailbreak. The Pinal County criminal investigator merely alerted Sanchez: "Subject Tijerina should be considered extremely dangerous and is known to be an escape artist."

Despite Sanchez's recollection of his incisive analysis of Tijerina's basic criminal intent at their first meeting, in 1966 the district attorney seemed unwilling to divulge his suspicions to a reporter.

"Right now it looks like he's taking these people for what they're worth," he said after the Alianza's Fourth of July march in 1966. "Yet, as far as I can tell, he's doing nothing illegal and maybe he can do some good. Our people are going to have to be awakened some damned day."

New Mexico Attorney General Boston Witt seemed no more certain of Tijerina's base motives. "We investigated his background with the assistance of the Mexican Government and the FBI," he told the same newsman. "We could not satisfy ourselves that he is either a Communist or a Communist sympathizer." Two months before the Echo Amphitheater incident Witt commented, "I do not at this time consider him an imminent threat in this state."

Some eight blocks from Sanchez's second-floor office in the pueblo-style Santa Fe courthouse, duplicates of the district attorney's data were filed for the governor's use. In 1966 the state Office of Economic Opportunity had in its advisory capacity gathered press clippings on the Alianza. It had also prepared a confidential memo of its own. Jumping from half-baked clue to hearsay, the string of handwritten notes reported that the Alianza was "said to be entering politics and to be seeking takeover of CAP [Community Action Programs] in northern New Mexico. . . . [Tijerina] talks about Cuba land reform. . . . Tijerina dropped from sight in '57, returned public view '62 or '63. In Arizona . . . apparent head of ring of thieves, leader of religious cult and called himself 'minister'. . . . In N.M. dropped title, now presents self as leader of poor . . . said to be speaker who can influence people to an almost hypnotic degree. . . . Sen. Montoya asked FBI to investigate. Check with them. . . ." The notes ended by citing Tijerina's "potential danger to maintenance of order" and the suggestion that he "may be controlled by accused and possibly actual Communists."

35

TIJERINA and the COURTHOUSE RAID

Jack Campbell, Cargo's predecessor as governor, had scribbled on the OEO memo, "I'll handle this from now on out." But little was done by the spring of 1967 to follow through on its intriguing leads.

On May 28 the Associated Press broke the news that the Alianza, having reorganized as the Confederation of Free City States, was planning a "national conference." The proposed date was June 3, the site was to be the tiny community of Coyote in southern Rio Arriba County.

The dispatch quoted Tijerina as threatening that his followers "will be ready to fight June 3 when they gather for a national conference" about sixty-five miles northwest of Santa Fe. "Tijerina said June 3 will be showdown day," the report added.

In addition the story said that the Confederation-Alianza's "self-proclaimed elders of the land grant" would vote to set up "ports of entry," presumably on Highway 84 and other roads in the vicinity, and "issue visas." Levying of taxes was also mentioned. Tijerina said he expected delegates from New Mexico, California, Texas, and Colorado for the Coyote gathering.

The story failed to explain that this was a return to the idea of reviving the San Joaquin del Rio de Chama grant. Although Coyote is said to lie within the old Piedra Lumbre grant, it bordered the disputed San Joaquin area. The nearby community of Canjilon, where many Alianza *valientes*—hard-core militants—lived, lay within a corner of the San Joaquin tract. It looked as if the governing council of Tierra Amarilla, elected two weeks earlier, would have to wait in line for land recovery.

It was also unclear whether the word "showdown" came from Tijerina's lips or was a journalist's attempt to capture his tone of ultimatum. Reporters subsequently testified that Tijerina himself had emphasized the word. In any case, it set the tone for the impending conference still six days off. The Alianza and the state of New Mexico were clearly on a collision course.

36

3

RACE
TOWARD
CONFRONTATION

When Tijerina divulged the news of the impending meeting at Coyote there was an ominous reaction from the U.S. attorney in Albuquerque. John Quinn warned that if the Alianza conference produced resolutions to occupy the San Joaquin grant again and erect entry checkpoints, it would be up to the National Guard "to keep the peace."

Also in Albuquerque, Judge Payne was waiting for Tijerina to appear before him by June 6 with the names and addresses of Alianza members. When Marshal Naranjo had delivered the judge's second order in Tierra Amarilla, Tijerina had said confidently, while presenting a copy of his resignation letter, "Now I have no responsibility to hand over the list." The court, however, was apparently ignoring his claim that he was "out of power"— Tijerina's phrase—and the Alianza's theoretical dissolution.

Again Naranjo drove north in search of Tijerina. He knocked without success on the doors of Alianza sympathizers and informants in Espanola, twenty-four miles north of Santa Fe. Then he drove a few miles further into the sad-looking suburb of Hernandez. In a frame house set on cinderblocks at the end of a dirt road he found Tijerina's niece, Josie, and Valentina Valdez. This was the Alianza's northern base and the occasional home of Anselmo Tijerina.

The girls were typing and mum. Naranjo returned south with the judge's order in his pocket. But his deputies served another copy at Tijerina's "usual place of abode," a three-room second-floor apartment over the Alianza's spacious, dingy meeting hall in Albuquerque. There Tijerina's nineteen-year-old wife Patsy accepted the copy. She was not helpful as to her husband's whereabouts.

Through the days and nights leading up to the conference, police cars stayed on the lookout for Tijerina at Espanola. While he kept himself scarce, the press fed public anticipation over the coming conclave at Coyote. Now the word "showdown" was quoted by the Santa Fe *New Mexican*'s Espanola correspondent, Doyle Akers. It was unclear where Akers had himself seen Tijerina, but he wrote:

"Tijerina called it a showdown, but didn't elaborate. He hinted that the group may attempt to take physical possession of at least one Spanish grant—the San Joaquin del Rio de Chama."

Near Coyote, residents found flyers in their mailboxes warning people who were not "citizens" of San Joaquin to evacuate. Federal employees at the large Abiquiu flood control dam east of Coyote and at the local Forest Service field station began sending their wives and children out of the area.

No one knew what the Alianza really intended—a fund-raising rally, an occasion to formally reorganize as the Confederation of Free City States, or another "occupation." Marshal Naranjo had conferred with State Police Chief Joe Black. Lawmen would adopt a wait-and-see stance. Naranjo would be in the Coyote region that Saturday for some "preplanned" trout fishing.

About now quiet efforts to import a crack mediation team from

California succeeded. The plan was to give Governor Cargo an emergency survey of the long-range problems and the volatile issues in the north. The governor gave lukewarm encouragement to the idea through his executive assistant, Lawrence Prentice. Others carried it out.

Don Devereux was at the end of his term as a field researcher for the Museum of New Mexico in Santa Fe. Slight of build, bearded, and habitually harried, the thirty-three-year-old Devereux had lived with a family in Vallecitos for over a year and had wandered through other northern valleys existing out of a pickup. Early in May he had reported to the Ford Foundation on the dangerous mood of the area. At the end of his letter he had proposed the "establishment for this critical period of a research program—conceivably to be staffed by a single social anthropologist or sociologist —to provide background and current documentation of the conflict—its manifestations, meanings and consequences. . . ."

In Santa Fe Devereux circulated his plan to friends close to Governor Cargo. Prentice had high hopes for it. At first Devereux enjoyed the support of the energetic young director of the state's Office of Economic Opportunity, thirty-two-year-old Reverend Robert Garcia. After leaving the seminary, the outspoken priest had come into the public eye for his work in northern New Mexico community improvement projects. Now he was on indefinite leave from church duties as one of Cargo's more daring appointments.

Another native New Mexico poverty official who helped sell Devereux's plan was Alex Mercure, the stocky director of the Home Education Livelihood Program (HELP). Operating for the past few years among the state's migrant worker population, HELP was a nonprofit corporation sponsored by the New Mexico Council of Churches but funded directly from the Office of Economic Opportunity in Washington. Mercure had joined a delegation in Cargo's office which urged professional troubleshooting in the north. "You find some guys," replied the governor.

The scope of Devereux's proposal to the Ford Foundation had narrowed by the time he talked to a California foundation which

39

specialized in Spanish-American social problems. "The governor wants someone who can help bring the peace," wrote Ralph Guzman of the Socio-Economic Studies Foundation in Los Angeles to a colleague upon receiving Devereux's urgent phone call. Guzman was also deputy director of the UCLA Mexican-American Studies project. "The Spanish-Americans are burning federal forests in the northern part of the state," his letter continued, "and, apparently, some private property. Racial tensions are mounting. Spanish-Americans want land they claim was stolen from them. They have an organization which is very strong and quite militant."

Guzman prepared to send Cargo two men for "the drafting of a recommendation for federal or private funding of a task force to resolve ethnic tensions and potential conflicts within the state." Thus Cargo's aide Lawrence Prentice defined the purpose of the projected Socio-Economic Studies team in his confirmation letter to Guzman. This letter had been requested by the team before they left California. It promised payment up to $1,500 for their "consulting" service.

The line was never explicitly drawn between the team's fact-finding job and any negotiating they might perform between the state and the Alianza. Perhaps Cargo was simply gambling that the key to avoiding trouble would be found in the hands of these "experts," as they were snidely termed in state house corridors. But their dual mission was already compromised. Since they were coming without any real directive it was unlikely that the team, on their own initiative, could prevent the law and the Alianza from clashing. As for providing an evaluation of the northern counties' ills, a history of unfulfilled recommendations for that depressed area had made cynics of most progressive-minded officials.

In recent years "northern New Mexico" has meant roughly a tri-county area. The label has taken on ethnic overtones: a large percentage of the predominantly rural populations of Mora, Taos, and Rio Arriba counties have Spanish surnames. The majority of the state's Spanish-speaking people (who constitute 26 per cent of the state's total population) eke out their living here. The identification has also become synonymous with economic deprivation and cultural isolation.

West of this 10,000-square-mile network of mountains and valleys, the rugged landscape changes into desert mesa and hardy cactus. Eastward, its forested slopes descend into grassland plains that sprawl into Oklahoma and Texas. On a map showing the layout of historic land grants the north is an extension of that jigsaw puzzle of huge tracts whose lifeline was the Rio Grande and its tributaries. As the state's guidebook says, the traditional residents of this upland region constitute "the only integral remnant of the northernmost fringe of the Spanish empire in America."

It is a contradictory realm of rich natural resources and poverty-stricken villages with memories of a self-sufficient pastoral economy. The political pattern has been one of patronage and exploitation. Caved-in adobe walls and boarded-up windows are an indication of the increasing lack of employment and the consequent annual departures for the rootless menial labor of the migrant worker.

But a handful of towns in the northern counties have been given second life by the breakup of the old peasant communities and the need for commercial centers to serve what remains. Featuring clusters of small drygoods and grocery stores, poverty war field stations, eateries with chile, beer, and *mariachi* music, these are the growing towns of tomorrow.

Bustling Espanola is already there. Between the twentieth century to the south and the nineteenth century to the mountainous north, it vies with Taos as the center of northern New Mexico's *manana* existence. In the late afternoon bumper-to-bumper traffic fills Route 84, its main street and Rio Arriba County's principal artery. It is the major shipping point for fruit from the Espanola Valley. Although not the county seat, it has become the political, recreational, and business hub of county life.

Northern New Mexico has long been the subject of woeful studies. Their recommendations for curing its complex ills have seldom been put into action. The first exposé of its plight was published in 1940 when George I. Sanchez, a native, wrote his *Forgotten People*. For the first time the orphaned north was described realistically:

"What has been said of education can be said with equal or greater force about other public services. . . . Health programs, the administration of justice, economic competition, and development, the exercise of suffrage, land use and management—the vital aspects of social and economic incorporation of a people were left up to the doubtful ministrations of improvised leadership. The New Mexican was placed at the mercy of those political and economic forces of those vested interests that could control the machinery of local government."

In 1964 an explosive investigation into the Rio Arriba County educational system was released by the National Education Association. It was boldly subtitled: *When Public Education Provides Patronage for a Political System.* Unlike other reports from Rio Arriba, its indictment of a "political stronghold" where "the talent and productivity of many people, not merely those presently of school age, have been sacrificed on the altar of political expediency," had the desired effect. The entire Rio Arriba school system was reorganized to make it less susceptible to political influence.

A comprehensive study of Rio Arriba and Taos counties was prepared in 1960 but it got no further than library shelves. An *Economic, Social and Education Survey of Rio Arriba and Taos Counties,* by Dr. John Burma and David E. Williams, unveiled the region for those who could perceive human beings between the statistics. In Rio Arriba 69.1 per cent of the forests and meadows were federally owned, mostly in the Kit Carson Forest area. Private ownership of the county's 3,750,000 acres amounted to 28.3 per cent, much of it within the old Tierra Amarilla grant confines. It was clear why subsistence farmers felt squeezed, and why 75 per cent of them now farmed only home vegetable gardens or raised only a few cattle on plots of between ten and forty-nine acres each. Rio Arriba's welfare rolls were greater than eleven other state counties combined. The Burma report commented, "It is no wonder 'chronic depression' prevails." Nor any wonder chronic resentment grew.

The Burma report began gathering dust in the state library because it was thought to discredit politicians of Spanish surname. In discussing the "fetish" of political activity in the county it used the descriptive words "vicious," "corruption," "obsession," "useful to create injustice," and "almost unbelievable in the United States."

The Burma report's section on education in the northern counties certainly had prodded the NEA investigation. But the state's cool legislative reaction to the report's forward-looking suggestions for economic development was a discouraging omen for the findings of the California reconnaissance team. Finally, Cargo's hesitant endorsement of the team's presence cast a shadow over their efforts to bring the opposing viewpoints into any negotiating situation.

On the morning when Lawrence Prentice dictated the final go-ahead for Robert Aragon and Hector Burgos, the members of the California team, to fly to New Mexico as confidential consultants, law officials were preparing their own response to the upcoming Coyote convention.

State Police Chief Black had already replied to Tijerina's quoted statement that his followers would be "ready to fight Saturday."

"There's no move we can make until they make their move," the chief stated. "We're prepared to handle any situation that arises."

But on May 31 a closed meeting of police leaders was held in Santa Fe to talk over "laws and orders" that could be used against the Alianza. Judge Paul Tackett's 1964 injunction against Rio Arriba County citizens carrying loaded firearms could be invoked. Potential charges ranged from felonies to misdemeanors. Unreasonably loud conduct and concealing one's true identity were mentioned. Unlawful assembly—thirty or more assembling to do any unlawful act—was to be kept in mind. Vagrancy—"loitering near any private grounds without the consent of owner and being unable to account for one's presence"—would often apply. There was the possibility of "sabotage" and "disloyalty." The uniformed men took notes in preparation for the weekend.

On this last day of May attitudes had alarmingly hardened. Tijerina had gone completely "underground." Marshal Naranjo made a scouting drive to the Coyote meeting site. He cruised around the fenced-in grounds of the old school where the Alianzans hoped to assemble. He was planning to have four deputies with him on the target morning, still three days off. "We do not expect any trouble," he added confidently. He acknowledged that he was co-ordinating plans with local lawmen. A newspaper story recalled the marshal's fishing trip near Coyote. Now, it predicted, "he will leave his fly rod at home."

The following afternoon the California team was in the air. Don Devereux and I drove from Santa Fe to pick them up at the Albuquerque airport. At this time Devereux wanted a newspaperman's involvement as observer with elastic deadlines. The day before I had been thoroughly briefed on the team's peace-keeping project.

Devereux had already urged on Cargo the need to maintain close contact with the law enforcement trio—Quinn, Sanchez, and Black—and keep them abreast of the mediation efforts. His worry about the governor's intrastate communications apparatus was well founded. Now that apparatus began to break down, allowing the administrative and law enforcement branches of state government to work at cross purposes.

During a drive beneath a stunning sunset, Devereux also filled me in on his knowledge of Tijerina. An hour later we were sitting in the airport lounge. He was answering the rapid-fire questions of a curly-haired young man named Robert Aragon.

Aragon had had Peace Corps experience in Chile. At this point he was suspicious of a journalist's presence. He was cool, unsmiling, and precise in his curt queries about the present crisis. His partner was shorter, quieter, and more relaxed, an older man named Hector Burgos. As a labor organizer Burgos had worked in the

Imperial Valley of California. In the 1965 Dominican crisis he had been sent to Santo Domingo with Mexican Government credentials to salvage liberals for the U.S. State Department.

Aragon took profuse notes. Then he made some calls from a pay booth. Within a half-hour three Spanish-American young men walked to our table and embraced the team warmly. A *chicano* grapevine was clearly in operation. Devereux and I returned to Santa Fe after arranging for the team to telephone Devereux the next day.

Six months later State Attorney General Boston Witt's investigation of this period was released. It erroneously said that *three* of us greeted the consultants at the air terminal. It correctly stated that Aragon and Burgos "proceeded to Santa Fe where they registered at La Fonda Hotel at 11:52 p.m." La Fonda was only the first stop in the hotel-hopping week that followed, when the team's arrival proved to have been too late.

4

SANCHEZ
MOVES
FIRST

It would be another week before anyone learned of Tijerina's movements that eve of the Coyote meeting. Then the armed might of northern New Mexico, civilian and military, would be after him. From a mountain hideout he would recall, "Since the state police was supposed to kill me, and later give the reason to the public that they shot me because I resisted arrest or had tried to run away, I started to stay in the background during Friday and Saturday." In the light of events after the courthouse raid, fears for his life might not have been unreasonable.

But on Thursday, June 1, 1967, newsmen scurried behind lawmen who were still trying to serve the federal order on the Alianza leader. They could only report that "Tijerina was in Espanola and not available for comment on whether any plans for the meeting had been changed since his earlier announcements." It may have been a journalistic distaste for doubt that made the reporter who placed him in Espanola certain of the unseen man's whereabouts. The only word we had was simply that he was "circulating."

Early on Friday morning, June 2, Devereux stationed himself in the imposing reception lounge of the governor's office. Beneath the state's bas-relief seal, amid the lulling piped-in music, he waited impatiently for the team's promised call. Sipping coffee he noticed a well-built, suavely dressed young man approach the secretary's desk. He overheard his name: Joe Benitez.

Benitez was a field representative with the VISTA program. Specifically, he worked out of the Center for Community Action Services located at the University of New Mexico, in Albuquerque. As part of his job to relate to indigenous groups, he had established relationships within the Alianza leadership. The land-grant movement represented the only present instance of a viable grass-roots organization without the traditional *patron* strings. Like Aragon, the California consultant, Benitez belonged to that budding generation of well-educated, urbanized young *chicanos* who empathized with the Alianza's purpose of regenerating racial pride.

The previous evening Devereux had heard his name mentioned as a valuable contact to guide the team to key northern militants. Benitez had driven to the capitol independently this morning to alert Cargo to the local bitterness building up over increased police activity. A press report had already described "beefed-up forces of state and federal officers" who were "prepared to meet any situation that might come about."

Introducing himself, Devereux informed Benitez about the mediation team's aims. They wanted to contact the northern Alianzans quickly. Benitez readily offered assistance.

But when the team finally telephoned, a prior matter of payment had to be settled. They asked for half their consulting fee right away. Lawrence Prentice dashed from the governor's office to a local bank, since a state voucher could not be processed fast enough. Borrowing $750 on his own signature, he gave the sum to the team when they appeared at the capitol. The understanding was that the Socio-Economic Studies Foundation would return the sum when it received total payment. About noon Benitez escorted Aragon and Burgos north for their first exposure to the temper of the troubled area.

47

TIJERINA and the COURTHOUSE RAID

The background Devereux had given me on the Alianza was as scanty and fascinating as the facts and conjectures in official hands. He was not sure how long the organization had existed. He thought Tijerina's birthplace was Arizona. Vague stories of Mexican sojourns during some mysterious pre-New Mexico period had come to him. He figured the Alianza's hard-core dependables numbered no more than 1,000. He considered their leader highly intelligent, an extraordinary orator, and thoroughly charismatic. He had heard of his Arizona law troubles.

During the pause that morning I did some spadework in the *New Mexican's* newspaper files.

The Alianza's protest march on the Fourth of July weekend in 1966 had been a lively affair. The sixty-two-mile hike from Albuquerque to Santa Fe took three days. Strung along the baking eastern shoulder of four-lane Interstate Highway 25, the sweating marchers trod against the impressive background of the craggy Sandia Mountain Range to the east and the ugly spread of gravel pits and highway equipment garages to the west. The heat hovered around 90 degrees, the skies were cloudless. Umbrellas shaded some marchers, others wore straw hats. Lagging pack automobiles bore tents, blankets, cooking wood, cardboard boxes with food, and loyal grandparents. A state police car took up the rear. Hecklers were ignored.

After the first seventeen-mile stretch the Alianzans wearily made camp alongside the highway. Blisters were examined and bandaged. During that first Saturday night, five gunshots clipped through the smoke of their campfires. "Wetbacks go home!" someone yelled from a passing car.

Among the signs carried by the demonstrators was a large cloth banner which read: "William A. Pile, Governor of New Mexico, destroyed Spanish archives." Pile was the state's seventh territorial governor, between 1869 and 1871. During a spring cleaning he told the state librarian to clear out an unfurnished room. Sold as curiosities and wrapping paper, its rubbish was popularly but erroneously thought to include the better portion of New Mexico's land-grant documentation. Now the Alianzans were walking to visit a different governor, Jack Campbell, but in their minds the historical context was not so far removed. They retained the pessimism that made "politician" a pejorative term in the north. And their fear and fury over wheeling and dealing in high places was acquired through years of bitter experience.

The war between the United States and Mexico ended in 1848 with American victory and the Treaty of Guadalupe Hidalgo. Although this agreement ostensibly safeguarded existing private holdings, the following half-century saw Spanish-Americans deprived of huge expanses of granted lands. Claimants to *ejido* (communally owned) acreages were cajoled, defrauded, and deceived into signing papers which Anglos considered title to terrain always previously understood to be community property. Anglos, it should be added, were by no means solely to blame for these events.

During the 1870's and 1880's a syndicate of prosperous, established Anglos known as the Santa Fe Ring deprived many Spanish grant settlements of their water, forest, mineral, and grazing rights. One member was reported to be the largest landowner in the nation, with interest in seventy-five land grants, personal ownership of nearly 2,000,000 acres, and part ownership of or authority as attorney for an additional 4,000,000 acres. These were the decades when hundreds of grant documents were mysteriously lost, sold, or burned. Surveyors appear to have used remarkably elastic measuring rods. As a result of collusion between lawyers in some cases, attorneys won prime grazing land as payment only to divide it with their adversaries. Land-tax laws brought sudden foreclosure on still more grant acreage.

This was almost recent history in the minds of such marchers as full-bearded, white-haired Jose Luis Sanchez, proudly astride a burro that Fourth of July weekend. When the footsore band of 125 finally entered Santa Fe on July 5 they were irritated to learn that Governor Campbell was in Los Angeles at an annual governors' conference. Tijerina, his face glowing with sun, promptly told two governor's aides appointed to meet him in a vacant lot near the capitol that his band would not budge until the governor returned. From the back of a truck he spoke the following noon to his frustrated followers and curious Santa Feans:

"I'm not a Socialist, nor a Communist, nor Red or Pink. I'm just a slave to justice."

After a mildly abrasive week of camping on the southern edge of town behind upright banners and nightly guitar-playing, Tijerina and his group were finally received in the governor's flag-draped private office. Campbell complimented their orderliness and interrogated Tijerina closely about the Alianza's infrastructure. The land-grant leader complained that Senator Joseph M. Montoya, of their own blood, had done little to advance his people's cause. The meeting ended amicably enough. Campbell said he would send requests to the President and the state's congressional delegation asking for an executive-level investigation of their land-grant claims. But a Santa Fe columnist had perceived the deeper disturbance which Campbell's gesture had not assuaged.

"Unless these thousands of New Mexicans receive some sign that someone does care about them," warned Mark Acuff in the *New Mexican*, "that growing feeling of bitterness is liable to explode."

In the activity surrounding the Campbell conference a respected historian's confidential memo to the governor was made public. State Archivist Myra Ellen Jenkins felt there was little basis for the Alianza's land claims. Indeed, she said, she had "examined hundreds of land-grant papers and many of the grants submitted were illegal under both Spanish and Mexican law. Many were encroachments on pueblo [Indian] lands always protected by Spanish and Mexican law."

Twice, Miss Jenkins said, the Spanish-American claimants had "had their day in court." She was referring to the activities of the U.S. Surveyor General's office from 1854 to 1890, and to the Court of Public Land Claims which "settled" many northern New Mexico land disputes from 1891 to 1904. In her private memorandum Miss Jenkins feared "outside influences which are reopening this old issue for pecuniary gain." Immediately the lady found herself slapped with a $2,000,000 slander suit from the Alianza for calling it "a con game." To date the case has not been pursued.

Next in the *New Mexican*'s tear sheets came the tale of the Echo Amphitheater takeover in October 1966. This bold strike for an original land grant, San Joaquin del Rio de Chama, had been decided upon during the Alianza's fourth convention the previous month. But local concern over the grant had been rising since 1940 when the San Joaquin Town Corporation was reactivated to "protect the society which is encompassed by said Corporation against the injustices and tricks of tyrants and despots, of those who insult us and seize our lands . . . to acquire, hold, possess and distribute through proper legal channels the rights, privileges, tracts of land, wood, waters and minerals which were deeded to and bequeathed by, our ancestors, the heirs and assigns of the Grant of the Corporation of San Joaquin del Rio de Chama. . . ." The Echo Amphitheater invasion was considered by the Alianza to be a "test case." It was also the debut of significant Alianza personalities.

On October 15, 1966, the 350 San Joaquin heirs and their ardent sympathizers became occupational forces moving into Echo Amphitheater. Electing old Jose Lorenzo Salazar as mayor, they voted in a governing council and dwelt in tents on the federal campground for several days. Thirty armed *vecinos*—settler citizens of a Spanish pueblo who can own a personal allotment as well as share the common grant range—stayed one more day.

"If federal officials, like forest rangers, try to throw us out," Tijerina threatened, "we'll throw them in jail for trespassing."

During the next uneasy week Forest Service personnel held worried meetings over the intimidation. Then the "revived republic" served eviction papers on astonished Regional Forester William D. Hurst at his office. He refused to accept them. Carson National Forest Supervisor Don Seaman announced that anyone returning to Echo Amphitheater would "absolutely have to be evicted" unless they showed camping permits. The Alianza was now suggesting that it might liberate a second ancestral plot, the San Miguel del Vado land grant twenty miles west of Las Vegas, New Mexico.

TIJERINA and the COURTHOUSE RAID

Then, on the chilly morning of October 22, a collection of state police and forest rangers were stationed anxiously near the Amphitheater's parking lot. First they heard car horns. Soon some 100 vehicles, honking and undeterred by the uniforms in their path, scattered lawmen as they skidded into the lot. Rangers Walt Taylor and Phil Smith were surrounded by excited Alianzans. Tijerina kept exclaiming, as the two were hustled off, "We take full responsibility, we take full responsibility!"

Suddenly Taylor and Smith were before a picnic table "court" and a portly, bald Anglo "judge" named Jerry Noll. As Noll presided, he was "nervous as a whore in church," Taylor remembers. Noll later explained, "Things happened so fast I barely had time to get to the bench before the defendants were brought before me."

The two rangers were promptly charged with "trespassing and being a public nuisance." They made themselves scarce after each received a "$500 fine" and "suspended sentence" of eleven months and twenty-one days.

Through another couple of days the "occupation forces" dwindled. Alianza teenagers patrolled wearing shiny deputy badges. They carried rifles and full holsters hung from their belts. Two carloads of FBI agents had been keeping the encampment under surveillance. Finally twelve state, federal, and forest officers cleared out the last squatters. The aged "mayor" was sitting in front of his tent boiling potatoes and coffee when the band was rounded up. A twenty-one-year-old man named Baltazar Martinez, in rakish beret and shirt unbuttoned to the waist, was relieved of his 30/30 rifle. The stenciled card that proclaimed the San Joaquin grant's restoration was scratched from where it had been pasted lopsidedly over the Kit Carson Forest sign.

Despite its anticlimactic end, the takeover was a powerful experience for the Alianzans. "I have never seen so much ethnic pride among the villagers before or since," a veteran observer of village society later said, "not to mention the obvious new knowledge of how much impact they could have through collective and determined action."

During the waning days of the occupation the Santa Fe *New Mexican* ran an editorial entitled "Not a Laughing Matter." It confessed, in part, "We can't laugh because our conscience is pricked . . . morally the case is far less clear . . . behind the legal technicalities we are confronted with the shameful fact that the United States of America made a solemn promise and failed, in many instances, to honor the obligations of that promise. People who were guaranteed the perpetual (and often tax-free) right to the use of ancestral lands have lost that right. . . . Land Grant heirs are asking that a federal commission investigate this situation and right the old injustice. Whatever the technicalities of the law, we think the national conscience would rest easier if this were done."

The Echo Amphitheater "judge" had been a relatively recent arrival. In Seattle Jerry Noll had read of the land-grant movement and written Tijerina a letter explaining his peculiar connection with the Alianza's claims. Then he had appeared at the Alianza's September convention, billed as an "historian of international law."

At the age of fourteen, Noll had been told by his father that he was the rightful "King of the Indies." His parents instructed him in an involved lineage which tied the Hapsburg family of Germany and Queen Isabella of Spain to a prophecy by Nostradamus. His parents told him how his younger nephew, "Don Marco Carlos de Castillo," had been kidnapped from his Seattle home in 1959 at the age of one year because of the threat he posed to the U.S. Government.

Noll had gotten into trouble with the law in Seattle. While in jail for one of his three convictions he was charged with stabbing a fellow prisoner with a dinner fork. Finally he had arranged with Tijerina to join the land-grant crusade. Tijerina was pleased to have his aid. Later, when Noll had proved his readiness to put himself in jeopardy for the Alianza, Tijerina would steadfastly refuse advice that he be discharged. "He's got his own pursuit and his own rights that he claims and I'm not interfering!"

A few months after the Echo Amphitheater stand, Noll penned a lengthy manifesto which was published in the legal columns of a local paper. A portion of it read:

"We shall commence to liberate our Kingdom, realms and dominions, and if the aggressors [designated as the United States of America] shed one drop of blood on any of our soldiers during the progress of this campaign, a state of war shall exist as of that moment." It was signed "Don Barne Quinto Cesar, The King Emperor." Attorneys preparing the government's Echo Amphitheater case shortly moved for a psychiatric examination of Noll.

Along with Noll, four men were arrested on federal charges as a result of the Echo Amphitheater incident, and released on $2,000 bail each. Cristobal, the youngest Tijerina brother, was one.

Since the Echo Amphitheater event had occurred within federal domain, Alfonso Sanchez's office had not been directly involved. But now, on the brink of the Coyote meeting, the site of Alianza agitation was within his jurisdiction. He meant to meet the challenge.

About the time that Aragon and Burgos were entering Benitez's car for their reconnaissance trip, listeners to local radio stations in the north heard a special announcement interrupt regular Friday programs. Sanchez was speaking from handwritten notes:

"As district attorney I wish to give notice to all Alianza members who plan to be present and participate in the meeting at Coyote tomorrow, that said meeting is versus the laws since it is planned to take over private property. Criminal charges of unlawful assembly will be filed against all persons who attend. Penalty is six months in jail. If you participate in taking over of private land, extortion charges will be filed against all who participate, and penalty is five years in the penitentiary. You are being misled by Reies Lopez Tijerina. You cannot take property by force without going to court. What he professes is communism and is illegal. Don't be misled and regret it later. Do not attend and stay at home."

Later, as a fugitive, Tijerina evaluated the sequence of events leading to the raid on the courthouse at Tierra Amarilla:

"Everything came to a head when the Coyote meeting was prohibited by Alfonso Sanchez. We don't know too much about law, but we do know that Alfonso Sanchez was violating all our constitutional rights . . . civil rights, especially the right to assemble peacefully."

Those not tuned into Sanchez's broadcast heard it by word of mouth. The punishment for being seen at Coyote ballooned in severity. Some understood the district attorney had vowed to "lock everyone up who went and throw away the key."

That Friday afternoon apprehension quickened. Espanola Correspondent Doyle Akers reported that Alianzans were supposedly holding rifle practice near Espanola. This was never verified. An absentee rancher with a 1,400-acre spread near Chama sent word to the police of cut fences and unknown cattle grazing on his land. He also complained of a sign tacked up on his property reading: "The U.S. is trespassing in New Mexico . . . all trespassers will be punished by law."

Then a call from the Santa Fe courthouse to the *New Mexican* requested a newsman on an "off-the-record" basis. Police were having a 2:30 p.m. secret meeting. Forty-five minutes later Reporter John Crenshaw returned. The "sober, serious" gathering had unnerved him.

About half a dozen men had sat in the district attorney's book-strewn office. They included a Forest Service representative and the head of the state police narcotics division. State Police Captain T. J. Chavez outlined the various charges prepared for key Alianza leaders, ranging from unlawful assembly to driving without a license and public drunkenness. These offenses were to be ready reference for officers manning roadblocks that would be erected that evening and stay up through Saturday. Blank complaints against the Alianza principals, authorized in advance by Sanchez, were also mentioned.

55

TIJERINA and the COURTHOUSE RAID

The officials gathered had clearly considered the Coyote meeting a test of their will. During the no-nonsense session Sanchez indicated that these strike-first tactics were being undertaken because "the feds aren't going to do anything." The word "Communist" came from Sanchez's lips in reference to Tijerina. "Black seemed to agree," Crenshaw thought.

While the lawmen were listening to Sanchez outline the official offensive, Benitez, Aragon, and Burgos arrived at the Alianza's outpost in Hernandez. Now it was heavily patrolled by state police. The dirt road winding off the highway was partly blocked by a Mountain States Telephone Company van. Pulling up to the house, Benitez led the team into a crowded room. All inside were angry, many were armed.

Dressed in fatigues, Cristobal Tijerina wore a sidearm. Before anyone would talk with Aragon, they insisted that the telephone truck pull back and that police surveillance be withdrawn. Burgos had noticed a lineman, protected by officers, working with tools on the building's telephone wires. Benitez called the governor's office to complain. Police later denied staking out the house. But within a half-hour the telephone man climbed down and police cars departed.

When the California consultants returned to Santa Fe around 4 p.m. their initial skepticism about the urgency of the situation had visibly changed. Their contacts in Albuquerque had not prepared them for the unsophisticated militancy of the land-grant forces and the primitive nature of the police response. With new respect for the imminent danger, they wanted Devereux to arrange a talk with Governor Cargo as soon as possible. During the afternoon Cargo had been in Albuquerque. When he finally returned he set up a 6:30 p.m. date for a conference with his consultants.

Afterwards Devereux gave me a rundown of their meeting. Cargo had opened with a ten-minute summation. He considered the Tijerinas "phonies" and financially motivated. He could not believe violence was really in the offing. Aragon felt obliged to restate why he and Burgos had flown to New Mexico: first to perform a reconnaissance toward negotiations, and second to draft a preliminary report on major areas of long-standing discontent. Then he gave Cargo the first idea anyone had of the Alianza's intentions for the approaching dawn.

A three-phase plan had been designed to meet any moves the police made during the Coyote gathering. Initially the Alianza would erect "token" roadblocks. Presumably this meant the promised "port of entry" signs merely indicating that visitors were now entering—or trespassing on—the San Joaquin free city state. If police interfered with this, functional roadblocks would seal off a section of State Road 96. Any "non-pueblo officers" (meaning state or federal lawmen) within the occupied section would be arrested. If police resisted this maneuver the Alianza would make an armed stand.

Cargo became interested. He discussed the report a little longer before Devereux let him know that the team was aware of the state warrants prepared for serving that night. Cargo confessed hearing that something of the sort was under way. Quickly the group stressed that arrests that night would speed up the phasing of the Alianza's response. Benitez believed that Tijerina did not want a confrontation but was committed to some face-saving course of action. If Cargo would personally meet with Tijerina, he suggested, there was a possibility of talking the whole thing down. Cargo tentatively agreed to the idea. In an adjoining office Benitez tried to get through to his Alianza friends on the telephone.

One prospect that had been discussed was a breakfast meeting between the two leaders in Espanola. This would require, however, an Alianza promise to keep the action at Coyote below Phase 1. Even the possibility of Cargo's going to a post-Coyote picnic was mentioned. When Benitez was unable to reach his northern contacts, Press Secretary Bill Privetti gave him the unlisted number of the governor's mansion. Devereux made a mental note of the digits.

Benitez's function during this period was highlighted in the attorney general's investigation document released six months later. Because Benitez worked with the VISTA program, his involvement was considered signal evidence of Attorney General Witt's thesis: complicity between the Alianza and the state Office of Economic Opportunity.

"During the week of June 5th and sometime prior thereto," stated this document, "Mr. Benitez, for reasons which are still not clear, took it upon himself to become 'intermediary' between the 'Alianza' hierarchy, the governor's office, the governor, and several other persons.

"It was Mr. Benitez who set up a diversionary telephone relay team which, at various times, moved from hotels and motels in Santa Fe, so that they could not readily be detected. Whenever a contact needed to be made, this relay team would then place a phone call to Mr. Benitez who was at his home in Albuquerque. The message would be taken and further relayed by Benitez to the Tijerinistas at their hideout. And outgoing messages from the Tijerinistas would be handled in the same fashion. The governor's calls were also handled in this fashion."

While Benitez was futilely trying to employ this "diversionary" scheme from the conspicuous center of the state capitol, Cargo himself made two calls. The consultants and Devereux heard only one side of his request to U.S. Attorney Quinn and District Attorney Sanchez to quash whatever warrants they had at hand, at least until the next day.

Someone had already informed Attorney General Ramsey Clark's office in Washington of the coming showdown. Apparently word had bounced back instructing the U.S. attorney's office in Albuquerque to cooperate with the governor. Possibly this was the import of Sanchez's earlier derogatory comment about "the feds."

When Cargo closed these phone conversations it was the impression of all in the room that both Quinn and Sanchez were going along with his plea. The governor had promised to call both officials first thing in the morning; it was hoped that by then communications with the Tijerina band would have slowed down the dangerous momentum of events. With a feeling of relief the visitors left.

Aragon and Burgos checked out of La Fonda. All went to the Inn of the Governors, a Santa Fe motel, for a thankful drink. There Burgos entertainingly recounted his escapades in Santo Domingo, describing a scheme of "deputizing the opposition" which Cargo might effectively use in the present situation: Place county sheriff's posse badges on the Alianza's marshals and put their desire for authority to peacekeeping advantage.

District Attorney Sanchez's recollection from the other end of the telephone line was somewhat different from the team's understanding of a willingness to halt the arrests. In response to the governor's request, Sanchez had told Cargo to check first with Judge James Scarborough, who had actually signed the warrants. "Don't ask me, Governor, don't ask me," he said. A little later, Sanchez recalls, the governor called the district attorney at his home, asking once more that the warrants be delayed. Again Sanchez insisted it was out of his hands, and proceeded to read over the telephone state police reports on the Tijerinas' troubles in Arizona and New Mexico. Then he mailed copies to the governor's office. He told the governor that he must read the material before talking with any Alianza representatives. The following morning, "at about 7:30 or 8," Sanchez remembers, he sent a state policeman to the governor's office with additional copies "so he'd know the kind of men he'd be dealing with."

Following his meeting with the California team Governor Cargo had lingered in his offices, telling newsmen that it was possible he would go north the next morning and personally speak with Tijerina. Then his secretary interrupted him with a personal call. State Police Chief Joe Black informed the governor that Cristobal Tijerina had been arrested on Sanchez's warrants.

"They did what I told them not to do," Cargo said. A few minutes later he departed for home.

TIJERINA and the COURTHOUSE RAID

About an hour later I was poring over neglected stories at my *New Mexican* desk. The local Associated Press correspondent burst through the door and dashed to his glass-walled cubicle.

"What's happening, Bud?" I asked.

"They're pulling in everybody up there," he said, clicking on his teletape cutter. "They've got Cristobal, Felix. They don't have Reies. Roadblocks everywhere."

5

CONFRONTATION AT COYOTE

The police roundup of the Alianzans on Friday evening began before the California consultants even entered Governor Cargo's office. While the team was urgently talking to the governor in the hope of stalling the lawmen's offensive, roadblocks were being assigned and patrol cars were heading for the addresses of known Alianza members.

The owner of a drygoods store later described opening his front door and being grabbed around the chest by a state policeman. He said the police first forbade him to take his eyeglasses and then wouldn't let him wear a hat. Juan Martinez had been pulled off his job as a janitor at the Tierra Amarilla high school. Manacled, he was rushed south to the Santa Fe jail before he could call his wife to explain why he didn't return for dinner. A third man told of hearing noises from his bed and starting to get up. He was arrested while pulling on his pants. "They never told me why," he said. Telephone lines soon hummed with tales of officials hammering on wooden doors in the night, hunting rifles confiscated, and mountain roads covered with darting police vehicles, their warning lights twirling.

Throughout the long night about eighteen men were actually jailed. One of them was the tall, gaunt great-grandson of the original recipient of the Tierra Amarilla grant. Jose Maria Martinez, with hands cuffed before him, was hustled to a Santa Fe city jail cell. Apparently some Alianza members were interrogated at their doorsteps and in the back seats of police cars before being released. Some days later Cargo was queried about the arrest procedures by a luncheon club of concerned Spanish-Americans. The governor recollected:

"I didn't order the arrests. I said if anyone is picked up in a car with munitions, such as tear gas, hand grenades, they were to make arrests. I told them if any arrests were made be sure you are on solid legal grounds." He admitted the timing of the arrests "left something to be desired."

He was answering with the benefit of hindsight. The big police catch that night was two vehicles driven by Alianza lieutenants Cristobal Tijerina and Lloyd Felix Martinez, respectively. Their car trunks held material which officials felt vindicated their precautionary action.

In 1960 Alfonso Sanchez, then a private lawyer, had been engaged by a supply house employee in Albuquerque who had lost two fingers when a block and tackle smashed his left hand. Two years later Sanchez at last won a $2,000 judgment from Judge James Scarborough for young Lloyd Felix Martinez. By that time Martinez had returned from a California trip to discover Reies Tijerina in his parents' living room, revitalizing their old land-grant fight. Later Reies was the minister at Felix's wedding. The judgment money won by Sanchez promptly funded one of Tijerina's trips to Mexico City in search of documents. Martinez went along. In 1964 Martinez was named vacuum-cleaner salesman of the year. Coming from the large Tierra Amarilla Martinez family, with its feisty local reputation, Felix was one of the Alianza's few under-middle-age activists. On this Friday night he looked strikingly like a cross between Cantinflas and Che Guevara.

When the roadblock four miles east of Coyote halted him that night, Martinez was questioned by State Police Captain Hoover Wimberly. Inside the car's trunk were stuffed eight new gas masks, a loaded high-powered rifle with telescopic sight, tear gas shells and "burp gun" ammunition, two revolvers, a walkie-talkie, clothing and a sleeping bag.

The car with Missouri license plates driven by Cristobal Tijerina contained a box full of curious rolled-up documents. A newsman said these were maps of the area showing designated places as prime objectives for seizure. He reported that Ghost Ranch, the Presbyterian educational center, was labeled No. 1. He also saw an "organization chart" laying out a chain of command including a president, a five-star general, a one-star general over each "army" to be created, regiments, battalions, companies, and platoons. In the trunk were ten account books showing Alianza dues for 1965 and 1966. Individual receipts ranged from $1 to $20. For one April there was a list of 112 donors. Several metal 3″ x 5″ card drawers containing membership lists were discovered. Looking under C police saw that "Cargo, J. A. Adelaida," the governor's wife, was in arrears for her 1966 membership dues. She still owed a balance of $6, half a year's worth.

"A lot of people," hinted Marshal Naranjo, "are going to be embarrassed."

Police also found a "black book" they said contained names of Alianza organizers in key localities. Each name had a code beside it. Finally a photograph of Fidel Castro, a copy of *The Rise and Fall of the Third Reich* and *Che Guevara on Guerrilla Warfare* were confiscated, along with a framed wedding photograph which sedately topped the trove.

As soon as Devereux, back in Santa Fe, learned of the mass arrests, he sped to the *New Mexican* office and dialed Cargo's number.

Meanwhile I alerted Aragon and Burgos to the about-face in developments. Desperately they tried to reach Benitez, who was now in his car heading for Albuquerque.

Cargo already knew what was going on. He returned an alarmingly high and exaggerated arrest estimate—between fifty and seventy—and seemed awed by the intensity of the police offensive.

Devereux asked pointedly, "Well, Governor, what's happening, were you doublecrossed?"

Cargo seemed anxious to get away from the telephone. He was heading for the Santa Fe city jail to talk with incoming prisoners right away.

Soon Benitez's home phone was overloaded with frightened messages from his northern contacts. In hiding, forty-seven-year-old Anselmo Tijerina reported police bursting into homes, apparently searching from a specific checklist. Anselmo wanted to speak to Cargo. Through Benitez the team told him to call the jail.

Now joining Aragon and Burgos at the Inn of the Governors, Devereux called Cargo again. The governor told him curtly that any meeting the next morning was impossible. Police would not allow it. Roadblocks were to remain through the next day. Cargo was busily getting the new prisoners in touch with their families. Many calls northward were also instigated by police in an effort to encourage prisoners' relatives and friends to boycott the Coyote meeting. Arrest was spelled out as the alternative. Constant questions were being asked about Reies Tijerina's whereabouts. Police seemed to feel that it was now or never to catch him.

Cristobal Tijerina was soon brought to Santa Fe in handcuffs, charged with unlawful assembly, carrying a deadly weapon, extortion, and injury to animals in connection with the Echo Amphitheater incident. Martinez was also charged with firearms violation. Already his father Juan and grandfather Jose had been arrested. After an hour-long talk with Cargo, Cristobal informed a police guard:

"I'll be out of here in three hours—your boss, the governor, will get me out. We got him 2,300 votes."

CONFRONTATION AT COYOTE

The unlawful assembly charge related to the meeting on May 14 in Tierra Amarilla. Sanchez told reporters that evening that other Alianza notables were being sought for unlawful assembly on April 14, when he understood the Coyote conference had been conceived.

Soon after midnight Anselmo Tijerina contacted Cargo, who was still greeting prisoners. Their few words were apparently of no consequence. About that hour what remained of the Albuquerque Alianza leadership asked Benitez for an emergency meeting with the governor. In the early hours of the morning it was arranged for them to arrive at the state capitol a few hours later, at 9 a.m. As yet, the Alianza had not officially called off the Coyote meeting.

Coyote is a fairly typical Rio Arriba hamlet. A quarter of its 250 to 300 residents receive welfare support. A handful of its family heads operate small farms or run a few head of cattle and sheep.

Within its collection of small, metal-roofed homes these Spanish-speaking men feel the emotions common to poor northerners. When they must retrieve their impounded cattle and pay a fine after the animals have broken into the 1,400,000-acre Kit Carson National Forest they become bitter. When they are forbidden to cut stove wood in the federal domain without a permit but witness large logging firms move into ancestral lands, they become frustrated. When they are told that their sheep cannot pasture in one location for two nights in a row, or bed down closer than 300 feet from a stream, they become angry.

They resent the Forest Service's concept of the greatest good for the greatest number of people when they cannot get it out of their heads that this "multiple use policy" is making them receive the loathed ten-pound brown paper bag of welfare powdered milk. Finally, they still carry the memory, difficult for an Anglo to understand, that this land was a Spanish pueblo's holding, never to be sold, always to be enjoyed and to yield communally.

"That is the feeling they still have in their hearts," explained a sheepherder near Coyote, "even if they don't say anything."

Many of the townsfolk have left for migrant work outside New

Mexico. The average family income remains less than $1,500 a year. The roads are mostly impassable in spring and fall. As daylight broke on June 3, 1967, the one paved turnoff to Coyote was seeing unusually heavy traffic.

Early Saturday morning police with riot helmets and shotguns were guarding roadblocks on most accesses to the village. The gate of the school grounds—site of the scheduled rally—had been chained and padlocked. Awake through the busy night, reporters were comparing arrest tallies.

As the time approached for Cargo's emergency meeting with Alianza spokesmen in Santa Fe, the Alianza members began trickling into Coyote. Outside the school grounds they mingled with an almost equal number of heavily armed lawmen. One young Alianzan found "state police and some guys who said they were from the FBI. . . . They started checking our cars because, they said, somebody tipped them off we had our cars full of dynamite, guns, ammunition. . . . They gave me a little white paper that said anybody who wanted to take over the land was a Communist."

Soon the crowd had grown to almost 100. Some strolled to an older structure behind the school. Another Tijerina brother, scholarly-looking Ramon, in from his home state of Texas for the meeting, had been picked up at dawn when his car was forced off the road. During the night police had not hidden their fervor to find Reies. Ramon said that his brother was close by, but afraid to come out because "two men have been hired to kill him."

Anselmo Tijerina, also picked up and held on a firearms violation that morning, gave no clues about his brother's hiding place. Marshal Naranjo and his son, Sheriff Benny Naranjo, said they had an idea which house he was holed up in, but they did not explain why they never descended on the site.

Rumors abounded that Reies had been secretly arrested, had run off to Mexico, or would leap police barricades by helicopter and be arrested in full view of his followers.

A quarter of an hour late, the white car bearing the Alianza representatives picked me up at the California team's motel in Santa Fe that morning. After Friday night's reversal the Alianzans had grown suspicious. My presence was felt to be insurance against treachery during their conference in the governor's office. And if policemen did come out from behind the drapes to arrest them, at least I would be obliged to report it.

True to Cargo's word, the car had encountered no roadblocks. In front were Benitez and his young wife. Crammed into the back seat sat Eduardo Chavez, Santiago Anaya, and F. M. Cassaus.

Treasurer of the Alianza until it technically disbanded, Chavez is a short, dapper bachelor with piercing eyes and a shining smile. He lives on the outskirts of Albuquerque with his eighty-seven-year-old mother, for whom he chops wood, draws water, and trims the oil lamps. Anaya wore work clothes and heavy boots from his maintenance duties at the Sandia Corporation. He had been the Alianza's vice-president. Cassaus was an elderly Alianza regular. His dark glasses, double-breasted suit, and garrulous glad-handing proved to be his trademarks.

It had drizzled during the night. We walked across the damp pavement to the capitol's locked metal doors. A small, old janitor opened them with his passkey. "Viva la justicia," he dared to whisper as we passed.

Cargo was in rolled-up shirtsleeves and without a necktie when we were all finally ushered into his office. He seemed professionally aware that his visitors belonged to the constituency which had placed him in that room. He told them to pull armchairs close around his desk. Then he noticed me, asked my business, and wondered if the Alianzans want me to stay. The New Mexico bureau chief of the Associated Press was already there with pad and pencil ready. Anaya said I was to remain.

Before the talk began, however, Cargo walked over to a cardboard carton. Extracting some objects with packing straw still dangling, he handed each of the Alianza leaders a glass ashtray as a souvenir of their visit to the governor's office. They thanked him formally. He took a breath and tried to appear relaxed, bantering about his "coyotes"—children of mixed Anglo and Spanish-American blood. A little agitated, Chavez stared at his clasped hands, then broke in:

"Well, Governor, what about this problem we have here, that is facing us?"

"If you have peaceable meetings, with no violence, I'll go, I'll sit right there," replied Cargo.

Addressing the governor as "Your Excellency," Anaya protested that the Coyote plans had been only to "put up port of entry signs, just put the signs up, there was no intention to make violence." He was particularly bothered by "the federal agents riding us. Your Excellency, what we don't understand is why they're looking so hard for Reies, why they're bothering his wife."

When Sanchez's name was mentioned, Cassaus burst out: "Is he the God of the world?"

Anaya formally noted Cargo's particular appeal to the Spanish-American people, and Cargo replied:

"I've done more for the Spanish than anyone in a hundred years. . . . I think that if you have no meeting this weekend the charges might be dropped."

"I don't care if I die!" Cassaus exploded. "If they want a revolution, we are ready."

The governor reiterated that if their meetings were peaceful, "You can yell as loud as you want."

A tentative agreement was finally reached for a cooling-off period through the weekend, and a meeting at 10 a.m. the following Wednesday with Cargo inviting Reies Tijerina. The governor also offered the three men passes to go north to disperse the crowd gathered at Coyote. They declined.

Then Cargo asked them to telephone to the north that he was not going to show up at Coyote.

"After Monday, then we'll see from there," he finished vaguely, seeing us to the door. Perhaps his mind was on his flight the next day to his home state, Michigan, and a scheduled conference with his friend Governor George Romney.

In Coyote the assembled police, Alianza members, and press heard Cargo announce on the radio at 10:30 that Saturday morning that he was not coming. He requested motorists "not to go into that part of the state." He revealed that he had undertaken an intermediary role and mentioned the possibility of a Wednesday meeting with the Alianza and its leader. The rain picked up again. Everyone started to go home.

Cargo explained his plea. "I don't want them to get into any violence. I know most of these people from campaigning around the state. A lot of them have been clients of mine."

One Alianzan at Coyote, Korean War medal winner Jose Madril of Velarde, said after the broadcast, "We are here peacefully. They who have confused this issue are the state police. They are armed, we are not."

Back in the capitol, State Police Chief Black had waited patiently in the reception lounge while Cargo met the Alianza representatives. He was pleased there had been no "incidents." He doubted that anyone of importance "got through the blocks into Coyote." In a later press report he thanked the people of Rio Arriba County and singled out his own captains "for bringing about this peaceful settlement."

Praise also came from Sanchez for the official handling of the meeting. "I can't say how proud I am of the state police." One of his investigators echoed much public feeling about Sanchez's strategy: "He had guts."

Another lawman was not so sure of the wisdom of the heavy fist. Sheriff Benny Naranjo leaned against a car as the Coyote crowd thinned out.

"I don't know," he told a newsman. "I think these arrests were a big mistake. Maybe they stopped something, but I don't know. Maybe we'll find out."

The abortive gathering at Coyote had in fact given rise to another less publicized get-together. One man who brought his family to Coyote discovered "a whole tribe of policemen blocking the entrance." He recalled that then someone from Canjilon had invited everyone to his *ranchito* where nobody would be bothered because it was private property. A barbeque and a swim were offered.

"He said we could go prepare the grounds and let everybody know of the change of scene. The people decided we should have the barbeque on the fifth of June, Monday, and that's how it stood."

Tijerina himself had been informed hourly of all these developments. Sanchez's announcement of three warrants outstanding for him, and his fears of assassination, kept him behind the scenes. In an interview in his hideout after the raid on the courthouse he went back over his memory of that Saturday:

"At this time I noticed that the people was furious like never before. By Saturday night we decided that we should not publish our activities anymore. In a short meeting attended by about seventy-five people we decided that we had to make a citizen's arrest of the person who was tampering and abusing our constitutional rights, Mr. Alfonso Sanchez.

"We had been told by a very competent lawyer from Washington, D.C., that we could as citizens arrest any officer, state or federal, whom we saw that was violating any particular law. We had in our possession official warrants of arrest given to us by said lawyer. . . . We had them at Coyote meeting but then they were taken back to Albuquerque by our people. . . . There was a great deal of confusion. The main leaders were being jailed and one of the members left for Albuquerque with the warrants. But we succeeded in getting hold of one for the person of Alfonso Sanchez."

Another source suggests that this warrant was already filled out, a plan devised before the Coyote gathering. If Sanchez had appeared there, "arrest papers" would have been served on him. Now, however, the San Joaquin grant's "Department of Vigilance" was preparing to select about twenty men, mostly volunteers, to serve the papers in a body. Sympathizers would act as scouts inside Tierra Amarilla. In a pickup truck, a Ford sedan, and a station wagon the chosen "officers"—armed with pistols, rifles, and shotguns—would leave from Canjilon Monday for their mission at the Rio Arriba County courthouse.

6

ILLUSION
OF
TRUCE

The eleventh-hour pacification truce effected Saturday morning between Governor Cargo and the trio of Alianza leaders appeared to have cleared the air of danger. The Alianza had apparently been pacified. This was a disastrous illusion.

The Friday night offensive had deeply wounded Alianza pride. The Alianza representatives who conferred with Cargo, as well as their jailed compatriots, had been further humiliated when they were pressed into telephoning friends and relatives to steer clear of Coyote. Anyone who believed that the tenuous agreement between Cargo and the elderly Alianzans would end up in a face-to-face talk between the governor and Tijerina had not learned two lessons of the last few days. First, the governor could not answer for his lawmen's decisions. Second, an entirely different mood and unreliable communications had separated the Alianza remnants in Albuquerque from their hunted comrades in the north.

At midday Saturday, Joe Benitez received a carefully routed message from Reies Tijerina himself. Reies was worried about

71

Cristobal. Was there any "political reason" why bond could not be posted for his younger brother? A call to Cargo brought the answer that bail was going to be set. Reies also wanted to know if the three warrants outstanding for him—two charges of unlawful assembly under the state's old anti-riot act, a third with three counts: extortion, unlawful assembly, and illegally shooting a deer and a cow—could be rescinded. He wished "to come into the open" on Monday or Tuesday.

Later Saturday afternoon Benitez telephoned Cargo again to ask his intervention in the matter of bailing prisoners and getting clearance for Tijerina to surface. The governor would do what he could, but cautioned that he had been "doublecrossed" before. He assured Benitez that he would remain in his mansion through the day in case Tijerina wanted to talk personally.

Tijerina had also said to Benitez that if things went badly he might like to meet a small group that included a journalist. These telephone conversations were arranged through a relay system. Reies's teenage daughter Rosa was presumed to be the courier, taking Benitez's answers to her father by car and foot, then returning a response by another phone booth.

Through the remaining hours of Saturday little occurred. Cargo prepared to fly for his meeting with Romney in Michigan. He had already disclosed that his wife and children were visiting her family in Belen, New Mexico, under "informal" police protection because five Alianza members lived nearby. Bail had been set for Cristobal and another man at $5,000 as both were already charged in connection with the Echo Amphitheater incident. About nine others were being held under bonds ranging up to $500.

Meanwhile another political figure in the state had quietly shown up in town: powerful U.S. Senator Joseph M. Montoya. Checking into La Fonda for his address Saturday night before the New Mexico Disabled American Veterans convention, he was noticed all afternoon in dining-room conferences with various local officials. Montoya stayed publicly aloof from the crisis over the Coyote meeting, but there is little doubt that he was following each step.

Cargo's inroads into Democratic northern bastions had been a thorn in Montoya's side. As the state's leading *patron*, Montoya's diminishing hold on his ethnic kinsmen signaled the possible end of an era. Montoya had once paid courteous attention to Alianza pleas, going along with the idea of a land-grant reevaluation. But he had reappraised the situation shortly after he was elected to the Senate in 1964. Now the leader of the creaking Democratic machine was lying low, getting readings on Tijerina's political influence from law enforcement confidants. Soon he would make his underlying concern apparent.

Those who believed the "cooling-off" period would be observed had also not appreciated the highly centralized nature of the Alianza's leadership. Whether because of Tijerina's own fury or that of his muffled followers, the furtive meeting was held in Coyote and the last-resort tactic unanimously approved: the "citizen's arrest" of Alfonso Sanchez. The Canjilon Ranger Station was less than a mile from the small ranch earmarked for the Alianza barbeque on Monday, and its personnel noticed unusual movements of people and cars that evening. Something was stirring. It was thought to be only the aftermath of the past night's excitement.

On Sunday morning Alianza sympathizers were having problems bailing their people out of the Santa Fe city jail. Over the next months bailing was to become an art for dedicated "outside" Alianzans. Obstructions this weekend were typical.

Before dawn the would-be bondsmen drove south from their homes to Santa Fe. They had already spent busy hours securing property bonds, certified deeds, and appraisals of property to be put as assurance that the prisoners would not abscond. At the jail they learned that either Sanchez or Sheriff Naranjo would have to sign the documents before the prisoners could be released. From locked office to unresponsive private home they drove as far as Ojo Caliente, forty miles north of Santa Fe, to no avail. By nightfall most of the prisoners were still locked up. Their bail seekers at last obtained Naranjo's signature. When they returned to Santa Fe at

10 that night, however, they were told they could not place more than one name on a single release. By then it was too late to revisit Naranjo's home.

Sunday newspapers played up the collapse of the Coyote gathering. The "ballyhooed showdown . . . fell flat." "Steam went out of the members of the Alianza Federal. . . ." Less than a fifth of the 500 predicted participants had showed up, and they had obligingly trickled home after Cargo's radio request. Editorials praised the authorities again for "quick action" which had "nipped in the bud Friday night the explosive situation at Coyote."

State police were lauded for having "beat Tijerina to the punch." Sanchez was credited with having designed the effective "bust." The round of backslapping did not include the governor, but his "fence-straddling" negotiation efforts bothered some conservative commentators. One with a dim view of the projected Wednesday meeting hoped Cargo "will avoid playing both ends against the middle and will emphatically make it clear that the Alliance should quit its theatrics."

Another Sunday story revealed that just minutes before Cargo's emergency session with the California consultants on Friday evening he had given his aide, Larry Prentice, a message: Major General John Pershing Jolly was to place one unit of the National Guard on standby duty. This story provided another example of the peculiar ambivalence that Cargo exhibited throughout these days. At 7 a.m. Saturday he was said to have announced canceling his coming meeting with the Alianza representatives. Perhaps to evade press surveillance during the touchy discussions, he told reporters then that he had no plans to talk to anyone. Two hours later he met the Albuquerque delegation.

In the midst of the Friday night mass arrests, Cargo had commented with exasperation, "They did what I told them not to do," referring to the zeal with which the police had acted. He had also alluded to strong evidence that civil rights were violated. But during a prerecorded radio broadcast on Sunday the governor was cautious as he tried to pour oil on the troubled waters. He fell back on the safe recitation of rural woes which could give rise to an Alianza.

"I can sympathize with the people involved," he said. "They are very, very poor." But he could never condone the Alianza's violence. He defended his reception of the Alianza protesters in April: An offer to channel their grievances did not "legalize" a hopeless cause.

The rest of Sunday was given to uneasy post-mortems. Cargo left at noon for Santa Fe airport in the company of a political opponent, State Representative Bobby Mayfield. Mayfield remembers that Cargo admitted hearing of an Alianza arms cache—automatic weapons, hand grenades, and machine guns. Six months later, as an aspirant for Cargo's office, Mayfield chastised the governor for being so positive that "these people won't do anything while I'm out of the state." The mysterious arsenal was to worry Sanchez later on, but it never materialized.

With Cargo airborne for Michigan, the next public development was arraignment for the Coyote prisoners. This had been scheduled for 9:30 on Monday morning in the Tierra Amarilla courthouse.

The seat of Rio Arriba County is named for the micaceous, glinty-golden clay which Spanish decorators brushed onto the lower portions of their whitewashed adobe rooms. Tierra Amarilla (Yellow Earth) was once the center for the Ute and Jicarilla Apache Indian agencies. Since 1880 it has been the county seat.

Its bastardized palazzo courthouse was built in 1923 for $46,000. The stolid structure would have been far the most imposing in town even if some whimsical painter had not painted light pink on its walls and baby blue on its window borders, colonnades, and molded floral wreaths.

On the morning of Monday, June 5, 1967, Judge James Scarborough was preparing to make the two-hour trip from Santa Fe to Tierra Amarilla to preside at the arraignments. Shortly after 8 a.m. the last four prisoners in the Santa Fe jail were brought downstairs to be checked out for transportation to meet him there. Griz-

75

zled and drawn, Cristobal Tijerina and his friends received their possessions from the booking desk. Most wore working clothes. A photographer focused in on Cristobal. "You'd better not," his subject warned. There was no idle talk. Escorted to the waiting police cars, the men were taken to Tierra Amarilla.

Settled in his office, Alfonso Sanchez was glowing as his work day began Monday. Considering the Tierra Amarilla arraignments a routine matter (he explained the next day), he had assigned his deputy, Norman Neel, to go north for the state. Again he hailed the "fast and forceful" police tactics.

Usually Sanchez would speak as an underdog driving his meagerly financed office to protect three counties from the forces of corruption. But this morning there was a strident confidence in his words. He recalled that Tijerina was still under federal order to appear in court the following morning.

"I just hope no one has told him not to show up," he said severely. "We can't bend the laws to suit the people."

Sanchez had little sympathy for conciliatory moves. "There can be no negotiations," he said of Cargo's Wednesday meeting. "You can't negotiate crimes. There can be no promises, not even from the governor. The sooner they find that out the better." The district attorney thereby clarified any confusion about who was responsible for Friday night's arrests.

"They've been coddled too much," he continued. "My job is to carry out the law made by the legislature. I will not tolerate people killed and property pilfered. That is Communism." He suggested that if the Alianza did not want to abide by court decisions, "they can go to Cuba."

But Cargo's conciliatory tendencies were still on his mind.

"I won't sit around and see anyone blackmail the governor. The law applies to everyone; there are no favorites. That's the reason this thing has gone so far. . . . My opinion has been that there is no jurisdiction on me or on anyone to forestall arrests."

For the moment Sanchez was reluctant to spread before the public the confiscated Alianza documents and arms. He would only pique curiosity by saying that his investigators were poring over the "six or eight foot-and-a-half-long file boxes of membership cards" and "finding many things."

Later it appeared that Sanchez's assurance was actually covering private anxiety. As far back as Saturday he had firmly believed: "I told them [state police], 'Until you've gotten Reies Lopez you haven't gotten anyone.' " Now, this Monday morning, he called Justice Department officials at about 10 o'clock. FBI Agent Ed Martin told him that Tijerina was known to be at Tobias Leyba's ranch in Canjilon. Sanchez wanted to know why they didn't pick him up on federal warrants still outstanding from the Echo Amphitheater incident. Quickly Sanchez phoned Chief Black. If the FBI information was true, he said, he wanted Tijerina arrested posthaste. Black replied that he would need warrants. "Pick him up," answered Sanchez, promising to have the warrants ready by noon. But, remembers the district attorney, "that's where Cargo came in."

Monday's newspapers sustained their endorsement of the weekend's hard line. The *New Mexican* emphasized that "meaningful discussions cannot be developed during a potentially explosive situation." Embittered northerners, it argued, "certainly can find some leadership which does not have to find a crisis to make themselves heard." But it disagreed with Sanchez on Cargo's capacity for mediation: the governor was in the "best position" for the task. It hoped the upcoming Wednesday encounter "will prove to be only the first of a series to explore the matter thoroughly."

Before noon on Monday Devereux ran into a "pale, rattled" Benitez in the governor's waiting lounge. He was disturbed about the "bail-bonding games" which had forced his Alianza friends to chase their tails with increasing irritation. It was Benitez's impression that a countermove was being prepared.

Throughout Sunday there had been more talk about Tijerina's interest in an interview with a reporter. A small plane, horseback, and footpath had been suggested as ways of getting to his hideout. On Monday morning I alerted my editor, Bill Feather, to this farfetched project. We exchanged "Now really" smirks.

The Canjilon picnic, spontaneously born when the Coyote meeting failed, had begun Monday morning. On a sloping pasture broken by sheep-rubbed tree trunks people began collecting for the barbeque before noon. They later told police they had not moved from the spot all day.

Apparently, despite Sanchez's information, state police were still searching for Tijerina, but Chief Black told newsmen, "I don't think he can be flushed out until after the arraignments today." Black had now withdrawn the twenty-five extra officers who had been on special duty since Coyote.

The land-grant leader later told me of his movements that Monday:

"At Canjilon people were selected by ballot to make the arrest [of Sanchez]. When they were trying to arrest him around Monday at 3 p.m. . . . ."

Interrupting, I asked Tijerina why at that hour.

"Because we heard on the radio that the arraignments would be in Tierra Amarilla. We had scouts in the Tierra Amarilla area who kept us informed of the court proceedings."

In Tierra Amarilla about forty spectators sat in the rickety courtroom pews as the prisoners were led before Judge Scarborough's bench. The hearing had been postponed from 9:30 a.m. to 1:30 p.m. because Sheriff Naranjo was late in coordinating transportation for the Alianzans. Inside the second-floor court chamber, the size of a large schoolroom, the rain on the old roof rattled so loudly that Scarborough had to halt the proceedings until it quieted down. Sheriff Naranjo served as translator. It was an uneventful procedure as the judge advised the prisoners of their rights, continued their bonds, and advised all but Cristobal to get attorneys—he was already represented by Albuquerque Lawyer Carlos Sedillo. Scarborough can recall "no unpleasantness at the hearing. I was told later there appeared to be a little hostility toward the court at the beginning, but this dissolved as it proceeded."

By midafternoon eight prisoners had been released. The audience of about forty had dispersed. Scarborough had said he would not be back up in these parts for at least three weeks. Sanchez's assistant, Norman Neel, was already on the highway to Santa Fe. Cristobal's lawyer, Sedillo, was chatting with State Police Officer Nick Saiz who was scanning the courthouse bulletin board. Judge Scarborough stood in the rear of the second-floor courtroom conversing with a son-in-law of one of the defendants.

Fifteen minutes after court had been dismissed UPI Reporter Larry Calloway put a dime into the courthouse's public phone. It was in a homemade booth with ordinary house siding up to the reporter's waist. Above that window glass enclosed him. Calloway was dictating a news story from notes of the routine session he had just covered upstairs. Behind him he heard a gunshot. He turned to see a drawn pistol and plunged to the wooden floor, still gripping the receiver.

"Some guy just took a shot at someone," he said to his editor, 150 miles south in Albuquerque.

"Who was it?"

"I don't know. I'm on the floor. They'll get him in a minute."

Calloway ventured a peek over his protective wall. Armed men "in work clothes or army fatigues" were filling the hallway. The pounding of heavy boots moved up the stairs. Yelling and gunfire broke out all around.

"It's a raid!" Calloway said. "I'm scared as hell."

He let the receiver fall back. His editor heard eight more shots before the line went dead.

In his state capitol office Executive Assistant Larry Prentice was called to the telephone by a secretary. He picked up the receiver and heard a male voice whisper, "They're shooting at us. Shooting live bullets at us. Under a table. Can't speak up . . . they'll kill me." It was Judge Scarborough's court recorder calling from behind two bolted doors. The first lock was about to be torn into jagged metal by carbine slugs.

At the *New Mexican* office Jim Neal, the news editor, picked up

his head at a bell clanging on the interbureau teletype machine.
Correspondent Doyle Akers was sending a bulletin from Espanola.

"Jailbreak!" exclaimed Neal.

Details were few. Gunplay in the Tierra Amarilla courthouse.
One wounded man at least. Very likely escaping prisoners. Akers
was off for a firsthand look.

A few minutes later Neal and I were speeding toward Tierra
Amarilla, about ninety miles to the north, to see for ourselves. I
copied the radio bulletins breaking in:

"One officer injured . . . Shiprock state policeman . . . men
holed up in court building . . . may be hostages in basement
. . . Chief Black sixty-five miles north of scene . . . started
about 3 o'clock. . . ."

7

AFTERNOON
OF
GUNS

The "TA Raid," as the courthouse attack became known, struck with shattering suddenness. Reconstruction of its ninety minutes remained problematic long after the alleged perpetrators were behind bars. Its fury concentrated within the chambers, stairways, and offices of the courthouse building and out onto the dusty parking area. Its action spread along the winding, dipping main road, and eventually drained out the town's two or three exits.

A somnolent, decaying village, Tierra Amarilla lies lazily picturesque just after you top a rise thick with ponderosas, as you come in from the south. From the highway you notice its spread of buildings just as you see the wooden historical plaque pointing to the fastest entrance into town. The sign informs you that some descendants of the Martinez who was first awarded the Tierra Amarilla grant still dwell here. On this particular day three of those descendants had just been arraigned in their home town's courthouse.

Fenced pastures soon break into smaller plots. Run-down farm machinery settles into high grass around frame houses with rusting roofs. You come upon the formidable antique courthouse from behind. Cords of fresh split wood stacked log-cabin fashion behind the bleaching pink and blue building and a gaping hole to its basement woodshed indicate the era of most of the town's appliances. Over an abandoned main street store facade the words "Billiard Hall" can barely be deciphered from flaking paint and wind-worn wood. On June 5, 1967, the garage-size movie house was advertising *El Fugitivo* and *El Rifle Implacable*.

Beside the courthouse stands one of TA's jewels, a boarded-up, thick-walled adobe hotel boasting the region's architectural specialty: mail-order "gingerbread" woodwork for second-storey balconies, stairways, eaves and gables.

"It was made for it," commented out-of-state journalists as they strolled the weatherbeaten street later, absorbing mood.

Trickling information from the besieged town pinpointed the arrival of raggle-taggle assault vehicles at 3 p.m. About an hour and a half later they departed with two bound hostages—heavyset Pete Jaramillo, Sheriff Naranjo's deputy, and young Larry Calloway, a UPI reporter—racing for the tiny hamlet of Canjilon twenty minutes away.

Throughout the ensuing five days frightened witnesses were to resurrect their fragmentary glimpses of what had taken place. Sensational testimony would be given during a hearing two months off. Further details would be added during an unusually long preliminary hearing six months later. A full year and a half after the shootout, it was hoped that the details of the raid would begin to fall into place during the first actual trial to examine it. But on that afternoon when outsiders were rushing to the town with their car radios going full blast, all the pieces were in the air.

Doyle Akers, the first reporter to arrive, turned off Highway 84 at the wooden plaque and flew down the grade into Tierra Amarilla.

"At the bottom of the hill," he later wrote, "I saw Deputy Pete Jaramillo's distinctive car coming towards me. I slowed and moved towards the shoulder because Pete and I seldom pass without stopping to exchange the time of day. . . . His car moved leisurely and at one point seemed on the verge of stopping, but I didn't see Pete inside. I could only tell there were three or four men. Well, perhaps he had loaned it to someone. . . . At that moment I was thirty seconds from the courthouse. Pete was in that car. An M-2 carbine was against the back of his head. A pistol shoved into his side. His own handcuffs bound his arms behind his back."

Akers, driving north from Espanola, had come upon the tail end of the action. Without knowing it he had passed Jaramillo and Calloway being abducted in Jaramillo's sleek green GTO car. Their captors were Baltazar Martinez, twenty-two years old, and Baltazar Apodaca, an even fifty years older than Martinez. They were picking up the rear of the vehicles from the courthouse.

As Jim Neal and I hurtled toward Tierra Amarilla from Santa Fe, news broadcasts described the raid's widening circles. Judge Scarborough had managed to get word to Santa Fe of a "jailbreak." Aides were desperately trying to find Governor Cargo in Michigan. Lieutenant Governor E. Lee Francis was acting in his stead. One of the two seriously wounded lawmen was Nick Saiz, a state policeman from Shiprock whose photograph had been prominent in the newspapers during the Coyote incident. Roadblocks were going up everywhere.

Riot-helmeted state police were passing us at tremendous speeds, sirens screaming and shotgun barrels visible out of windows. Now came a bulletin that the National Guard, in full field gear, was being called out. From here on it was dead radio air. Rain clouds and high clearing sky alternated over the mesas and distant mountains. It was 4:30 in the afternoon.

About that time Akers was entering Tierra Amarilla, perplexed about the lack of recognition from Jaramillo's car. The deputy sheriff had in fact tried to signal him.

"I shook my head," he told Akers later. "Didn't you see me? I tried to warn you."

He and newsman Calloway had just been taken on a hair-raising tour of Tierra Amarilla by their two captors in a pickup truck, during the occupation of the courthouse. When the raiders had cleared all office workers from the courthouse rooms, apparently everyone had been herded into the County Commission office at gunpoint. The deputy sheriff and the reporter were selected as hostages by the two Baltazars, who then made their survey of the town. After appropriating Jaramillo's private car, they followed the route out of town their friends had taken about fifteen minutes earlier. But first they stopped for gas. Martinez looked at the filling station attendant, Mike Romero Jr., and showed his carbine and pistol.

"This is the first time I ever had a gun pointed at me," Romero said later that night. "I was so nervous I couldn't find the dipstick to the engine."

"Your best gas and oil," Martinez ordered. He took a $20 bill from Calloway's wallet, packing the returned change into the reporter's coat pocket.

When Akers pulled into the parking area before the courthouse, it was eerily deserted. Then he noticed the police automobiles. "Cars 26 and 27 looked like hand grenades had gone off inside." Walking around with his camera, he noticed to his right another riddled police car, its tires shot flat. There was blood staining the sidewalk below the sheriff's office and a bullet hole through the glass of the front door.

The blood had been spilled when the courthouse janitor and jailer, Eulogio Salazar, was shot while in the office with his boss, Sheriff Naranjo. A courthouse employee who had leaped from a window saw the jailer "staggering out. He was bent over and moaning. There was a guy behind him with a rifle ready to give it to him again." Salazar had been hit in the cheek as he hurled himself through the window of the sheriff's office. Staggering around the parking lot, he was shot a second time before lurching to the safety of a relative's house. He had been carried in the bouncing bed of a pickup truck to the Espanola hospital sixty miles away.

Akers warily advanced into the building. It was "like walking into a tomb." The halls and the offices were empty, but most of the doors hung wide open. Akers pulled at the closed door of the County Commission room. "Twenty pairs of frightened eyes greeted me."

For almost an hour and a half the office workers had been sitting stone-silent. Some of their fellow employees in the assessor's office had made the ten-foot plunge over the windowsill and now were behind the locked doors of private houses in town.

"Have they gone?" A voice broke the silence.

"Who?" Akers whispered back.

"Anybody upstairs, downstairs?"

Akers saw Sheriff Benny Naranjo, wobbly from an earlier blow on the head. The sheriff said, "Judge Scarborough, he's upstairs."

They sped to the second floor.

Court had been cleared and Scarborough was conversing in the rear of the courtroom. From downstairs he heard a noise "like a pistol shot, or a plank being dropped." This was probably the shot that knocked State Policeman Nick Saiz to the floor, a .45 bullet in his chest. Mrs. Monroe Fox, the wife of a blind attorney, rushed back into the courtroom with her husband and his seeing-eye dog.

"Then I heard the noise of shots, lots of commotion, loud talk, and scuffling."

Escorting the Foxes and Court Recorder Mike Rice into his private chambers, Judge Scarborough saw Undersheriff Dan Rivera in the courtroom. Did Rivera want to come with them?

"He didn't answer, just went out the door." The undersheriff had already latched the main courtroom entrance. Scarborough then locked an antechamber door as well as the bolt to his own office. Inside they were very quiet.

"Every time someone coughed it sounded like it was tearing the house down."

From the corridor outside someone shouted, "Come out! Come out!"

"Then they cut loose with a machine gun at the door," Judge

85

Scarborough said. "I've heard a machine gun and fired one, and this sure sounded like one."

The raiding party had reached the antechamber, but advanced no further. Apparently the silence from behind the inner chamber door deterred the searchers.

Undersheriff Dan Rivera's head had snapped around at the sounds of two shots. Leaving the courtroom, he saw what looked like a drunk down the stairs. Then he quickly walked into the jury room, locking it behind him. He fell back as the door was shot open. Discovered within, he was knocked to the floor with a rifle butt. As he was moved downstairs and ordered to open the jail cells, blood from his broken nose and gashed skull smeared the plaster. Stepping over Sheriff Naranjo on the floor, he picked up the keys and stepped back over the prone form. He opened the basement jail and then was told to join the others in the County Commission room. At his pleading, he was soon released for medical attention.

Judge Scarborough cracked open his door. The jamb and lock of the antechamber were shot to pieces. Mike Rice snaked his way to an adjoining office and dialed two Santa Fe numbers. He couldn't get through to the state police. About 3:30 p.m. he had Lawrence Prentice on the line and, in Scarborough's words, "told him we were beleaguered and embattled."

Outside the courthouse, according to the judge, "cars kept pulling up and the occupants would call to the men inside, talk to them a minute, and then drive off." About this time Martinez and Apodaca were making their tour of the town with their two captives. Citizens of Tierra Amarilla stood disbelieving while Martinez, in his red battle beret, sighted his carbine at the bubble lights of the police cars. A shot over their heads shooed them home. In houses all along the street families crouched fearfully behind bolted doors or peered through living room curtains.

The judge and his friends endured a seemingly interminable wait until Sheriff Naranjo and County Manager Joe Branch came up the stairs. The raiders had gone.

86

Akers remained at the courthouse interviewing dazed employees. "I don't know what happened," one official mumbled. "They came in here and shot a state police officer right there." He pointed to a blood smear on the floor near the antique steam radiator in the main hall. "Then someone called an ambulance from Parkview [a nearby settlement] and I helped put him on a stretcher and into the ambulance."

After lying on the floor for nearly an hour, Saiz had been rushed to the Espanola hospital for emergency treatment. There he was still conscious and described getting hit:

"This bunch came up and stood around me. I did not even know they had guns. This guy pulled the gun and says, 'Give me your gun.' I went to give him my gun and he shot me. I fell down. I told him, 'Why did you shoot me? I was going to give you my gun.' I should have shot him."

Saiz's lung and left shoulder bone had been pierced. He was of two minds about his assailant.

"I did not run from no son-of-a-bitch. He just walked up and shot me." He would not reveal the man's name. "Don't worry, I'll get him." Then, from his stretcher, he went on:

"This guy that shot me was pretty nice. He got me an ambulance. He could have left me there to die. The first shot went off was at me. Then they started shooting up the courthouse. They took my bullets, my handcuffs and my gun. It was a $135 gun. I bought it myself. That's what hurts, you know."

A frightened clerk from the assessor's office would only tell Akers, "We heard the gunfire and jumped out of the window."

Naranjo, his western-style white shirt splattered with blood from his head wound, remembered:

"Shots were fired through the open window of my office. I hit the floor, but Eulogio [Salazar] jumped out the window. That's when they shot him, I guess."

The slender, crew-cut young sheriff had torn off his shoulder patch and hidden his metal badge.

"They came in here and ordered me out. They knocked me

down and then made us go into the Commission room."

For much of the time Naranjo had lain face down on the wooden floor, a rifle butt slamming him whenever he raised his head a few inches.

Finally Akers strolled outside for more photographing. "The town was still deserted. Nothing moved and there was that gnawing feeling that maybe it wasn't over yet.

"At that instant, two cars turned the corner down by the school. I only saw the barrels of guns sticking out the windows. I dived behind one of the huge columns in front of the courthouse, then chanced another glance. The cars were state police."

Mike Rice's telephone call from Judge Scarborough's chambers had brought the first news of the raid to the governor's office in Santa Fe. His few words caused instant consternation. Nobody knew the number of assailants, but rumors made up for the lack of facts—hostages in the courthouse, released prisoners, tommy guns, grave shootings. Naturally exaggerations were more attractive: At one point at least fifty people were said to be holding the entire town of Tierra Amarilla.

After the initial shock, Acting Governor E. Lee Francis rallied a group around him for a conference. A call was immediately placed to Governor Cargo in Michigan, but he was meeting with Governor Romney and attending a reception. The call did not get through to him till 5 p.m. It appeared that the state police were aware of the shootout half an hour before Rice ever reached Prentice, however. Prentice later told me that when he telephoned the state police with what he thought was the first news of the raid, he was taken aback to learn that Chief Black was already on his way to Tierra Amarilla.

District Attorney Sanchez was in his Santa Fe office at about 3:30 p.m. when he was notified by telephone of the shooting in Tierra Amarilla. With his assistant, E. E. Chavez, he drove north immediately, stopping briefly at the Espanola state police headquarters. From there he sped to Tierra Amarilla, where a woman leaned out of a window and yelled, "Get out of here, you son-of-a-bitch!" Then he drove to where the action had moved, Canjilon.

Acting Governor Francis had assembled Prentice, Secretary of State Ernestine Evans, and Father Robert Garcia, the state OEO director. Devereux listened in on their discussions. Other officials and secretaries were rushing in and out. The lieutenant governor contacted General John Pershing Jolly, commander of the New Mexico National Guard; the Guard's basic northern units had already been alerted. Soon Police Chief Black's voice came over the police radio requesting National Guard assistance. News from the "battle zone" was fragmentary, but a state police walkie-talkie was brought in and Francis was able to speak directly to Black. Jangling phones kept nerves on edge. New people were anxiously milling through the governor's office. The reports from the north were sufficiently disturbing, Francis decided, to justify Black's request. General Jolly was called again and Francis told him to take whatever steps were necessary.

Later there was question over the sequence of these requests. Did Francis have Black's direct request before telling Jolly to move north? Most accounts suggest that he did, but that he had not conferred with Governor Cargo when he made the actual decision. Another says that Governor Cargo telephoned the order that the Guard should not be called until state police on the scene deemed the step necessary. Still a third has the governor, calling from Grand Rapids, approving Francis's ordering the Guard mobilization but demanding they remain on standby until he hurried home.

Once the move had been taken, Francis was relieved. "The main job," he now felt, "is up to Black and his men and Major General Jolly and his guardsmen."

"There were really no more decisions to be made," Prentice agrees.

Another approach to the crisis was being promoted on the same floor of the capitol, however. Father Garcia, his staff, and Devereux instigated the most controversial aspect of the developing raid

89

story. They urged Acting Governor Francis to use his emergency powers to summon sociologist Clark Knowlton from his office at the University of Texas. Knowlton, a forty-eight-year-old specialist in northern New Mexico village history, had known Tijerina since the summer of 1965 when Tijerina had walked into his office at El Paso asking for a copy of Knowlton's paper about the Spanish-American land loss. Since then Knowlton had spoken at every major Alianza gathering and had acquired Tijerina's confidence. With this background, Garcia and Devereux argued, Knowlton offered the best chance of ascertaining Tijerina's intentions.

The acting governor had not made a secret of his desire to establish a "dialogue" with the rebels. "I told them we're ready to talk," he said to a reporter. "I am in constant contact. I've talked to a couple of people up there—not members of the Alianza—to try to get things settled down."

Prentice later described Garcia and Devereux as "underfoot, to put it mildly. When someone's shooting at you, it's no time to start a conversation." Garcia and Devereux, however, had exactly the opposite view. Direct communication with a group that was now undeniably "insurgent" was both defensively and constructively imperative, they tried to persuade Francis. In any case, Knowlton arrived later that night in a state-owned airplane.

"At least to my knowledge," said Prentice, "Francis did not authorize it." Later, when this episode became a political hot potato, the lieutenant governor denied ever granting Garcia permission to clear the aircraft's use. It was Devereux's impression, however, that Francis had provided the go-ahead signal.

Father Garcia now began making covert telephone calls to northern New Mexico and elsewhere. Asked whether his office was contacting an "Alianza backer," Garcia replied, "I wouldn't call him a backer, no. But he understands these people. He can talk to them. And that's what we need now."

Already Prentice had spoken with a housewife in stricken Tierra Amarilla. She gave him a blow-by-blow description of the raid. He considered a flying inspection. But thunderheads, visible even from the state house windows, ruled out any inspection of the troubled area by plane.

Earlier that morning Aragon and Burgos had entered a car with Alex Mercure, director of the migrant-worker HELP program. They were starting a survey of HELP anti-poverty centers in the north. With them was a HELP employee experiencing his first day on the job.

In the far-flung northern communities the four visited various HELP stations. Here villagers with a history of seasonal departures for migrant produce-picking jobs were taking adult education classes in practical mathematics and English. Listening to northern complaints, the team was making investigations under the long-range aspect of the contract that had brought them to New Mexico.

The four men drove into Canjilon about 2:30 p.m. and talked with more local people about their differences with the Forest Service. Then they went on to Tierra Amarilla.

The streets were strangely quiet. They parked and Burgos wandered around taking snapshots. From the courthouse a woman threw open a window and yelled to Aragon to tell her husband not to come for her. Then Jaramillo's car whisked by them and somebody waved from inside. Mecure started driving off and came to a newly erected state police roadblock. Three nervous policemen were sighting guns at his car.

Neal and I still had not managed to get into town. At the historical marker on the highway, Santa Fe Sheriff Eddie Escudero emerged from the cover of his car and ordered us to pull over. We must have unknowingly passed Jaramillo's car with the hostages speeding in the opposite direction. Each time a vehicle came down the road Escudero and his deputy clicked off their rifles' safety catches, and we crouched behind a fender. A few minutes later I saw Devereux screech to a stop in a rented car which Garcia had personally secured for him. He had been sent to give a report from the scene and was allowed to pass through.

TIJERINA and the COURTHOUSE RAID

In town Devereux halted near a "mass of police and police cars." Officers were angrily cramming the courthouse plaza. He noticed the stains of Salazar's blood in the dirt outside, the torn doors of police cars yawning open.

"Everybody looked scared, panicked. There was a feeling of a shock wave in the air," he said. Within the building, firearms bristled. Only one telephone had not been ripped out; it was monopolized by incoming reporters. The interior damage included a mangled safe and a two-way radio transmitter smashed all over the floor.

Devereux meandered down the street in search of an unoccupied telephone. Knocking at a private home, he gained entrance only by promising not to reveal the call's origin. Three terrified families watched him with wide eyes as he called Garcia to report, "It's all over in TA."

Still at the turnoff point, I was paying close attention to the police radio monitor. Escudero and his deputy halted more cars, poking the barrels of their rifles through camper curtains. We heard that Judge Scarborough had been taken to nearby Chama for safety. Concern shifted to the two hostages. We did not know it, but at that moment Jaramillo was walking down a country road with a cocked pistol held to his head by Baltazar Martinez.

Next we learned that the first National Guard contingents from Espanola were readying a convoy for Tierra Amarilla. The raiders were supposedly regrouped near Canjilon. We heard that the police had both Calloway and Jaramillo in sight.

Escudero got in his car and raced southward to the Canjilon turnoff, ten miles away. I gave chase over the dipping road to the small ranching community.

8

ROUNDUP
AT
CANJILON

In Canjilon the cookout planned during the Coyote conference had been in progress since Monday morning. Actually the Alianza parents and their children had been satisfied with sandwiches for lunch. But the host, Tobias Leyba, father of seventeen children, had earmarked a sheep for an afternoon barbeque. Wearing his army fatigue work clothes, he had a sharpened hunting knife ready for the slaughter.

Canjilon was an understandable reserve of Alianza strength. An old community within one corner of the San Joaquin land grant, some of its inhabitants are reputed to be descended from New Mexico's seventeenth-century conquistador hero Don Diego de Vargas and his band, who liberated Santa Fe after Pueblo Indian revolts. Through the years it had become a trading center for farmers and sheep raisers. To outsiders it is a pass-through point for the trout-stocked Canjilon Lakes ten miles away. Residents watch the Anglo fishermen cruise past their homes on weekends to cast freely from banks where they are forbidden to graze livestock.

93

TIJERINA and the COURTHOUSE RAID

The hamlet's population has dropped from about 600 in 1953 to 125 at present. Many of its citizens of working age travel beyond New Mexico in search of produce-picking work because they cannot live year-round under the Forest Service's grazing restrictions. By spring 1967 Canjilon had suffered the loss of 1,000 year-round cattle permits to graze on federal pastures. It had lost twenty free milk-cow grazing permits, as well as all free pasturage for horses and bulls. The total reduction of usable land since 1947 has been 31 per cent. In addition, the treasured Mesa de las Viejas has been denied to local use, even with federal permits. Reseeded, it is believed to be open only to ranchers with extensive cattle operations.

Rival *moradas,* the politico-religious meeting houses of a Catholic fraternal organization, the Penitente Brotherhood, have kept the community of Canjilon in a state of disunity. Finally, the placement of a forest ranger station like a frontier fort on the settlement's outskirts has suggested the presence of a restrictive force.

Canjilon's nucleus is a gas-and-grocery store, a miniscule post office in a private home, and the nearby ranger station. Leyba's *ranchito* occupies a gentle rise about three-quarters of a mile away. His is the last one-storey adobe house before the land swells into wooded hills. During the gathering on the morning of June 5 conversation centered on the weekend's arrests, the frustrating bailing efforts, and today's arraignments. In the early afternoon some men left the picnic for Tierra Amarilla, "to find out what the bond was" for their eight fellow Alianzans, they said.

A schoolteacher named Ruben Dario Salaz, from Alameda, New Mexico, later interviewed twenty-two eyewitnesses in the basement of the Alianza headquarters. He published transcripts of his taped talks in a 15,000-word tabloid called *Tierra Amarilla Shootout.* Salaz gave no names, but his accounts were echoed in depositions taken by the Justice Department and the American Civil Liberties Union.

Two vehicles left Canjilon, according to two of these transcripts.

A car bearing three men arrived in Tierra Amarilla first. Entering the courthouse, the three men "asked to see District Attorney Alfonso Sanchez about the bond money." Just as they were told that Sanchez had not come, "six or seven men entered with black silk masks covering the bottom of their faces. . . . Some of them were wearing straw hats while others wore those little caps with brims at the front. One of them had on a knit shirt."

Dispersing throughout the courthouse, the masked men were soon heard shooting. The three "visitors" from Canjilon and the clerk who had talked to them hit the deck. From that vantage point one of them recognized some Alianza members rushing in. He yelled for them to find cover too. Crawling to the phone booth, he found it occupied "by some sort of reporter" (probably Larry Calloway). Inching back to his companions, the man saw a raider he knew fire his gun until it clicked empty. The gunman said he was using blanks to make noise.

Another gunman made two people kneel while he ran off. The informant saw somebody lying on the floor, then heard window glass shatter over his head. Raising his eyes, he saw masked men on the stairs "bringing down a man who was all bloodied up."

At that he leapt through a window, almost landing on another fugitive. An "automatic weapon" opened up at him and two companions who had joined him. All scattered, the informant running for an arroyo where he cooled his head. He saw two policemen running for the mountains, chased by two other men. Bullets kicked up the dust. Then more masked men ran from the courthouse toward the mountains.

When he got back to the car his friends were huddled underneath. Driving away quickly, they speculated that the invaders had been members of the Mano Negra.

When the second car from Canjilon drew near the courthouse, the shooting had already started. The newcomers went in through the swinging door. They recognized some "Alianza people" and saw other men they did not recognize. At that moment bullets came

95

in their direction. They turned but found themselves trapped by a police car that was disgorging officers who lifted rifles to their shoulders.

Retreating into the building, they too jumped out of windows. Hitting the ground, they made for their car. Rifle fire followed them. Running around a corner, they came on an unoccupied police car full of firearms. "I'm gonna defend myself," one said, and grabbed a gun. His companion followed suit. When another state police car approached, the two "pumped bullets" until it ground into reverse.

The two men then threw down their guns and "ran towards some bushes with the hope of hiding until we could get to our car." When the shooting abated, they went back to their car and took off for Canjilon. Turned back by a roadblock, one of them got out and tried to circle around to Canjilon by walking "in the mountains for maybe five or six hours." Overhead he saw police helicopters circling.

The testimonies taken by Salaz are shot through with half-fact and cover-up. However, apart from those portions where witnesses are clearly trying to avoid incriminating themselves, they provide the best feel for that hysterical afternoon. It does appear that some people came to the courthouse unaware of the action planned. It also seems probable that others were late for the arraignments held that afternoon, or had come to take home those being arraigned. Identification of the various groups that arrived at the building at or about 3 p.m. was never definitively made, down to the very individuals who comprised them. The emotions of revenge, fear, and surprise on the part of both police and visitors—whether innocent or implicated—made the afternoon almost impossible to reconstruct. The overall tale that emerges from Salaz's "case studies" is not a fabrication.

By the time I had followed Sheriff Escudero's car into Canjilon, a collection of armed state policemen were blocking the muddy, rutted dirt road weaving past farmhouses toward Leyba's home. They had just caught up with the vehicle carrying the two hostages, Reporter Larry Calloway and Deputy Sheriff Pete Jaramillo, away from Tierra Amarilla. They were now handcuffing Baltazar Apodaca, one of the two abductors. The heavy-browed, frowning First World War veteran glared at photographers. Calloway stood apart from him, his fingers trembling as he brought a cigaret to his mouth. Then Calloway walked over to Joe Baldonado's gas-and-grocery store. His voice was shaky as he phoned his recent experiences to his wire service in Albuquerque.

Calloway's wrists had been bound with an electric cord torn from a courthouse coffee percolater when Martinez and Apodaca took him, along with Jaramillo, from Tierra Amarilla. In the commandeered GTO with Martinez at the wheel the four men headed out of Tierra Amarilla for Canjilon. Calloway worked at loosening his wrists. Martinez passed a police car and swore as it spun in a U-turn to pursue him. Another boxed him in from the front. Spinning into a soft mud shoulder, the green GTO bogged down. Martinez and Apodaca switched armaments and split up, each taking a hostage for cover.

As they moved off on foot the police tracked them through gunsights. Apodaca jammed a military model .30-caliber carbine against Calloway's nape and guided the reporter by one arm. Across the drenched courtyard of an old adobe church, Martinez moved Deputy Sheriff Jaramillo at the point of his .38-caliber pistol.

"If you shoot me, I'll kill him. I won't go into the gas chamber!" Martinez yelled at the police crouched behind their cars. Soon the two groups were beyond each other's view. Calloway, his wrists now unbound, pretended to stumble and suddenly turned on Apodaca. He got his hand securely on the rifle stock, but Apodaca released two shots into the wet dirt before Calloway tugged the gun free. Police leaped fences to overpower the old man.

Calloway also remembered the earlier moments under fire in the courthouse's telephone booth. From where he hid he heard the

TIJERINA and the COURTHOUSE RAID

wounded policeman, Nick Saiz, moaning. Calloway's fingers pulled the booth's fragile door closed. Then another body on the floor tumbled against it. Sticking his head up above the wooden partition of the telephone booth, Calloway saw Reies Tijerina, black gun drawn, commanding, "Vamonos, muchachos!" ("Let's go, boys!") Discovered by three armed men, the telephone was torn out from above the reporter's head. Grabbed and hustled down the hall, he was placed with the building's collected office workers in the County Commission room. On his way he had noticed the blood everywhere. He had seen the downed policeman's eyes following everything that happened.

For almost twenty minutes Calloway remained in the same fearful state as his fellow prisoners, silently staring straight ahead. Then Baltazar Martinez sallied in, picked out the reporter and Deputy Sheriff Jaramillo. Approaching the front door, Martinez stepped back and blasted at the lock with his carbine. He missed by six inches. Angry, he kicked it open, and then pushed his prisoners into the daylight. Martinez and the aged Apodaca headed for a pickup truck with a plastic crucifix glued to the dashboard.

On the way Martinez let loose with what Calloway guessed was about fifty rounds of carbine bullets, shooting flashily from the hip at three parked police cars. Two blocks further a nervous group of onlookers in front of the old pool hall scattered as Martinez shot over their heads. Martinez jimmied open the trunk of one of the shot-up vehicles. From another he and Apodaca hauled out rifles and shotguns, tossing them into the truck. Driving back to the courthouse in the pickup, they transferred the guns into Jaramillo's own car. Then the escape ride to Canjilon began, interrupted by a detour to display the hostages. A woman spat and said in Spanish: "Trespassers! Take them out and hang them!"

Calloway had a strong impression at that point that Tierra Amarilla's streets were held by rebels. "My God, they've got the whole town," he whispered to Jaramillo.

By the time Calloway had freed himself and called in his story, the

98

sky over Canjilon was murky. A damp chill was in the wind. Now only Jaramillo remained in danger. Young Martinez had maneuvered his human shield onto another farm road and toward a parked car. From out of nowhere the gunman's birdlike mother appeared. Weeping, praying, pleading, she wanted her son to let the deputy go.

Inside the car idling in the muddy trough of the road sat two teenage boys. Baltazar Martinez drove off with them, Jaramillo, and his mother. Two miles south of Canjilon he suddenly slammed on the brakes, jumped out, and ran into the woods taking Jaramillo with him. In her oversize threadbare coat his mother traipsed after them.

State police at the Canjilon roadblock were getting very uneasy. Dusk was fast coming on and storm clouds loomed overhead. Slightly in the background stood two clean-cut men in overcoats leaning impassively against a car: the FBI was available for advice. Deputy Jaramillo was the first concern of Police Chief Black and Captain T. J. Chavez. They were also worried about the passing time, which was allowing the raiders precious minutes to filter deep into the hills.

Chavez sent reinforcements to pursue the car that had come to Martinez's aid. Apodaca, handcuffed, sat in the rear of a police car. New units of lawmen continued to arrive. The carbine used by Apodaca was passed from officer to officer and profusely photographed. Policemen paced impatiently around their cars, whose radios reported the minute-by-minute movements of Martinez and Jaramillo. Tobias Leyba's house was presumed to be the regrouping place for the Alianza escape caravan from Tierra Amarilla. But an advance by the police awaited Jaramillo's rescue and the arrival of the National Guard.

One policeman helped Apodaca drink from a can of soda. A fellow officer said, "Don't give that old bastard anything, let him die."

Replacing his film, a news photographer whispered to a policeman that Apodaca was working his hands free. Apodaca was yanked from the back seat and his wrists were locked behind him while the photographer clicked his shutter.

Then came the word that Jaramillo was in the clear. He had been forced to jog deep into the woods until Martinez had told him to lie on the ground. When Jaramillo dared to look up, Martinez had disappeared into the brush. As he walked back through the trees, Jaramillo met Mrs. Martinez trudging after them.

"That guy's nuts," the deputy sheriff said with relief as he emptied a bottle of soda down his throat.

At this time the imminent arrival of the National Guard was all that delayed a sweep of the target area east of Canjilon. A paddy wagon with the troops was going to be necessary. Up the muddy road, bordered by a sagging wire fence, a cluster of houses seemed all the more inscrutable for the sudden attention focused on them. Farthest away was Leyba's house, its white window frames standing out against a backdrop of forested hills. Police Chief Black began ordering his men to move from home to home along the wet roadside. They sprang into action, sheriff's deputies, state police and cattle inspectors running in spurts, dropping down with guns ready, peering through binoculars.

"Look, they're sending kids out," someone said. A child bounced like a rabbit through the pasture grass fringe. It disappeared into one of the corrugated-iron-roofed houses. Another little figure ran toward the house highest on the rise. It was about 7 p.m.

Exasperated, the police chief could wait no longer. Behind a protective car, crawling in first gear as slowly as a tank, the parade of policemen began their sweep up the slippery road.

In Michigan, news of the raid had forced the rescheduling of a Republican fund-raising dinner. Cargo and Congressman Gerald Ford were to appear half an hour earlier so the governor could leave in a jet training plane offered by the Michigan National Guard. Cargo was doing everything he could to speed home. "I assume we can get the situation in hand," he said, feeling very much in the dark as to exactly how. "I hope we can. It's a very explosive thing; very difficult to cope with." The red tape involved in clearing the loan of the plane made Cargo's flight home take longer than if he had boarded a commercial plane.

In Santa Fe his office was still tense and chaotic as the police began their advance at Canjilon. Acting Governor Francis made bilingual appeals over most radio stations north of Albuquerque "for all concerned to lay down their arms." Motorists were once more cautioned to stay away from Rio Arriba County.

Father Garcia had by now reached Professor Clark Knowlton in Texas and informed him of developments. Plans were still alive to use him as a mediator. The men in Santa Fe discussed ways of arranging this.

At about the time Black's men were avoiding muddy puddles as they walked toward Leyba's house, someone at the state capitol suggested relocating their operations center. The National Guard armory on the highway out of Santa Fe had an emergency civil defense room in its stoutly constructed basement. Shortly dubbed "the war room," it was supposed to facilitate statewide communications and coordination of strategy. The lieutenant governor and two carloads of aides and staff drove to the new building two miles away. According to Larry Prentice, the National Guard communications system under the direction of Colonel Edward J. Hamilton turned out to be "lousy." Switching back to the reliable state police portable radio was the only way to find out what was happening in the north.

A large map of New Mexico on glass hung on one wall of the conference room in the armory. The military atmosphere was enhanced by rows of desks displaying official department titles on nameplates. Although most decisions were being made at the scene of action in the north, the newly arrived officials felt "psychologically pretty well in touch with the situation."

Back at Canjilon, the yardage between the advancing police and Leyba's house was shortened by the minute. Chief Black hiked confidently ahead of the police car. His men fanned out to check homes along the way, rapping doors with rifle butts and ordering people to show their faces.

Soon a cluster of pickups and cars could be distinguished in the grove behind the house. Police jumped irrigation ditches, vaulted rusty wire fences, and came toward the strangely immobile vehicles from three sides. One detachment followed the road directly to Leyba's door. Another came from the south side, watching the house on the skyline and the grove nearby. Two officers filtered back into the trees, clearly intending to surround the grouped vehicles from the rear.

From the woods darted a tiny form, little legs churning to get ahead of the police. It was Baltazar Martinez's mother again, her long hair uncoiling from its nest on top of her head. She was shooting fearful looks over her shoulder at the police weapons. I actually heard her mumble in Spanish, "When they are children you can look after them, but when they grow up they follow their own road."

Then the two policemen emerged from the woods behind the collected cars.

"All right, hands up. Come on, let's go."

Their words shook me into realizing how silent and suspended life had seemed for the last five minutes. By their vehicles, the Alianzans had for a moment seemed to be in a tableau. Leyba came first, joking with the policemen nearing his door, waving his open hands. Seeing their guns, he threw his arms into the air. Behind him slowly moved a stream of women, bundled babies, teenagers, and men with their hands over their wide-brimmed hats.

The arrival of the police was later described by one of the rounded-up Alianzans:

"We were chatting inside the house at 5 p.m. when some of the ladies called me to come outside. I went out and saw all these policemen coming toward us. At the time, climbing up the hill like they were, they looked like ants, there were so many. . . . Then the state police arrived as if it was their own playground. They drove in a cloud of dust. Those on foot jumped fences. They pointed guns and rifles as if they were in the jungles of Vietnam. I was getting ready to butcher a sheep when the invasion first attracted my attention. I walked over to a group of police, told them to put their guns away, that I personally insured their safety. One of them said, 'Come over here.' I did, extended my hand to shake his, and as he took it I felt something hard pressed into my back. I turned to see the blue steel of a rifle barrel."

9

THE TANKS ARRIVE

Foremost among the "picnickers" filtering out of the oaks and junipers of Leyba's back pasture was a straight-backed girl in tight jeans with raven-black hair tumbling over her shoulders. Her right hand gripped a young man's hip pocket; his hands met atop his curly head. Reies Tijerina's nineteen-year-old daughter Rosa was strikingly beautiful as she led the slow surrender procession. The surrounded Alianzans walked under the determined scrutiny of police with firearms trained on them. Young girls wearing their fathers' cowboy hats giggled softly with each other. Their elders passed relaxed, low-toned comments. A few youngsters directed their brassy, disdainful slang to the stony-faced officers holding tightly to their guns. Some babies whimpered. There was an odd resignation in the air. Passively they grouped where they were told, in a yard between Leyba's house and garage shed.

All thirty-nine men, women, and children were lined up against the adobe wall for name-checking. Patsy Tijerina, Reies's wife, was identified with her five-month-old infant Isabel, named for the queen of Spain.

"I don't see what all the fuss is about," she complained. "We're just up here for a picnic."

Police also noticed fourteen-year-old Danny Tijerina, the land-grant leader's son by his first marriage. Misty drizzle had begun to fill the air. Patsy was escorted to a police car for her baby's shelter. Plainclothes Officer Freddy Martinez moved along the people pressing against the adobe wall to get shelter beneath the eaves. In a palm-sized pad he took down each name. Newsmen arrived and more policemen, among them a handful of Jicarilla Apache officers from their reservation to the west. The children and teenagers stared bemusedly at the police guns.

The rain grew heavier. Leyba had already been relieved of his hunting knife. A search of the garage turned up a carbine and a shotgun. More rifles were discovered in a nearby outhouse. Then the prisoners were squeezed into the garage, which was already occupied by a car. Police settled into their cars or huddled under the dripping roof overhang. They smoked cigarets and listened to the crackling monitors.

From Tierra Amarilla Alfonso Sanchez had come to Leyba's *ranchito*. He stood shielded behind some policemen in the shelter of a skimpy tree. He heard a prisoner's name. "Mi primo" ("My cousin"), he said half to himself and shook his head. Crossing his arms he muttered,

"Now what do I do with these people? How do you do this and not make them bitter all their lives?"

That dilemma was making police anxious for the prisoners' transportation to arrive. Sanchez was advised, for safety's sake, to hurry to Santa Fe. It was just starting to dawn on everyone that the day's fury had represented something more than an attempted jailbreak.

Although members of Tijerina's family had been identified, Tijerina was not one of Canjilon's "ten adult males," as police broke down the list of captives. The net had been drawn too late. The principals had flown. News reports now latched onto a sensa-

TIJERINA and the COURTHOUSE RAID

tional mistranslation of the fugitive leader's name: "King Tiger."

Near the focus of activity east of Canjilon a spotter plane zoomed low over treetops. Already police helicopters were racketing overhead in the dusk. The second stage of the search got under way.

The National Guard had not shown up by the time I walked away from the darkening, somber scene at Leyba's homestead. Avoiding mud puddles on the way into Canjilon I noticed the broken line of parked official vehicles that seemed caught in the midst of some holocaust, contrasting with the calm, clear rushing of irrigation water through the *acequias* (ditches).

In a living room behind Canjilon's tiny post office I came upon Sheriff Benny Naranjo, still in a blood-spotted shirt. Shaking from chill and shock, he was preparing to talk to Albuquerque television newsmen in the glare of a portable facelight.

Reporter Larry Calloway had placed Tijerina at the raid, gun drawn, "looking every bit the revolutionary leader." Although Calloway's story had been weeded by a bureau chief on guard against libel, this disclosure had remained. Now Naranjo delivered the first indication of the raid's basic motive.

"I heard a shot and my jailer [Eulogio Salazar] ran into the hallway. Then there was a lot of shooting. I was held face down on the floor and every time I raised my head they rammed a rifle butt on my neck, saying 'Stay down, stay down.' "

Before being ordered to join the other courthouse employees in the County Commission room, the sheriff had heard gunmen repeatedly demand the whereabouts of Alfonso Sanchez.

"But it wasn't a jailbreak like you guys said." Naranjo wanted to correct the first reports. "That's all wrong. They came here for Al."

The sheriff had heard the insurgents yelling, "Reies said not to hurt nobody, Reies said not to hurt nobody."

"The raiders had it in for Alfonso Sanchez," Naranjo emphasized.

106

Alianza members remained expectedly close-mouthed during the uneasy next days. They stuck to their story of the "picnic" and provided no clues to the reasons behind the raid or the location of their fugitive comrades.

The official Alianza version of what happened came out two nights later, in a mountain shack where, after elaborate secret preparations, Tijerina met a clandestine delegation from Santa Fe. He alternated between a formal militaristic account—"The arresting party went throughout the various rooms of the courthouse but Alfonso Sanchez could not be found"—and a subjective synopsis —"So apparently that Monday came to a sad conclusion. Then the arresting party left. To our dismay the area was covered with state police, but they all ran like coyotes. As I was told, New Mexico doesn't have much of a state police force, or at least that's the way it looked. . . . If they really thought we were criminals they should have made a good stand."

But he was evasive about his own participation.

"There was someone in command—it wasn't me—that apparently wasn't capable of controlling all the armed men."

In his view Saiz and Salazar had caused their own injuries by "resisting." To the direct question of whether he had been there, he spaced his phrases thoughtfully:

"I will leave that up to the public. I don't want to say no because I don't want to make people feel that I'm ashamed to count myself among our arresting party, nor yes to incriminate myself and please my enemies."

Following the raid, Tijerina revealed, there had been a switch of cars at Canjilon, with some men continuing south to Espanola.

Wherever they had scattered, the courthouse attackers were certainly not around the floodlit Canjilon Ranger Station. Transformed into the manhunt's command center, the damp road entrance, small parking lot and modest building had taken on the bustling flavor of a nighttime football game. Through the foggy weather state police were pouring in to receive new patrolling assignments. The first National Guard contingents were arriving in

107

growling quarter-ton troop transport vehicles. Bewildered young men from Espanola and Taos emptied out of them in starched fatigues, holding M-1 rifles they were about to use in earnest for the first time.

Once before, in 1881, a New Mexico territorial governor had been obliged to dispatch a general to Tierra Amarilla to restore the peace. Ike Stockton, a local badman, had been raising hell in the San Juan region ever since a posse gunned down his brother earlier in the year. He caused so much commotion that Governor Lew Wallace, the author of *Ben Hur*, sent General Max Frost to Tierra Amarilla to gather the militia and end the outlawry.

The Guard had also been called out to patrol New Mexico's borders in the wake of Pancho Villa's attack on Columbus in 1916. It had seen duty during a miners' strike in 1951-52, when a courthouse had also been the focus of agitation. Now, in "tactical convoys" mobilized out of sixteen units in Santa Fe, Espanola, Taos, Albuquerque, Belen, Socorro, and Las Vegas, it began filling the highways pointing north.

First to pull into Canjilon were units drawn from the towns closest at hand. At about 9:30 p.m. two contingents brought in a pair of M-42 "duster" tanks, the kind employed during the Korean conflict. Transported from the Espanola armory on flatbed trailers, one had been too large for Canjilon's concrete bridge and had smashed a side wall. Ammunition for their twin 40-mm cannons, however, was left behind in an ordnance warehouse.

The final Guard units would bring troop strength to about 350 for the coordinated search in the coming dawn. Another 400 men would remain on standby during the "activation" period. At midnight on Monday, June 5, the last canvas-covered trucks were rumbling through Santa Fe's quiet streets en route to the "disturbance area."

In charge of the multiplying manpower at Canjilon was Adjutant General John Pershing Jolly. A large man in a duffel coat with unzipped hood falling back, wearing his general's hat with oakleaf clusters on its brim, Jolly barked orders. He tried valiantly to create order out of "the mammoth posse" which was descending upon the Canjilon Ranger Station. Jeeps, a troop-loaded bus, the army-green convoy trucks, a mobile medical van complete with two white-clad doctors, the flatbed tank trailers—200 transportation and support vehicles had to be situated for the night. Supply depots had to be set up and command centers established. After some consideration, Jolly turned down a Michigan state offer of a jet to help in the hunt. Finally steel-helmeted troops had to be bivouacked for an unlimited period in strange wet fields.

Jolly held constant conferences with his grim-faced subordinates. His guardsmen soon pitched encampments at Canjilon, Vallecitos, and Tierra Amarilla—where some units had been sent directly to ring the courthouse. The building was to be closed up for a week while investigators went over every inch of its space and every page of its record books, but just now Police Chief Black wanted the Guard to cordon it off because he feared Tijerina might launch a full assault on the town. From a secondary Guard "headquarters" at the Presbyterian Church's Ghost Ranch, Personnel Officer Colonel Glenn Lovett told reporters that his men would remain there "as long as needed."

General Jolly, too, was ready for a long siege. His guardsmen had brought about 20,000 rounds of ammunition. But the general radioed Fort Bliss for an additional 20,000 bullets. "Twenty thousand rounds won't last very long," he said sternly, "if we start shooting."

Adding to the congestion were idle state policemen waiting to form nocturnal patrols which had to be deployed according to General Jolly's ideas for uncovering the Tijerinistas. FBI observers, state Fish and Game officials, and lawmen of every stripe were mingling with newsmen like buffalo swarming to find a leader. The understandably confused guardsmen stayed tight-lipped and obedient.

Within the ranger station itself back rooms were used for the occasional interrogation of Canjilon suspects thought to have been at the raid, for sorting radio communications, and for private strategy meetings. The front receiving office had been turned over to the burgeoning press. Television newsmen, stringers for large western papers, and journalists from every local paper and wire service dozed on floors and desks, waiting for an unlikely opportunity to get "outside" on Canjilon's continually clogged telephone circuits.

At Leyba's *ranchito,* meanwhile, incidents began to take place that created another controversial element in the raid story. The manner in which the Alianza families were detained there formed the basis for a subsequent civil rights suit, with Chief Black and General Jolly named as defendants.

A few weeks after the raid the American Civil Liberties Union held open hearings in Albuquerque and Espanola. The Canjilon prisoners said they had first been held inside the garage with the rain blowing in. Two hours later a paddy wagon had arrived and fourteen people were told to get in it. Three or four had to sit on the floor. Then another wagon showed up, presumably for the rest of the group.

"During this time," claimed one witness, "the National Guard also arrived on the scene with drawn rifles and drawn bayonets, but it was the state police who actually gave the orders." Then there seems to have been a change of plans. "After several hours the people were told to get back to their tents or vehicles . . . not to make any large fires, and to be in bed not later than 11 p.m." The police announced that they would hold roll calls that night and the next morning of the names they had collected earlier.

Thus began the "cattle pen" incident. The east became incensed over it two days later when a photograph from Canjilon vied with the Arab-Israeli war on the front page of the *New York Times.* The first reports indicated that men, women, and children were corralled in a split-fence stockade for closely penned hogs. Actually they were told to return to the back pasture, fenced with barbed wire, where they had first been surrounded. There four pickups, a sedan, two smoldering fires, a baby's kiddycar, and scattered cooking

110

utensils awaited the Alianzans. It was true that Leyba commonly used this enclosure, 50 x 100 yards in size, for sheep and cattle.

The Alianza families were held here overnight and through the next day "for their own protection." This was one state policeman's explanation. One of the thirty-five guardsmen "protecting" the compound confided, "They're bait. The brass expects that that Mexican will come back in here tonight to try to free these people."

Shelter for the night was provided by makeshift lean-tos, pickup truck beds, and two tents. It was the understanding of the prisoners that they "could neither leave the premises nor communicate with anyone outside," contended the ACLU brief. "They were held incommunicado, although no arrest had been made, nor did any firearms or weapons of any kind ever show up after a complete search by state police and/or National Guardsmen. There were no warrants served, either against the person or search warrants for the vehicles." Except for the discovery of arms in the garage and outhouse, this statement agreed with the reports of my fellow newsmen.

For toilet facilities the "detained" were told to hail a guardsman to escort them to the single outside privy. One man swore that a guardsman advised him to keep twenty feet away from the army sentinels that night or he would be shot. Another complained that when he was plagued by his bladder ailment he had to urinate in front of women and children. The next day, still in their "protective" limbo, the Alianzans allegedly suffered more indignities.

Back at the command center at the ranger station, Chief Black was briefing an "at ease" lineup of his uniformed and plainclothes officers. The soggy parking lot was a jumble of men and machines, stark electric light, and deep shadows.

"No rough stuff," Black warned, during the pursuit patrols that night. All major highways, secondary roads, and back country cow trails were to be secured. As he was assigning specific perimeters, Captain T. J. Chavez interrupted him. A white 1965 Ford Galaxie was supposedly bringing Alianza guns and reinforcements. The squad cars were to keep on the lookout.

Now his men headed for their cars, checking ammunition supplies. Everyone was making foraging visits to Baldonado's store. The proprietor was doing a land-office business in lunchmeats, sandwich bread, and dimes for the pay telephone. Before dawn he had sold his last potato chips, which newsmen spread with peanut butter.

At the National Guard encampment eight miles north of El Rito, commanding officer Captain Boesflug was giving instructions to jeep patrols searching the area between La Madera and El Rito.

"If you have to shoot," he said, "don't shoot to kill. And the best way to do that is to shoot at their legs. But I want to repeat, don't shoot unless you are fired upon."

In Santa Fe that evening a car containing three of the Alianza hierarchy from Albuquerque was picked up after a brief chase. Victorino Chavez, Santiago Anaya, and Camilo Sanchez had been under surveillance since the police first learned of the raid. Now they were held on suspicion of coming north "to incite a riot." Each was being held on $5,000 bail.

Joining state police unit 23 at Canjilon, I settled myself in the back seat. Through the unusually chilly night the car cruised over a maze of hill roads. Our "scout" was a local cattle inspector. Ready for bear, he described the coming gunfights with gusto. Excitedly the other officers concurred that Baltazar Martinez would probably not allow himself to be taken alive. Our patrol car halted at many homes rumored to be related or favorable to the Alianza cause. The police held quick conversations between cracked doors or through partly opened bedroom windows. Between stops we munched cold sandwiches, kept our ears tuned to the progress of other cruisers on the monitor, and sipped whiskey for warmth. I witnessed none of the breaking and entering reported later by homeowners in the region.

One woman said six state police stamped through her rooms with drawn rifles but with no search warrants. A man charged that police displayed two warrants for other houses as they went through his closets. He was taken to Tierra Amarilla, then to Santa Fe, where he was released three days later because no charges had been filed. His employer fired him for lost time. Another man was taken on a search of his garage. All the while an officer held a gun to him, warning, "If anyone shoots at me, I'll let you have it."

Hours later our police cruiser slogged out of a wagon road where we had crept up to some red taillights. They belonged to the unnerved owner of a horse trailer. Returning to the El Rito Canyon Road, a speeding white car was caught for a split second in our headlights. Giving chase, the police cruiser braked as the white vehicle swerved suddenly off the road. It groped its way up a logging path before bouncing to a stop. Flushed out were eight wild-haired, raggedly dressed young men whose average age was twenty. While they were spread-armed against the car and searched, the trunk was opened. Wire cutters, fuses, dynamite caps, four loaded hunting rifles, and a pistol were inside. A bottle of sweet wine was poured into the dirt. One boy's wisecrack was cut short by a threat. Two state police cars took them all to El Rito. Another police car met us there and transported them the last lap to the Santa Fe city jail. This was the extent of the night's haul. The next two days would hardly be as successful.

Around 11 p.m. in Santa Fe that Monday night, State Corporation Commissioner Murray Morgan was pulled from bed by an urgent telephone call. He was soon talking to Stewart Hatch, an OEO official under Father Garcia. The plan for bringing Professor Knowlton from El Paso to New Mexico was becoming a reality. Hatch wanted Morgan's approval for use of the state Corporation Commission's own single-engine plane for the job.

"Hatch told me," Morgan later recalled, "that he was calling for the governor's office and that they needed an intermediary to get to Tijerina. He said they have a man in El Paso who is the only man Tijerina trusts."

When Morgan asked what office Hatch was calling for, Hatch

replied, "This is the Office of Economic Opportunity. We do these things for the governor." It was Morgan's understanding that Dr. Knowlton's mission was "to prevent further bloodshed in northern New Mexico. That sounded like a good idea to me and in such a case use of state resources would be okay."

Lawrence Prentice was with Acting Governor Francis in the "war room" when word came that the Knowlton project was in operation. The plane had been gone an hour. "There was not much I could do about it," Prentice remembers. According to him, Francis was "a wee bit perturbed." A little later the armory vigil broke up for some sleep.

The Michigan trainer jet bearing Governor Cargo landed at Kirtland Air Force Base in Albuquerque about 2 a.m. An armed guard stood at the gate and there was an increase in roving patrols on the base. The governor was met by his personal bodyguard, "Red" Pack, who hastened him north to Santa Fe. On the way into town Cargo stopped briefly at the armory and encountered a few lingering reporters.

"Every person involved," he promised, "is going to be charged with a felony. Every person who took part is equally liable whether he pulled a trigger or not."

Cargo swept aside hopes for a Wednesday meeting now. "I thought that by having them come in Wednesday it would give us an opportunity to get everything straight and on the record." Now, he felt, this was out of the question. "You can't sit down and negotiate with Jesse James, and that's what it amounts to."

There were reports that the governor was irritated by the transfer of operational control to the "war room" in the armory. It smacked of military control over state affairs. By morning the governor's office was working out of the state capitol once again.

About an hour after Cargo landed, Pilot R. F. Kirkpatrick brought the SCC plane safely into Santa Fe airport. With him were OEO "Information Specialist" Charlie Cullin and Professor Clark Knowlton. The sociologist checked into the Desert Inn Motel near the capitol building. There he began conferring with Aragon and

Burgos, who had returned from Tierra Amarilla late Monday afternoon.

The courthouse raid was yet veiled in Monday night's darkness. Its controversial offshoots were still the state's own problem. By Tuesday morning, however, the situation was under the critical scrutiny of the nation. The famished news media, political propagandists of varied allegiances, officials directly touched by the incident, and a vociferous state citizenry would make it their own property.

By sunrise the event would be history. The tanks would tip off their flatbeds in Canjilon. The massive hunt would in fact never loose its impressive firepower. Tijerina's band would scuttle through the mountains. As the wake of the raid widened, the forces of the law sought who had done it. Others, preparing to rebound against the raid's shock waves, searched for who to blame.

10

THE
HUNT

With Cargo home the spotlight shifted to Santa Fe. The intrinsic conflict between his and Sanchez's approaches to the Alianza problem flared into a bitter public duel.

The governor touched off the open exchange by suggesting that the Coyote arrests had been based on flimsy warrants. He now felt that accusations of "Communist" and bailing obstructions had backed the land-grant followers into a corner. Sanchez's radio broadcasts through the weekend had "stirred the people up again," after he (Cargo) had "quieted things down" on Saturday.

Sanchez was wearing the small hip revolver he kept on his belt for the rest of his days in office. Throughout this week he was flanked by a stocky bodyguard from the Santa Fe Police Department. He lashed back that Cargo's "holding hands" with the land granters had given them a mistaken idea of their rights.

On a local radio program Tuesday morning Santa Fe State Senator Edmundo Delgado joined the fray by placing the responsibility for the raid at Cargo's door. "He gave the people who have been duped false hope."

Delgado continued, "Those of us who have been around here

116

for a long time and who are from old Spanish families would have made claims on that land long ago if we had thought there was any legitimate claim." Delgado articulated the embarrassment of many established Spanish-Americans who felt their racial image smeared "because some good people had been led into a conspiracy against law and order."

Cargo held a Tuesday morning press conference to parry. Sanchez's job "is to prosecute. He's not primarily a radio announcer," the governor retorted. Cargo doubted that a personal survey of Tierra Amarilla would do any good because Sanchez's and Delgado's comments on "the explosive situation" had refired tempers.

While he talked the capitol's loudspeaker system was tuned in to a radio broadcast and Delgado's satin voice came over the air.

"Damn him," muttered Cargo. "If we could get them off that radio long enough we might do something. They're going to stir them up again. The other night I got them agreed to leave and then there's old Al Sanchez on the radio, stirring them up again."

But the governor was firm in his warning that the Alianza steer clear of further violence. He said the raid "borders on insanity." As to Tijerina, Cargo felt he was "a guy that's a little mentally unbalanced—there's no question of that."

The governor took this opportunity to mention that his office had been advised by the State Department in Washington that "there was no real basis to land claims" of the Alianza. A State Department legal adviser had personally discussed the question with Tijerina during their winter meeting. Although told that the United States Government did not recognize the Republic of San Joaquin, Tijerina had received the appointment to discuss the Treaty of Guadalupe Hidalgo. "He was informed," the legal adviser had said, "that the State Department did not see his problem as an affair involving the foreign relations of the United States." Tijerina had then been referred to the land division of the Department of Justice.

If Cargo was only half on the spot it was because he had been

117

only half in the driver's seat. His responses to the growing Alianza problem had vacillated. His personal sympathy for the northern social dilemma was constantly balanced by his instinct for political self-preservation. He was always accessible but always ambivalent. This prevented him from maintaining effective chains of command within his own offices, much less among law enforcement agencies. He had pulled back from his support of the California SES team. Those now attempting to deal constructively with the situation in subtler fashion than by deployment of tanks began to keep the governor's office out of their confidence. Cargo had said during his news conference, "There isn't any dialogue I can open with them now." His former informants became more careful in protecting their contacts when they tried to reopen lines of communication with the grass-roots north.

When the sun lifted Tuesday over stricken Rio Arriba County, the northern "campaign" was in progress. Chief Black had vowed a "search of every bush, trail, cabin, and canyon." The five-man crews of the two M-42 tanks had spent the night inside their iron fortresses. Now they clanked along farm roads, children gaping at their deep tracks. Their armament consisted of ammunitionless twin 40-mm cannons and .50- and .30-caliber machine guns. Helicopter teams, their officers leaning out with automatic weapons visible, maintained contact with twenty jeeps below. Mounted patrolmen, trucks, and squad cars joined in the gigantic 2,500-square-mile stake-out.

Although the raiders had had the long night in which to escape, Chief Black felt the coordinated dragnet would snare them.

"I don't think they can get out right now," he said. "We've got them socked in."

His subordinate, Captain T. J. Chavez, was worried that the raiders' numbers had swelled. "There's no telling how many joined them during the night," he said. In rumpled suit and tie, Chavez had been tirelessly coordinating his plainclothes state police patrols with the National Guard troops and other searchers since the previous afternoon.

In total about 500 men participated in the hunt. Some were sent to El Rito to bottle up that side of the mountains. Others were held at Ghost Ranch in case anyone left the shelter of the forest for the highway. A haystack-by-haystack probe of the terrain between Canjilon and Tierra Amarilla came up with no suspects. All day the piney hills were covered with soldiers with orders to shoot if anyone resisted arrest. Piecemeal reports of the military strategy were slightly confusing. The search from Canjilon to Tierra Amarilla seemed sensible. Jolly believed the raiders had moved north of Canjilon just before dawn. But the allocation of 250 troops to head from Vallecitos toward El Rito and also north from Ghost Ranch seemed to underestimate the insurgents' concern for their own skins.

Appointed area commander of El Rito, Major George Treadwell said the job now was to keep the fugitives on the run. An electrical engineer at Sandia Corporation, Treadwell believed that fairly soon they would be forced to come out for food and rest. Black also was counting on "cabin fever." But a colleague, Major Tom Taylor, with Korean and Second World War experience, allowed that "securing" such a huge area was a "massive undertaking. The chances of us finding these men are very remote, but we might be lucky. . . ."

Roadblocks on all major arteries were thorough affairs. Every vehicle was stopped; all licenses were carefully checked. Trunks and cargo compartments were scrutinized. Some Espanola newsmen successfully passed through six such blocks before being halted by a jeep with four armed guardsmen 200 feet from the TA courthouse. Under guard they were allowed to see for themselves that the heavily protected building was indeed vacant and bolted shut.

Tips kept police hurrying from hamlet to cow camp. Large stores of ammunition and arms reportedly brought into Coyote were never located. A tank backstopped that search. An anonymous call

that Tijerina had gone south to Hernandez drew police and guardsmen. They uncovered neither Tijerina nor the arms he was supposed to be picking up. A rumored raid on Chama never materialized. At Kirtland Air Force Base near Albuquerque an anonymous
caller the night before had threatened to blow up the base's landing strips. Armed guards at the gates were swiftly doubled and
parked cars not displaying the Air Force decal were checked. The
caller said he belonged to the Alianza. A similar threat was phoned
to an Albuquerque radio station Monday night. "You think
they're having trouble up north," a voice warned. "Wait until
tonight." The caller said he was "one of Reies Tijerina's followers."

One state police car drove fifteen miles up the wild Chama Canyon to the Benedictine Monastery of Christ of the Desert. The
police asked the monks if anyone had requested sanctuary. Told
no, they were given a tour of the four-year-old retreat and shown
the glass and adobe chapel just built. The following Sunday the
policemen returned with their wives and three old *santos*—wooden
Spanish religious figurines—which had been gathering dust in their
homes. One of these, restored, became the church's crucifix.

Local residents were shocked to find their homeland virtually
under martial law. Espanola city police had been rerouting north-
bound traffic off U.S. 84 and through Ojo Caliente. Only essential
delivery trucks could use the major highway. Some fishermen returning from the Canjilon Lakes stared with disbelief at the tanks,
soldiers, and weapons of every caliber and description.

"What happened," they asked, jumping out of their cars. "Have
we gone to war?" The Vietnam analogy was not missed by some
veteran guardsmen.

Captain Edward DeBaca had returned home to Santa Fe from
Southeast Asia a year before. Leading one patrol through mountains east of Canjilon, DeBaca used movements he recalled em-
ploying against Vietcong guerrillas. But perhaps the greatest
similarity between the two campaigns was, he felt, "It's hard to
recognize the enemy."

At the same time Espanola Valley residents rallied to distribute aid. The Rio Grande Cafe contributed food. The Espanola chapter of the Red Cross served sandwiches and coffee. The Espanola hospital provided a fifty-gallon thermos of coffee which was carried north. Volunteers helped with the impromptu commissaries. Ambulances from Espanola funeral homes were dispatched to the area. Local doctors stayed on around-the-clock call.

The searchers had a mental checklist of wanted principals. Cristobal Tijerina had been released by Judge Scarborough minutes before the courthouse was struck. Although he had been presumed to be on his way home, he did not turn up during the strenuous attempts to rejail him.

Anselmo Tijerina had been arrested on the morning of the deflated Coyote meeting. On the morning of the Monday when Tierra Amarilla was invaded he was released from the Santa Fe city jail. After cleaning up the office in Hernandez he had driven north to Canjilon, but was intercepted by police once again. They advised him to get back home "or you might be arrested again." Officials did not seem sure of how to deal with him. He was picked up and released again. Finally he and his daughter camped on a knoll behind the Hernandez house because he said the Guard was breaking in so often.

Not surprisingly, the hottest search was for Baltazar Martinez. The young kidnapper and alleged "dynamite carrier" was unofficially characterized as "the most dangerous nut in New Mexico."

Martinez had been described as appearing quite young as he stood in the doorway of the County Commission room with what looked like a dynamite stick in one hand, a lighted cigaret in the other. "You are good people," he had told the twenty terrified courthouse employees. "We don't want to hurt you. Don't make us hurt you." He later testified that he had actually been carrying flares, and he showed the jury how he had wrapped them in pink paper marked "dynamite." (Martinez was acquitted for his role in the raid on the grounds that he was temporarily insane.)

The twenty-two-year-old Martinez had moved to Canjilon soon after his father died in Utah. He lived with his ninety-year-old grandmother, younger brother, and mother, and corresponded with a third brother fighting in Vietnam. Although he had only gotten through the eighth grade, Baltazar had acquired a love of drawing. To avoid high school he had left home for potato-picking in Colorado, then tried the U.S. Army. Even after eight months, language difficulties put him literally out of step with military requirements—"So the platoon would go one way and I would go the other." He stopped eating and was soon deemed "unsuitable" for army life but was given an honorable discharge.

After returning to Canjilon he shortly got into trouble for brandishing a pistol at the Canjilon schoolhouse polling booth when he was told he was too young to vote. Handcuffed, he escaped from the police, removed the handcuffs, and returned them to the police the next day.

Storekeeper Robert Quandt of Canjilon remembers Martinez as "a quiet young man who fought a lot when he got drunk but paid his bills. . . . I never considered Baltazar a good leader. He is a good follower." According to Quandt, Martinez had become an Alianzan "for the same reason that a kid would drop out of school. Everybody has to join something—something that captures his imagination." Now stories were passing through the moutain homes about Baltazar's escape artistry: his footsteps in the mountains were said to measure fifteen to twenty feet apart.

Tuesday's hunt did pull in one Alianza stalwart, Tijerina's unlikely lieutenant Jerry Noll. He had been in hiding before the raid, evading the federal warrant that had been issued when he refused to appear for psychiatric examination after the Echo Amphitheater incident. The police reported that Noll was seen fleeing from Tierra Amarilla with Reies Tijerina. In Cebolla, a community on the highway between Canjilon and Tierra Amarilla, Noll said he was being sheltered by friends when he learned of the raid. "I grabbed my tortillas and ran." He was clambering out of Navajo Canyon, near Echo Amphitheater, as a police car spotted him near the highway. Unshaven and exhausted from stumbling all night in the hills, Noll claimed he was beaten on the ride to the Santa Fe jail.

News photographers were making the most of tanks bearing troops alongside horses ridden bareback by black-haired farmers' sons. But they were neglecting the house-by-house methods of other searchers. A "war zone" immunity seemed to prevail in some instances. While I saw no door or window smashing by troops, the word-of-mouth reports were too numerous to be discounted. A few weeks later, on a raid follow-up assignment, I was taken to three homes with cardboard window patching and splintered doors displaying signs asking officers please to leave the place alone.

In Leyba's back pasture the families arrested the previous evening were still under "protection." Some additional pup tents had been put up for them. Guards were described as having their rifles pointed towards the people mingling inside the stockade, preventing anyone from coming closer than fifteen feet to the barbed wire. It was alleged later that a pond at the lower end of the slope was the only available water supply. Intended for sheep and cattle, it was pictured as "stagnant, green and muddy." In one case it was used to mix a baby's formula. By noon Tuesday the picnic supplies were all used up. Jolly ordered in two canvas trailers of C-rations, which the Alianzans refused. Officers expressed concern that the prisoners were growing "very restless."

General Jolly had first displayed bewilderment when asked why the prisoners were being held. "That's a good question," he said, "I really don't have an answer." He did try to emphasize that they were not exactly arrested. Captain Adelino Sanchez of Belen, New Mexico, a U.S. Department of Agriculture employee when not on Guard duty, said that "one old woman" had tried to escape from the pen twice that day. "I believe she's the mother of one of the men we're searching for." At the muddy intersection near Leyba's field one tank had been deployed so that its cannons pointed down a road leading to the men, women, and children.

TIJERINA and the COURTHOUSE RAID

At one point General Jolly was asked just what species of confinement this was. He was short with the reporter.

"Let's don't get involved in civil liberties. None of them has complained."

Before the Canjilon compound was dissolved about 5 p.m. Tuesday afternoon, there were stories of families split up by the mass detention. Some children were reported hungry in isolated homes where they awaited parents or relatives.

In Santa Fe everyone waited on the progress of the hunt in the north. Word that Eulogio Salazar, the wounded jailer now in St. Vincent's Hospital, might talk to an enterprising reporter began a barrage of calls. It was unlikely that Salazar, his mouth blown apart, could have talked to anyone. He made it known he would first have to check with his courthouse working mate Dan Rivera. The undersheriff himself was recuperating from his blackened eyes, concussion, and severe bruises.

In Albuquerque Policeman Nick Saiz remained in critical condition at the Bataan Memorial Methodist Hospital, where he had been rushed Monday night. A compound fracture of the left arm and a punctured lung were giving the young officer much pain, but he was "holding his own." Also in Albuquerque, a federal judge made the symbolic gesture of dismissing charges against the fugitive Tijerina. Judge H. Vearle Payne was in his court to follow through on his order instructing the land-grant leader to "show cause" by June 6 why he shouldn't be held in contempt for failing to deliver the Alianza's files. But the order had been issued before the weekend turned northern New Mexico upside down. Squads of police now staked out the federal building. Judge Payne went through the formalities of dismissing the order because District Attorney Sanchez had turned over the confiscated complete roster of Alianza members to the U.S. attorney's office.

In Washington, D.C., news of the raid was of special interest to the OEO's civil rights division. Anthony Tinajero, a native New Mexican and personally acquainted with Tijerina, prepared to return to the state immediately. When the OEO's attempts to mediate came under investigation later, Tinajero's presence was questioned. His Washington superior said he felt at the time, "If he can contribute in a meaningful way to solving the problem that would be fine." On Tuesday Tinajero placed his name in the pool of individuals willing to meet secretly with Tijerina in the mountains. Governor Cargo had written a confidential "to whom it may concern" letter on his personal stationery authorizing Tinajero "to contact leadership of the confederation of Free City States in order to further my efforts to maintain law and order in New Mexico."

Additional first-hand glimpses of the raid itself were still coming to light. Journalists pouring into the area throughout Tuesday ferreted out new facts like pieces to a jigsaw puzzle.

Carlos Sedillo, Cris Tijerina's attorney that Monday, remembered chatting with Nick Saiz minutes before the gunfire broke out. From the security of his Albuquerque office he described hitting the dirt beside his car as trenchcoated raiders dashed past him. After hearing their shooting he saw Eulogio Salazar stagger towards him dripping blood. Someone struck Salazar from behind before the slight jailer wandered off. Slipping into his car, Sedillo tore out in reverse when he noticed a "submachine gun" pointed at him. Other men with rifles began firing. A bullet smacked into his rear bumper as he spun his car free.

The absence of other state policemen in the building was due to an accident on the Chama highway nearby. Unaware of the courthouse firefight, State Policeman Juan Santistevan of Tierra Amarilla drove back to the building to find "six men standing in front of the road firing at me."

Two bullets ripped into his car. One smashed through the windshield inches above his head.

"They shot hell out of my car. I ducked down and threw the car into reverse." Two police cars following him made whirling U-turns. One escaped across an open field. But as Santistevan was turning around he entered the line of fire. Abandoning his car, he ran off on foot. The memory was unpleasant as he talked to a reporter.

125

"If any of those sons-of-bitches get in my sights, they're dead. I'll kill them."

Following the courthouse takeover, state police hung back. For over an hour they grouped at a roadside cafe, making no attempt to plug up the town or re-enter the dangerous plaza in front of the occupied building.

The flight of the state police was the object of Alianza hilarity and scorn that evening. Land-grant sympathizers also mimicked Sheriff Naranjo's slurred pronunciation on television that night, laughing till they cried. Still upset, the sheriff had been describing the downing of Undersheriff Rivera. "So they hit my undershirt, and my undershirt hit the ground." But for a civil strife, such displays of malevolence were at a remarkable minimum.

The bravery of Rio Arriba County Commissioner Nick Salazar was cited. Disobeying an order to stay put, Salazar assisted some other TA citizens in lifting Saiz's stretcher into the ambulance. All the while a rifle pointed at his head. Driver Angie Zamora refused an armed man's demand for the ambulance keys. She then drove the seventy miles to the Espanola hospital in forty-five minutes.

Local newspapers were vaguely indignant on Tuesday. "There is just one word for the outbreak of violence at Tierra Amarilla yesterday—revolution," opened the *Albuquerque Tribune's* lead editorial. But then the paper felt around for a sounder stance: Everyone involved had done their duty in restoring order. Only Cargo's "kid gloves" were gently slapped. The *New Mexican's* initial reaction alone included a measure of social concern. The raid was "the bitter fruits of neglect." The paper missed its own irony when it described the Alianza's attempt to perform a citizen's arrest on the district attorney as an "attack upon a bastion of American justice." But it did explore the "insurrection" as a product of poverty, ignorance, and alienation in northern New Mexico.

On Monday night at about 10:30 Patsy Tijerina had finally been transported to the Santa Fe city jail and booked for "conspiracy," the usual holding charge in those days. Her infant daughter had been placed in the care of the Child Welfare Department. A mustached Albuquerque reporter in the guise of an attorney was allowed by city police to interview the Alianza leader's wife. The heavily guarded jailhouse was noisy. The two were allowed to talk in a secluded room before she was taken to her cell. This "exclusive" was published that afternoon—a string of winsome, painful anxieties about her future and her husband's and baby's welfare.

Before the Canjilon prisoners had been let loose, the menfolk had been carefully screened. Some individuals were picked out, charged with conspiracy, and shuttled to jail. About twenty-four hours after they were first rounded up, Tobias Leyba's ranch was returned to its owner, although he was in jail.

On Tuesday afternoon the possibility of the secret visit with Tijerina became more likely. With Joe Benitez I took a preparatory trip to Anselmo Tijerina's home in Hernandez. We sat in the kitchen of the house where the California consultants had first met Cristobal.

At this point Anselmo was Reies's shadow. He is a quiet, ruggedly handsome man, loose-limbed, with whitening curly hair and the Tijerina hypnotic hazel eyes. He enjoys a drink, unlike his abstaining visionary brother, and is said to be a fierce man in a fight. He calmly told us about his harassment during the last days.

Benitez had relayed some hastily gathered grocery funds for a particularly needy family, ten children whose parents were somewhere in jail. Then they discussed the delicate subject of locating Reies. Anselmo looked me over while Benitez talked. Yes, he replied, he had been in touch with his brother in the hills. But it was very risky. Reies was moving all the time. For some reason, however, Anselmo seemed to feel it vital that the meeting be chanced. I was first perplexed that the Tijerinas were ready to put themselves in such jeopardy. It was surely in part because Benitez had informed Anselmo of Knowlton's arrival. Also, Reies had made known his desire for other contacts. For a while Tinajero, the OEO adviser, had been a possible choice. I soon got a strong impression that Anselmo and Reies understood the real peril in the present noncommunicative state of affairs and wanted to do something about it.

Anselmo was ready to try to devise some transportation scheme for the proposed interview. He promised to notify Benitez. Our meeting had been low-key. I had come to Anselmo and his daughter as to an enemy delegation. I had watched the fragile beginning of trust as they listened attentively to Benitez attempt to convey in Spanish our appreciation for their risk. The trip to Tijerina's hideout was tentatively scheduled for the next night.

The Alianza's first public protest was a three-day march from Albuquerque to Santa Fe, the state capital, on the Fourth-of-July weekend in 1966. Reies Tijerina, the Alianza's leader, strode along beside a burro at the head of the caravan to present his movement's demands to the governor.

Reies Tijerina's next maneuver was not so peaceful. In late October 1966, a honking caravan of one hundred Alianza vehicles burst through a guard of forest rangers and state police to invade the federal campground of Echo Amphitheater in northern New Mexico.

At the recreation site the Alianza membership staged a "camp-in," symbolically reviving the old land-grant community of San Joaquin. Among their elected officials was a "mayor," old Jose Lorenzo Salazar (in black hat), a direct descendant of the grant's original recipient.

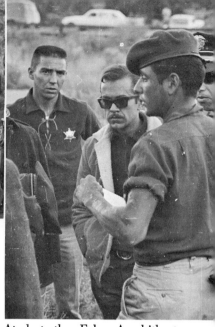

At last the Echo Amphitheater takeover was brought to a close by a force of police and federal officials. With Rio Arriba County Sheriff Benny Naranjo (wearing star) looking on, Baltazar Martinez (in beret) was the last man relieved of his rifle.

During the winter of 1966 plans began brewing at the Alianza's headquarters in Albuquerque for new activity in the spring. First would be a meeting with the newly elected governor, David F. Cargo.

When Tijerina (standing) finally led an Alianza band into the state capitol dining room to speak with Governor Cargo (seated, right), his movement's mood had grown insistent.

(Below, left) One of the Alianza leaders arrested before the Coyote meeting was Jose Maria Martinez, a descendant of the Spanish settler who was first awarded the Tierra Amarilla land grant.

(Below, right) Two days later, three carloads of armed raiders descended upon the crumbling courthouse in Tierra Amarilla. Sheriff Naranjo, still dazed from a head wound, stood in front of the building after the attack.

RAY CARY

(Above, left) As the waves of attackers rushed into the courthouse, two lawmen were shot. Out of this window jumped Eulogio Salazar, the jailer. County Clerk Padilla (with glasses) and Sheriff Naranjo look out in the direction that Salazar limped off.

(Above, right) The police caught and handcuffed one of the raiders, World War I Veteran Baltazar Apodaca.

Baltazar Martinez shot out the window glass and red bubble light of this state police car. The courthouse is in the background.

RAY CARY

Deputy Sheriff Pete Jaramillo was led into the woods at pistol point by young Baltazar Martinez. Here, just after he was set free, he gratefully downed a bottle of soda and described his two hours of captivity.

RAY CARY

Now nothing delayed a police sweep of the small ranch near the hamlet of Canjilon where it was believed the raiders had regrouped. Checking homes like this one along their route, to be sure no Alianzans were hidden inside, the lawmen moved up.

Advancing on the ranch, the foremost policemen pointed their rifles at Tobias Leyba (in fatigues), later identified as one of the raiders. He was promptly handcuffed and put under heavy guard.

RAY CARY

RAY CARY

In a fenced grove behind Leyba's home about forty men, women, and children were discovered. Although they claimed they were having an Alianza "picnic," police herded them out of the trees.

Police took down the names of their new prisoners. Reies Tijerina was not among them, but his daughter Rose (center) was.

RAY CARY

Tijerina's pregnant wife, Patsy, was also identified among the group and handcuffed. The families remained in their "protective" compound for twenty-four hours.

The National Guard was called out. Commanding General John Pershing Jolly (left) conferred with his officers about how to hunt the Alianza leaders who had escaped the police net at Canjilon.

Immediately the stricken courthouse was ringed by jeeps and state police reinforcements. General Jolly and State Police Chief Joe Black feared Tijerina might rally followers for another attack on Tierra Amarilla.

On the day of the big hunt two tanks, the "duster" type used during the Korean War, backed up the searchers. Ammunition for their twin 40-mm cannons, however, was left behind.

News photographers made the most of tanks bearing troops alongside horses ridden by the local farmers' sons.

Helicopters also aided the manhunt. One officer "rode shotgun," peering into the green blanket of trees and holding a submachine gun. The parallel to military operations in Vietnam did not escape notice.

Thirty-five members of the New Mexico Mounted Patrol helped to comb the county of Rio Arriba and its far-flung hamlets for Tijerina and his band. (Note the tank in the background.)

Foot patrols covered miles of high-country fields and hiked up overgrown logging trails, poking their bayonets into isolated haystacks. They turned up no one.

After a full day's unsuccessful hunt, the National Guard was sent home. Tanks rolled back up on their flatbed trailers and pulled out of the temporary command center which had been established at Canjilon.

News of the raid spread across the nation. From Denver came Rudolph "Corky" Gonzales (left), one of Tijerina's fellow militants, for an impromptu talk with Governor Cargo on the state capitol steps.

Five days after the raid Tijerina was captured when a gas station attendant recognized him. He was hastily taken to prison.

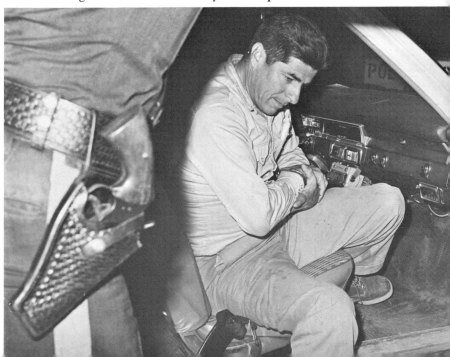

Another fugitive was Reies's younger brother, Cristobal (right). Here he is shown near his hideout, arranging a complex surrender with Alianza Lieutenant Felix Martinez.

At an Alianza convention in 1967, Tijerina with (from the left) Hopi Leader Tomas Banyacya, SNCC Representative Ralph Featherstone, and Maulana Ron Karenga of the Afro-American group US.

Four of the brothers at the convention. (From the left: Cristobal, Reies, Ramon, Anselmo). A fifth brother, Margarito, was behind prison bars.

KARL KERNBERGER

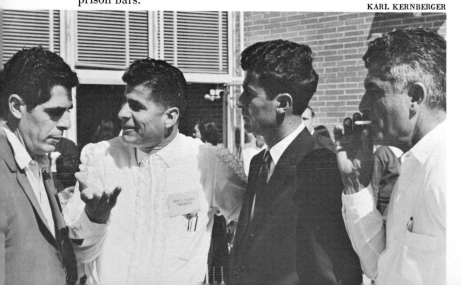

In January 1968 the slaying of a key figure in the court-house raid brought State Police Chief Joe Black and District Attorney Alfonso Sanchez back to Tierra Amarilla.

Found in his car with his face beaten beyond recognition was Eulogio Salazar, the jailer who had been wounded during the raid. An identical conclusion swept official circles.

RAY CARY

Among the Alianzans rounded up within twenty-four hours after Salazar's body was discovered was Jerry Noll. A staunch Tijerina supporter for the past two years, Noll believed that his personal claim to the title of "King of the Indies" was in line with the Alianza's land demands.

Leading the relatives who picketed against the reimprisonment of Tijerina and his followers were Reies's first wife, Mary, and her two daughters.

RAY CARY

RAY CARY

Tijerina's appointment as head of the southwestern portion of the Poor People's Campaign in 1968 caused bitter local friction. Archbishop James Peter Davis nevertheless joined in the Albuquerque segment of the march.

When the first trial for the courthouse raid was held in the winter of 1968, Tijerina was "advised" by California Attorney Beverly Axelrod (left) and Mississippi Lawyer William Higgs (fourth from left). Higgs stayed on to become his right-hand man. Tijerina was joined by his son Reies Jr. (second from left) and wife Patsy (right).

RAY CARY

Soon after the Poor People's Campaign a homemade bomb was thrown at Tijerina's living quarters atop the Alianza meeting hall in Albuquerque. It shattered windows and Tijerina's wife became fearful for her baby, born while she was in Washington.

Neither threats to his life nor new legal trials on the horizon deterred Tijerina from broadening his crusade in 1968-69. Now fully in the national arena of social protest, he accused the Albuquerque Board of Education of discriminating against the Spanish language and culture.

11

JOURNEY
TO THE
HIDEOUT

The strategy of saturation search began to look futile Tuesday
night. The following morning Chief Black called for a huddle with
General Jolly. From their talk came Black's announcement that he
was going to send the Guard home. Governor Cargo learned of
Black's order for demobilization with obvious surprise. He quickly
checked with the police chief and was told about the change from
blanket hunt to selective search.

"I think if we move out," Black explained, "my people can get
to our informants and we might pick Reies up. We have got to
contact other members of the Alianza for information."

Cargo was less optimistic. "I'm afraid as far as finding these
people . . . we're not going to catch them right away. We might
find them by air . . . but not by the military."

It had been the largest mobilization, General Jolly recalled, since
he had assumed command of the New Mexico National Guard in
1959. He thought it was probably the largest in the state's history.
His soldiers had performed like dutiful beaters in a tiger hunt—

long and noisily and hard. During the marches through overgrown logging trails, dewy pastures, and high ponderosa forests one guardsman recited an apt ditty: "Ten thousand Swedes went through the weeds chasing one Norwegian."

In retrospect the Guard was not dismayed by the $19,039.87 bill for the maneuver, even though it was four times Jolly's estimate that morning. The money had paid for three days' work by 750 guardsmen—more than half on standby—gasoline and food. As tanks rolled back up ramps, troops piled into trucks and buses picking burrs off their socks, and the portable hospital went back to its garage, the Guard wrote off its contribution to the unsuccessful hunt as a positive exercise.

In its biennial report submitted to the governor a year later, the Guard immodestly summarized:

"The alert and operations during this incident proved to be of great value to the training of National Guard troops. The operation was conceived in a state of confusion due to lack of intelligence and information. The sudden show of force made by the New Mexico National Guard forced the armed band into hiding, preventing further outbreaks, and establishing calm in a troubled area."

At least the Guard fared $1,000 better than the state police. Chief Black was to estimate "direct expenses" resulting from the entire situation after June 5 as about $20,000 for "damaged police cars, lost, stolen or damaged equipment, living expenses for the extra men." Also there were "indirect expenses," such as increased patrolling during Alianza rallies after the raid and the injury pay to Officer Nick Saiz. When Black pleaded for an emergency allocation of $14,328 to help cover these costs, the state Board of Finance boosted the amount to $31,000 "just in case" and tacked on a commendation for the police effort.

With the Guard gone, however, that effort was limited to twenty-five specially assigned state policemen. Black had also sent most of his emergency forces home and did not lament the Guard's withdrawal. "I feel we can gather information better by moving freely in the villages, working through informants, rather than under a military-type operation," he reiterated.

Actually the arrests of four suspects Wednesday did not take place in the northern villages. Forty-four-year-old Ramon Tijerina was apprehended at the home of the youngest Tijerina, Cristobal, in Albuquerque. All the raid charges were thrown at him, plus a bewildering count of attempting to damage property with dynamite. Now the publicly announced "wanted" list was for five men. Reies Tijerina and Baltazar Martinez vied for the top position.

"Martinez is our number one boy," felt Black. "He is more dangerous than Tijerina. His actions proved that."

"Wanted" posters included the information that young Baltazar was possibly wearing his red beret and had "dynamite sticks" on him. Anselmo and Cristobal Tijerina and a young man named Moises Morales were also sought.

The "occupation" atmosphere lifted. The north tried to pull itself back to normal. Its lifeline, U.S. 84, was reopened to normal traffic. Most of the checkpoints were taken down. But it was still nowhere near business as usual. The usual summer influx of pickup campers was steering clear of the recreation spots in the area.

"I've had ten cancellations this past week," fretted the owner of a large Chama motel. "My last tourists pulled out this morning. Chama looks like a ghost town and the fishing has never been better."

"People are just not coming in, and you can't blame them," another motelkeeper complained. "There was too much nationwide publicity on this Tijerina thing."

An AP reporter, muddy and soaked from two days' continuous coverage, was greeted at a Chama gas station Wednesday night by a pistol barrel. "Get moving, boy," the attendant muttered. "I mean it."

The third phase of the manhunt began the same day that the raid's legal history started. On Wednesday, June 7, the courtroom chapter

131

of the courthouse attack was inaugurated in fine western style. At the Santa Fe County courthouse Judge James Scarborough opened the tangled series of prehearing hearings, arraignments, preliminary hearings, motion hearings, and trials which would build up as confusing a legal layer cake as New Mexico had seen in years. But it was Scarborough's next-to-last involvement with the mountain of litigation. He would shortly be removed from the case because of his unusual involvement in it.

By the time Scarborough's black robes had settled around his elevated seat in the high-ceilinged courtroom, sixteen people were under charges stemming from the raid. Alfonso Sanchez had not found it easy to draw up specific complaints based on the turmoil. I watched him look up the definition of "kidnapping" in his legal volumes, then telephone pistol-whipped Dan Rivera who had returned to duty after medical treatment.

"How bad hurt are you, Dan, great bodily harm?" After a moment he repeated, "Concussion, broken nose, black eyes—we have them on the death penalty. Thanks, Dan."

Each of the sixteen defendants was charged with two counts of kidnapping and three of assault with intent to commit murder. Officer Saiz's lung hemorrhaging had stopped; he had "definitely improved." Jailer Salazar was in satisfactory condition now. There would be no homicide charges resulting from the raid. But Sanchez was to amend his complaints many times before the charges reached their final form in any trial.

In the courtroom five armed officers stood against the walls. Guarding the judge, they nervously eyeballed the jammed visitors' aisles. The strict security extended to the red tile-floored hallways. Half a dozen armed police watched bystanders and carefully frisked anyone entering the courtroom. Between his robes a small holster was visible on Scarborough's belt. And a derringer was said to hang from his shoulder holster. Seated below him, his court recorder Mike Rice was similarly protected.

Scarborough appointed two "friends of the court," Albuquerque attorneys Charles Driscoll and Lorenzo Tapia. Exhibiting further judicial caution, Scarborough paid special attention to the presence of the civil rights observer, Anthony Tinajero. He meticulously waded through all steps of the signing of warrants, the receiving of complaints, and ended up remanding seven of the sixteen defendants to New Mexico State Prison for safekeeping. At each pause he glanced at Tinajero. The civil rights controversy over the "cattle pen" detention at Canjilon was having its impact.

When the seven were named for incarceration, the heavy sobbing of Rose Tijerina and her mother caught the judge's attention. The court's "friends" objected to locking her up. Sanchez argued quickly that he wanted "particularly the young lady in view of her relationship to the head of the movement." Scarborough relented. Father Robert Garcia went into the corridor with Mrs. Tijerina when her weeping became too much for the judge.

It was revealed that Garcia had organized a "Citizens' Committee for Human Rights," with Tinajero and Professor Knowlton. The OEO head had been one of many who were aghast at the situation in Canjilon. The Citizens' Committee had been hurriedly created, as its press release stated, "to seek to secure proper legal protection for the people involved and their families as are their rights as Americans."

Garcia had also resumed his quiet efforts to communicate with the Tijerina forces. With Tinajero he visited the prison after the prisoners were transported there. He had helped Tinajero obtain the governor's written approval to contact the Alianzans at large. Other parties were putting in their bids for personal interviews with the fugitive leader. Cargo himself said he told an unnamed Alianza intermediary that Tijerina "will not be harmed if he gives himself up." But the governor added, "He will be prosecuted." That afternoon Cargo had received in his office F. M. Cassaus, who had conferred with him before the raid, and Ruben Dario Salaz, an Albuquerque high school teacher. These self-appointed spokesmen urged the governor to grant the same kind of general amnesty the California consultants had suggested the day before. But Cargo would hear of no sweeping pardon. His visitors warned that if Tijerina were harmed, "things are going to be a lot harder to handle."

Behind-the-scenes communications were the order of Wednesday afternoon. At a hastily called news conference late in the day Cargo revealed that an hour and a half earlier he had received a message through Garcia's office: Tijerina might surrender. The governor had guaranteed safe conduct. For about an hour Cargo and Chief Black conferred. One observer said they were disputing over which one of them would actually bring in the land-grant leader. Then Cargo received a second communiqué from Tijerina's representatives. When he called in newsmen he was fuming.

"They told me that he was not going to surrender now—to this office or to anybody. The state police have been told that he's to be apprehended."

Anselmo Tijerina, for the moment unharassed in Hernandez, discounted the surrender offer. "I don't think anybody is in touch with my brother." Anselmo admitted, however, that some people from Washington had called to make secret contact with Reies.

The week certainly had not been easy on Alfonso Sanchez. On Monday at the Tierra Amarilla courthouse three or four carloads of men had tried dramatically to get their hands on him. Various next steps were rumored to be in the back of their minds. The first was to shoot him outright. The second was suggested by a militant Alianzan a month after the raid. Leaning against a rusty car resting on its wheelless belly in a northern village, he speculated:

"What would they have done if they'd have found Al? They'd have gotten him out there and they'd have asked him to say yes or no to the question whether he had told the Abiquiu Corporation to cut the barbed wire and let their cattle graze in the national forest. If he'd of denied it, a plug between his eyes."

Possibly an Echo Amphitheater-style "trial" was considered, but the third notion is more imaginative. Since Sanchez had been understood to vow to lock up anyone who appeared at Coyote and "throw away the key," it would be fitting to shuttle the district attorney from mountain shack to mountain shack until he died of old age.

On Tuesday, with the raid and his contest with Cargo preoccupying him, Sanchez had been pained to learn that a judge had dismissed some indictments dear to his heart. For months the district attorney had been spending long, hard days on his strong case of misappropriation of funds in a scandal involving the New Mexico Highway Commission. The judge described Sanchez's homework as "fatally defective" and threw out the indictments purely on technical grounds.

Now, on Wednesday, the governor's office was obligingly ignoring a cloak-and-dagger enterprise which would rub salt in Sanchez's wounds: our clandestine meeting with Tijerina. For a while it appeared that Tinajero, with his "pass" from Cargo, would be one of the group. For some reason, however, he was not among the trio—Benitez, Knowlton, and myself—who were making arrangements to be led to Reies that night. It was later reported in the attorney general's investigation that this was because the civil rights observer was "no longer acceptable" to Tijerina, possibly because of his connection with the federal government.

Intermittently all day Benitez had been telephoning north to firm up plans for our trip. The value of risking it was clear. Knowlton could provide the governor's office with an indication of what Tijerina was thinking. In sheer tactical terms this was vital for the state's intelligence. I could try to uncover what had actually happened, and why. At this point a number of different explanations were given for the raid, and no one knew which was true. That it was to free the Coyote prisoners did not hold water because they had already been out of custody for fifteen minutes at the time of the raid. Perhaps, then, a botched jail bust? Unlikely. Another theory, that the raiders wanted to destroy land records in the courthouse, seemed baseless. Two hours was certainly sufficient time to light matches. A violent reaction of stung pride? Certainly, in part. But Sheriff Naranjo's abbreviated version—that the raiders were after Sanchez—needed verification.

135

TIJERINA and the COURTHOUSE RAID

The emotions which had short-circuited that Monday also needed analyzing. The event obviously had a social and historical dimension which could not be ignored. Cargo appreciated this and it was the reason why, in a pivotal role, he became so indecisive. Reies Tijerina, now being described by the police as *five foot ten inches tall, with wavy black hair, weighing a hundred and seventy-five pounds, with hazel green eyes and usually wearing black horn-rimmed glasses,* had to be given a voice as well. The raid did not fit into a cut-and-dried format of crime and outlaws. It had too many human dimensions and social ramifications for that—as the dilemma of the "protection" camp at Canjilon had amply illustrated.

Late Wednesday afternoon I left the newspaper office and climbed a hill behind my apartment and watched Santa Fe's rooftops turn golden. Close to 6 p.m. I saw a white car pull up my driveway. As arranged, Benitez was picking me up for the first leg of our trip into the hills. Inside the car Professor Clark Knowlton was already sitting, a bearlike man wearing glasses beneath an expansive, shining forehead. This first relay was only four blocks to a parking place near the Hotel La Fonda. We walked up to Room 444, loaned to Devereux for the night by a California doctor passing through town. With growing impatience we waited until 9 o'clock. A few minutes after the hour the black telephone rang like an alarm clock.

"Si," whispered Benitez after a moment. Hanging up quickly, he faced us. Usually the young man displayed the carelessly preened composure of a Latin movie idol. Now his hair was mussed and he looked tense like the rest of us. "Frontier Motel, in Cuba," he said, then gave a faint smile. With visions of Herbert Matthews locating Fidel Castro in the Sierra Maestra I grabbed the portable typewriter that Devereux had brought.

First I walked out. Then Knowlton left the room, and finally Joe. We tried to saunter naturally. Noticing an inconspicuous side exit, I turned and sidestepped a garbage can. The door wouldn't budge. Retracing my steps, I sent the lid of the can clanging to the floor and rebounded heavily off Knowlton's startled bulk. We grinned,

136

then tried valiantly again. In ten minutes we were carefully observing the speed limit on the highway to Albuquerque.

The state attorney general's probe into our excursion, made public six months later, surprised me with its near accuracy. Indeed, it cleared up a few minor points. "Their car left the La Fonda Hotel and headed toward Albuquerque via Highway 84 south; at Bernalillo they took State Road 44 to Cuba where they were met by another car at the Frontier Motel. They then were transferred to the other car and proceeded north via State Road 96 and State Secondary Road 112 to the rendezvous place. During this entire phase both cars and horses were to be used. It is not known whether horses were, in fact, used."

Unfortunately we never saw horses. Driving through darkened Cuba, we slowed down in front of the Frontier Motel. From a parked car a face briefly noticed us, then pretended to be kissing a girl. Stopping behind some buildings, we transferred to the back seat of the other car. Once out of town I was shifted to the front seat and handcuffed, and the three of us were blindfolded.

The driver ripped out. The car raced, made lurching U-turns, backed up. Cold air hissed as a window was rolled open. When approaching carlights glowed I was told to fall into the girl's lap. Knowlton made a nervous joke. I asked for a cigaret and it was placed between my lips. We were on a paved road, we changed to gravel. It seemed hours before we stopped.

Chilling night winds flushed in as the door opened. Steps soon returned. A hand clutching my arm escorted me into another vehicle, high off the ground. We seemed to be crammed into a truck cab. At the silent driver's side the butt of a handgun pressed into me. Now the road was very bumpy. I believe we changed vehicles again. I received the impression that there was signaling with cigaret lighters to points ahead. At last we braked. My blindfold was undone.

It was too dark to recognize those around me. A dazzling spread of stars was overhead. Single file we were taken to a hill, then be-

137

gan descending it through the outlines of trees. A black hillock grew into a shack. Approaching the door we suddenly saw Reies Tijerina illuminated in a burst of light. He was standing on a chair twisting a bulb into a ceiling fixture.

The Alianza chief was wearing a khaki-colored western shirt that appeared to be just ironed. His hair was combed. He looked remarkably groomed and in control for an outlaw. He and Knowlton had a fond *abrazo*. Then they went outside with Benitez for some private words. I watched the men left guarding me in the shack turn with disbelief the pages of newspapers we had brought. Lookouts had been posted and they frequently relieved each other to get out of the cold. I was ignored as they kept scanning photographs of tanks and police roadblocks. They looked young and weary and all bore rifles. It appeared that the cabin was only a stopover for the interview. When Tijerina returned, we established ourselves across a kitchen table covered with, an oilcloth.

I said my newspaper would print nothing libelous, no diatribes. Tijerina nodded automatically, then laboriously began a historical defense of the Alianza's land claims. I was incredulous.

This man was in flight from the largest mass of armed power ever focused on an individual in the state's history. Had we placed our lives in each other's hands so that I could become versed in the legality of his cause? Cutting him off, I tried politely to make it clear that present events were my professional interest. He sighed, and waited for my questioning. The people who had transported us, along with provisions and new footwear, sat around the small room or leaned against the wall. I asked Tijerina where he had been hiding before the Coyote meeting.

Close to two and a half hours later a guard whispered worriedly to Tijerina. Dawn was near. I took some photos of him sitting against an unidentifiable wall with a John Kennedy portrait on a calendar. We shook hands formally.

Climbing back up the hill, I noticed the eastern glow illuminating a long, high ridge which loomed immensely. Later speculation was that our meeting had been near Mesa Poleo, not far from Youngsville. The cabin was supposed to be a rendezvous for village lovers.

Wearing only the blindfold, the ride back seemed more direct. At the Frontier Motel we picked up our car. From a highway cafe I called Devereux, who had been chain-smoking all night in Room 444 of La Fonda. At about 8:30 a.m. I was let off at my house. Goodbyes to Knowlton and Benitez were understandably final. Knowlton had to report and get lost. We had to forget our knowledge of each other for some time.

In the newspaper office I began typing: "By the hum I could tell when we were on asphalt." After contriving a story to explain the origin of the venture without compromising anyone, I simply copied our question-and-answer session word for word, omitting a few unessential exchanges. My thirteen-page piece ended: "Before my blindfold was untied I was told not to look around but to move straight ahead. At about 8 a.m. I walked into the city of Santa Fe, which was surprisingly still there, and still in the twentieth century." Then my editor, Bill Feather, and I waited for the expected phone call as soon as the story hit the streets.

We were not disappointed. Alfonso Sanchez began calmly, hurt that he was not notified of the preparations for the rendezvous.

"Why didn't you tell me, why . . . I could have got that guy." Then his injured feelings hardened. He wanted me at his office right away. With Feather on an extension it was suggested that our conversation might better be held at the newspaper office. An afternoon appointment was set.

This was Thursday, the most trying day of all for Sanchez. Still another new angle to the ongoing newspaper coverage of the raid was a story which must have caught the district attorney's eye soon after our telephone conversation. Father Garcia had confirmed that he had "a person in direct contact" with Tijerina, but refused to say more. The same reporter located Knowlton. The professor would only prick curiosity by saying that his purpose had been "to

139

really cool this thing." He did reveal that he had been asked to testify the following Monday at a congressional subcommittee hearing in Washington which had decided to hold special sessions to dig into the Spanish-American discontent which had peaked in Tierra Amarilla.

To further infuriate Sanchez, the article emphasized that Garcia was actively working with the civil rights Citizens' Committee looking into the Canjilon "cattle pen" incident. Apparently the district attorney rearranged his day. Postponing his appearance at our office, he rushed over to the state capitol with his bodyguard. Emerging from the elevator on the top floor, he was fully prepared to arrest the youngest state governor in the United States for "aiding and abetting."

12

CAPTURE
OF THE
CHIEF

On Tuesday the sheer shock of the attack on Tierra Amarilla and concentration on mass search for the culprits had kept reactions relatively fluid. But on Wednesday the National Guard pulled out. This admission of the attackers' successful escape changed the picture. In the failure to track down the principal raiders, the feud between the governor and the district attorney developed virulently.

Both Cargo and Sanchez were understandably on edge Thursday. The Alianza kingpin, whose charismatic influence had been emphatically demonstrated a few days earlier, was on the loose. His unpredictable, invisible presence began to fill every fearful cranny. This anxiety ignited a new round of charges and countercharges over the responsibility for the raid.

Not long before, Cargo and Sanchez had been mutually wary politicians of opposing party membership. One Sunday during the campaign year of 1966 Cargo was on the stump in Tierra Amarilla. He came upon fellow lawyer Alfonso Sanchez hammering nails into one of his pieces of Main Street real estate. For a politically appropriate number of minutes the two men used the tools side by side.

Both men had left their mark on the Rio Arriba mountain settlement of Canones. As district attorney, Sanchez had filed suit in 1964 against parents on strike about the poor roads their children had to travel to school. Cargo, on the other hand, had made the townlet a symbol of his rural Spanish-American emphasis. His pilgrimages to Canones, one in the company of *New York Times* columnist Tom Wicker, were replete with promises of roads and schools and job opportunities.

Now Sanchez was insisting that it had been a grave misjudgment for the governor to talk personally to the Coyote prisoners that Friday night in the Santa Fe city jail. Cargo's "dallying" and "holding hands" and "coddling" had placed "my life in danger," the district attorney charged. In defense of his pre-raid policies Sanchez maintained that he had not labeled the Alianzans Communists, "but I told them that what they were practicing is a form of Communism." There also appeared in Sanchez's comments a distinct shift in his feeling toward the state police since their previously praised suppression of the Coyote meeting. It had been their fault, the district attorney now maintained, that outstanding warrants for Tijerina were not served before Coyote.

The governor responded with like defensiveness. He had gone to the jail that night to persuade the prisoners being booked to telephone relatives and discourage the Coyote gathering. The state police were most certainly looking for Tijerina before Monday.

"What does Sanchez think they were doing in Tierra Amarilla," Cargo asked with irritation, "looking for Little Orphan Annie?" The governor reminded the district attorney that before flying to Michigan he had made radio pleas for no violence and no Coyote meeting.

But the crux of their differences lay in Cargo's contention that the district attorney could have rounded up the troublemakers beforehand. Sanchez was complaining bitterly that he had three warrants ready for Tijerina's arrest that Friday night but the governor had "asked me to hold up on the warrants until later." So

far this agreed with what those of us observing the efforts to forestall confrontation had witnessed. Then Sanchez painfully admitted
that although he had *not* suspended the warrants as had been requested, Tijerina simply could not be located Friday night.

Cargo lamely had the last word in this self-protective exchange.
"I didn't ask him to hold up on the warrants. I told him not to
get just part of the family, but to try to get all involved, or at least
to try to get Reies first." The governor grew scornful. "Al Sanchez
told me he could have picked him [Reies Tijerina] up any time he
wanted to." Referring to his April conference with the land-grant
leader, he asked, "Why didn't he [Sanchez] arrest him the day he
came up here armed, if he was so dangerous?"

Cargo's disavowal of his request to Sanchez to suspend the Friday offensive certainly contradicted what listeners to his side of his
phone calls to U.S. Attorney Quinn and the district attorney had
understood.

Sanchez shrugged off suggestions that hope of political advantage was behind his strong attacks. "I am running for nothing," he
said. "What would a little peon like me do in the governor's
office?" Actually the state attorney general's job had been rumored
to be more on his mind. When he stalked into the governor's office
on Thursday, however, it was with the authority of an occupant.
Sanchez had been "thunderstruck" by the newspaper story that
the governor's office now admitted being in "direct contact" with
Tijerina. At all costs, he was determined to unlink the chain to the
land-grant leader's whereabouts.

Storming into the OEO offices down the hall on his way to
Cargo's quarters, the district attorney engaged in a tough-worded
conversation with Father Garcia. The OEO director would reveal
only that the governor had talked directly to the "contact" on the
telephone. Sanchez wheeled around and made for Cargo's office.

Taking his bodyguard into the room, Sanchez told the governor
that he had sworn an oath of office and intended to fulfill it. He
recited an "aiding and abetting a criminal" statute. According to
the district attorney, Cargo began "hemming and hawing," but in

143

the end he gave up two names. All evidence points to his revealing Benitez's key liaison role. The governor was also said to have delivered the name of Benitez's principal Alianza contact, the same emissary who had entered Cargo's office under a white flag the previous Saturday morning, Alianza Treasurer Eduardo Chavez. Shortly afterward, official dogging caused Benitez to move his family to Phoenix, Arizona, his original home. It was widely rumored that Cargo's private secretary, a young Spanish-American girl who had been at his side since private law practice, quit soon thereafter to protest this "betrayal." Whatever name or names were revealed by Cargo, they apparently were not "direct links" to Tijerina. But Sanchez conveyed them to state police on the spot.

"Thank you, governor," he said, turning to leave. "That's all I wanted."

Sanchez next visited the *New Mexican* office in his continuing search for individuals to lead him to Tijerina. The publisher's plush second-floor office had been readied for him. Inside sat a lawyer, stenographer, tape recorder, Newspaper President Walter Kerr, Editor Bill Feather, and myself. Sanchez looked suspiciously at the machine.

"What's that for?" For the record, he was informed. "We don't want any record," he snapped. "We just want to talk."

As the tape spools wound steadily, Sanchez formally requested the names of my contacts. First he came on soft.

"Just one, that's all I need, just one."

He listed all the lives that remained in danger with Tijerina at large. Grimy and tired, I stuck to the fabricated story of how I had gotten to the land-grant leader. Finally Sanchez was distracted by our attorney's comment that my story was tantamount to Tijerina's confession. He brightened and seemed to forget his threats of arrest. But he demanded my film and original manuscript.

The negatives had come out of the darkroom tanks solid black. The yellow typed sheets I had ripped into shreds and deposited in the newspaper's back shop bin. For the next hour and a half Sanchez, his Sancho Panza bodyguard, and State Police Captain

T. J. Chavez waded into the mounds of newsprint, to the amusement of black-aproned printers working around them. At last, laid on the floor, were the thirteen jigsaw puzzles of my story.

My report certified that a "citizen's arrest" of Sanchez had been the motive behind Monday's shootout. It provided a glimpse from the enemy camp of the days leading up to the raid. It restated Tijerina's awesome resolution. There had been no begging for understanding. When I asked how long he felt he could hold out as an outlaw, Tijerina had replied calmly:

"I've got a thousand places, there are tens of thousands of families to whom I'm a faithful representative." As less than ten such followers watched him in that mountain shack, he had spread his arms and continued.

"If I'm a fugitive to the federal government or to some poor state officials, to my people I'm not a fugitive. On the contrary, my people have developed a new faith, a new courage and determination. . . ." In replying to my direct query of whether he would undertake guerrilla action, he said cryptically:

"We will reduce our activities to the boundaries and rights of the various free city states."

It later came out that this question had also been bothering Professor Knowlton.

"I went to find out if guerrilla warfare was planned," he said. "To find out if the Tijerina men had automatic weapons and to find out if there were any Cubans in the group." He discovered "none of these."

I later heard that Knowlton's presence had helped to dissuade Tijerina from thoughts of taking over a local radio station. The professor reassured Tijerina, during their private conversation in the dark, that his wife was safe. But her miscarriage after she left the Santa Fe jail was attributed to the strains of this period.

With the disclosures resulting from our trek to Tijerina's hideout, the fat was in the fire at the OEO office. Father Garcia occupied the hottest seat. A state employee who joined a civil rights group was annoying to right-leaning newspapers and politicians alike. When it appeared that the OEO office had somehow taken part in sending intermediaries to insurgents in the mountains, a whiff of treason was in the air. Using state funds to fly a rebel sympathizer (Knowlton) to the state was the last straw. Now the OEO received the brunt of the pent-up desire for revenge for the raid.

Cargo's "riot experts"—the California team—were sneeringly mentioned in news stories. Father Garcia accepted full responsibility for summoning Knowlton, but not for dispatching the professor north. Knowlton later explained:

"There were all sorts of rumors going around Santa Fe and no one knew what was going on. Father Garcia didn't know I had gone until I was back. I went on my own. I then advised him of what I had seen and asked him to pass it on."

As the man responsible for the "OEO meddling," Garcia was besieged for explanation. In defending Knowlton's role he said:

"The roots are sociological. I intended Dr. Knowlton to assist me with his advice in the causes of the insurrection. . . . He knows a great many of these people and groups in northern New Mexico. These people trust him. . . . They communicated with him. . . ."

Reporters hammered at the man. He acknowledged that the "communications" he was referring to had been by telephone. He said it was not within his province to urge those still at large to surrender, but added, "Of course we relayed the governor's messages to them."

Then Garcia was prodded about reports that his office had asked for a general amnesty.

"Let me put it this way," he tried to explain. "We asked the governor at the very beginning if he would give safe conduct passes to those people so he might meet with those people without their being arrested."

"The governor refused, did he not?" a newsman shot back.

"I would have to go back and determine who backed off," answered Garcia. "The final answer was, since it would be almost impossible to keep the district attorney from making an arrest, they finally decided this was not considered to be feasible."

Pressed for his opinion, Cargo said he was "not very happy" about the secretive goings-on. He emphatically denied that his office had ever requested a plane for Knowlton, whom he shortly thereafter characterized as "a broken-down old professor." He said he couldn't think of any reason why Knowlton should have been brought in, adding, "I wish they had asked me about it."

While the OEO controversy was starting to boil over on Thursday, the governor was attempting to settle other brush fires resulting from the raid. He was publicly optimistic about the "revolution" being over. But Police Chief Black advised him not to extend his confidence to a visit to Hernandez, where Tijerina was believed to be hiding. The governor's wife had remained on Mackinac Island, Michigan, with Governor and Mrs. George Romney, but her name in the confiscated Alianza files forced him to explain.

"My wife is not much of a joiner but is an heir of the Atrisco land grant," he said, referring to an Albuquerque suburb that is still under the heirs' control. "These people kept after her to join. About three years ago, she gave them six dollars. I guess I could deny it because she gave them the money in cash, but she gave them money." Cargo put a quick stop to the association. "I think people should attack me and not my wife," he added. He said the only time his wife had attended an Alianza rally was when they ran into Tijerina addressing a gathering on a drive to Taos a few months before. During a dinner party at La Fonda later, Cargo would sink into his chair a little as his wife gaily teased him: "And all that time he was sleeping with an Alianza member."

On Thursday Mrs. Mary Escobar Tijerina, Reies's first wife, came to ask the governor's help in releasing her daughter Rosa from prison. After promising what little he could, Cargo discussed with a *New York Times* correspondent the factors behind the violence:

"Little chance for education of the children. Poverty. Poor roads. Disputes over park boundaries, and the people being refused permits to graze cattle in the national forest."

TIJERINA and the COURTHOUSE RAID

Later that day the governor's attention was again abruptly diverted from any perspective of the raid's causes and effects. Albuquerque news media had received a 1,500-word typed letter signed by Tijerina and mailed in Espanola on Tuesday. Written as a communiqué from one sovereignty—the "free city state" of San Joaquin—to the state of New Mexico, the document appeared to be a combination of the royalist jargon of Jerry Noll and the impetuous pronouncements of Tijerina. Throughout its haughty wordage Cargo was severely castigated. But what caught the governor's eye was this sentence:

"The officers and agents of the U.S. Government and of the state administration should realize that their families are in a vulnerable position, since most of them reside within the territorial jurisdiction of one of these free city states, and these free city states are fully determined that these persons are not going to do their dirty work and hide behind their office. . . ."

Federal officials immediately appropriated the letter to investigate possible violations of postal regulations in its wording. Cargo felt personally challenged.

"If he wants to come to my house, let him," the governor dared. "He has threatened my family and I'll meet him in the front yard, and he won't get a chance to explain."

At the same time the governor obtained extra police for the front yard of his mansion to protect his wife and two children when they got back from Michigan.

The two consultants, Burgos and Aragon, had lain low since their return from Tierra Amarilla Monday night. Their work since then had been awkwardly conducted in the midst of the very turmoil they had been hired to clarify and prevent. They recognized that their most practical contribution had come during their Friday night discussion with Cargo. But even its benefits had been negated at the very moment they were advising him. Now all they could hope to achieve was some written summation of the second half of their mission, an analysis of the frictions in the north. On Thursday they checked out of their motel and flew home to California.

148

Knowlton waited until Friday, still insisting to the reporters who got to him that he had not come to investigate civil rights matters. "I was brought up," he said, "because it was thought by some people in Santa Fe that I might be able to help in securing information and give advice on the situation."

Knowlton's emergency summons to New Mexico had cost Garcia's office $157.50, paid to the state Corporation Commission for the use of the plane and pilot. Out of his own pocket the professor bought his air ticket home to El Paso on Friday.

Knowlton's justification for appearing in New Mexico after the raid was words in the wind. Such criticism poured onto the OEO offices that the state's attorney general began considering an investigation into "alleged complicity" between the Alianza and the state Office of Economic Opportunity.

By Friday Cargo was a little calmer about his family's safety. He revealed that he had received a second communication from Tijerina. This was a postscript explaining that the first letter was not meant to apply to the governor and his family. In Cargo's words, "He meant it for everybody else but me."

But others were still highly incensed about the immediate results of the raid. Voicing indignation at the Canjilon incident, Bernalillo County Democratic Chairman William J. Byatt demanded the facts.

"It was a vicious violation of civil rights to haul these innocent people from their homes without warrants and haul them into barbed-wire pens like cattle," he told party officials at the end of their meeting Friday night. "Regardless of Tijerina," Byatt said, "I demand a full investigation of what went on in Rio Arriba County. These people weren't in the courthouse."

During the first days after the raid, representatives of the American Civil Liberties Union had kept their distance. Now Byatt said that the New Mexico chapter of the ACLU was meeting Saturday to discuss the entire Canjilon episode.

In Denver, Colorado, the guest who never came to Coyote was also talking with great fury about the Canjilon incident. Rudolph

TIJERINA and the COURTHOUSE RAID

"Corky" Gonzales, the nearest militant leader from another state, had led a Crusade for Justice contingent to New Mexico on Thursday for a first-hand appraisal of the situation. Returning to Denver Friday night he drafted a telegram to President Lyndon Johnson, Attorney General Ramsey Clark, Director of the Civil Rights Commission William Taylor, Governor Cargo, and District Attorney Sanchez. His wire read:

". . . It is with great concern that we ask your immediate consideration and attention to afford fair and impartial administration of justice to those individuals arrested and now in custody . . . areas of concern are fair and reasonable bond, legal aid and a thorough investigation of the legality of all arrests, warrants, interrogation, search and seizure procedures, etc. . . . It is of imperative importance that the incidents, long standing problems and complete disregard of the law [the Treaty of Guadalupe Hidalgo] be thoroughly studied, evaluated and acted upon in order to prevent future problems and misunderstandings. . . ."

Meanwhile the U.S. Department of Justice had been forced by the New Mexico turmoil into restating its attitude toward the landgrant claims. The Alianza's demands, one Washington official said, "are so fantastic that it's difficult to form a defense in reasonable words." Another spokesman felt "there's an element of racial feeling that's being played on," and quoted a paragraph in the Alianza's twenty-page pamphlet which asserted, "The Spanish people do not want or seek to integrate with the Anglos. They want to be left alone." If the Alianza ever took its arguments into a court, the Justice Department believed, a recent southwestern decision would hamper its case. A southern Colorado court had ruled in a dispute over the Sangre de Cristo grant that rights under Mexican law did not survive U.S. occupation and that if there were violation of the Guadalupe Hidalgo Treaty, this was for courts to investigate further.

Gonzales's telegram to the President was dispatched only after a sympathy rally on Saturday in Denver's Sunken Gardens. The athletic young leader called for "dedicated and concerned members of our community . . . not only in Denver but in the entire southwest . . . to support a just and honorable cause." Gonzales had been unable to fulfill his own desire to meet the fugitives in the hills. By Friday night Tijerina still had not been apprehended. State Police Chief Black vowed to keep his men on double duty as long as "the big prize remains at large."

Shortly after midnight Friday I was yanked from my first real sleep of the exhausting week by a telephone call. An anonymous tipster had brought about the capture of Tijerina and his son on a road near Bernalillo. The newspaper office wanted me there immediately in case someone thought I had leaked the leader's whereabouts.

About two weeks later Tijerina was sitting in the glassed visitor's cubicle at New Mexico State Prison. He was pretending to talk to his blind attorney, Albert Gonzales, for whom I was disguised as a seeing-eye secretary. My two-and-a-half hour interview yielded a fascinating account of Tijerina's upbringing and philosophy. I launched our conversation by asking him about his capture.

In the well-fed, recuperative ease of prison Tijerina recalled a gas station attendant at San Ysidro staring at him with sudden awareness.

"That man that saw me, I saw him recognize me, because he looked startled. . . . I was going to tell my son and Ubaldo [Ubaldo Velasquez, a HELP employee and the third man in the car] to let me off before entering Bernalillo, but honest to God, I fell asleep. I was going to Albuquerque to report $200 raised in San Mateo. And I had in my mind to ask Cargo through negotiators to drop all the charges of the men who had been arrested for unlawful assembly and I would turn myself in to clarify the whole question.

"The officer who arrested me said in the papers that I hadn't shown no surprise, no resistance. But, honest to God, I had fallen asleep. I knew it. I knew it then. That's why it was the will of God."

151

TIJERINA and the COURTHOUSE RAID

According to Velasquez, Tijerina and his son had come to him Friday afternoon wanting a ride to Cuba. Apparently the three had changed their route that night after spotting police on the highway. The "anonymous" call to Albuquerque state police headquarters had described Tijerina as appearing "very, very thirsty." His stomach was hurting from bad water he had drunk in the mountains, Tijerina believed. He had been spitting blood. The attendant's shock of recognition came as Tijerina leaned over to drink from the station's hose. As soon as the brown 1960 Ford driven by Tijerina's son was out of sight he rang up the police. Over two-way car radios crackled the alert: *Tijerina heading south on State Road 44 with two other males.*

At quarter after midnight an unmarked state police vehicle located a car fitting the given description within Bernalillo's city limits. Radioing ahead, a marked car flashed the Ford off the highway. When plainclothesmen cut off an escape to the rear, an officer walked up to find young Reies Jr. in the driver's seat "acting casual as though it was a routine stop for a traffic violation." The youth was recognized. A flashlight beam fell on Reies himself, lying down on the back seat. A loaded Spanish-made Llama .380 automatic pistol was found in the right rear pocket of his trousers.

"He said nothing whatever," recalled the arresting officer, "except that he had a stomach ache."

Meanwhile other patrol cars had rushed to the scene. The three men were handcuffed, taken to separate cars, and six squad cars with sirens wailing and lights flashing raced at eighty-five miles an hour to the Santa Fe jail. There Tijerina was held on two counts of assault to commit murder, two counts of kidnapping, one count of destruction of state property, and one more count of possessing a deadly weapon.

When he was searched, another pocket was found to contain a much-folded tearsheet from the previous Sunday's *Albuquerque Journal*. It was an account of the swift police action that had nipped the gathering at Coyote in the bud. The headline read, "Land Grant Showdown Fails."

152

News of the arrest threw State Police Chief Black into metaphor: "A jewel that dropped out of its setting," he proclaimed, "and we picked it up."

"Tijerina got a little too bold," mulled Cargo. "I was really happy to hear he was caught. Joe [Chief Black] did a beautiful job." The governor's warmth towards his police chief grew. "He knew the people well. He knew pretty much how they thought. If you know something about these people you can sort of predict what is going to happen in certain instances." Presumably Cargo was referring to the fortuitous arrest and not to Monday afternoon in Tierra Amarilla.

District Attorney Sanchez was no less elated. "We're very happy Reies Lopez Tijerina was caught." His understatement became officially charitable. "We're happy no one was injured, including Reies Lopez Tijerina." The state police were back in Sanchez's good graces. "I think the public should be justifiably proud of the work done by the state police."

"His own people are the ones turning him in," Sheriff Naranjo said on learning of the capture. "They don't trust Tijerina any more. They're frightened." Then Naranjo was taken to the Santa Fe city jail where he formally identified Tijerina as present at the raid. The sheriff asked Tijerina point-blank about his brother Cristobal and Baltazar Martinez. "If they're still in my county I want to know about it." Tijerina looked at him and said nothing. Naranjo felt that if these two men were apprehended, "that would break the whole thing."

Tijerina was ready to discuss other matters, however. He got his chance at noon when he was taken by patrol car for the four-block ride to the Santa Fe County courthouse. As with Wednesday's courtroom appearance, the precautions were impressive.

At the Santa Fe city jail officers had been stationed at windows with rifles. Here in the courtroom, Judge Scarborough again wore his trusty tooled leather holster and armed officers stood at each shoulder. Over thirty additional police swarmed around the building, directing traffic, not hiding their sawed-off shotguns, .30/.30

carbines, and sidearms. At the wooden doors to the court, the police searched all who entered.

At mid-Saturday's formal reading of the charges Judge Scarborough advised the three men of their rights, then read through the counts. Tijerina was still wearing the snap-buttoned western cut shirt which had seemed so neat in the hills. Now it looked lived-in. But Tijerina himself seemed relaxed and almost relieved as he heard the death-penalty charges of kidnapping read out loud. Although Sanchez had drawn up these charges, his assistant Norman Neel did not believe the first-degree kidnapping would stick. The exact definition of the "great bodily harm" which distinguished the first- and second-degree kidnapping counts would be disputed during later court appearances.

Earlier in the morning the state police had obtained a new statement from UPI Reporter Larry Calloway, one of those abducted after the raid. Now Calloway revealed that he had seen Tijerina's son carrying a gun in the besieged building. The same charges made against his father were brought against Reies Jr., with the difference that instead of being accused of carrying a deadly weapon the youth was charged with aiding a felon. Sanchez had to provide Scarborough with an argument for thus incriminating the young man in black T-shirt and tanker jacket who seemed bored with it all. "He had a gun, rifle, or deadly weapon," Sanchez testified, "and participated in all the proceedings as a principal or as an aider or abettor." It was enough.

But before the short session got under way Tijerina had been permitted to talk freely with newsmen. When he had been taken to the jail that night, he complained, he had not been advised of his rights and was given trouble when he tried to make a phone call. He was not bitter, however, as reporters crowded around the defense table where he sat with Albert Gonzales.

"You can't help these mistakes," he said of Monday's raid. "It is like Vietnam. You can't blame President Johnson when soldiers kill women and children."

Where was he on June 5, 1967? That was naturally the first question asked. Tijerina maintained he had been in San Mateo, near Grants, in the morning, and then had driven to a friend's house somewhere around Coyote. Throughout the hunt for him, he said, the house was never searched.

Wouldn't his arrest hurt his cause?

"Of course not!" Tijerina hurled back. "It strengthened it. You can now see the success of leaders working on the minds of the people. The state made a very big blunder in calling for the confiscation of property and mass arrests for unlawful assembly. You don't even find that in Russia." He said his capture would be a "spur for the people" to organize.

To summarize the value of the raid he used the same word he had used to assess the Echo Amphitheater incident:

"Publicity," he said. The shootout had been the only way his followers "could get their yell across the country and the world."

The plan to arrest Sanchez had been made the day before the raid, he continued, but now he placed the decision-making meeting in Albuquerque. He admitted signing the letter to the news media, but said he had not written it himself. He had been upset when he learned it had been interpreted as a threat; the unnamed scribe had only been instructed to state the Alianza's claims and complain about the trouble at Coyote.

"I felt very, very bad," Tijerina said. "I'd like some day, if my future permits, to offer my apology to the governor."

Tijerina felt that Larry Calloway had been unfavorable to him ever since the reporter had covered the Echo Amphitheater incident. "He'd like to see me behind bars." Questioned about the gun he was carrying when captured, Tijerina said it had become a habit "because the state police have a plan to get rid of me for good." As in my interview with him, he denied claims that he had involved himself in the discontents of the northern counties for personal gain.

"My confederation has an income of from $300 to $500 a month, and it doesn't go into my pocket, except for some expense money."

Before he was led away to prison, Tijerina gave his forthright summation of the courthouse raid:

"It was a terrible but terrific success."

13

REVERBERATIONS FROM THE RAID

Even amid the din of war in the Middle East, the shots fired at Tierra Amarilla were eventually heard around the world. The little episode with its anachronistic ingredients seemed to justify many foreigners' preconceptions about America's actual age. France in particular gloated over having its stereotype of Wild West primitivism borne out. The Paris edition of the *New York Times* revealed that *le western* was not a cultural myth.

To Americans as well the raid contained all the elements of the latest vogue in western movies. Recently the cowboy formula has been carried south of the border, adding a dash of Mexican chili pepper flavoring: *bandidos, rurales,* flamboyant costuming, revolutionist trappings, crumbling Spanish colonial locations. Here it was brought to life in the thrilling raw. A *New York Times* editorial irresponsibly played up the cinematic similarities. In mock scenario format it described the developments up to, through, and after the courthouse raid. It described The Shootout, The Chase—with

TIJERINA and the COURTHOUSE RAID

"Jolly's raiders" pursuing the brigands—and tried to mitigate its flippancy with a hollow final chord of social concern.

Not all eastern response to this western event was so superficial. In the chambers of a Washington subcommittee House legislators would probe the "why" of the raid from flown-in witnesses. And, inevitably, cliches would be mouthed to explain, and hopelessly confuse, the network of human relationships which had short-circuited that traumatic Monday afternoon. The Right started to ascribe the raid to Communist agitation and "outside" rabble-rousing. The Left began capitalizing on the enthralled audience to bring forth accusations of enslaved minorities and police states. The Center talked glibly of social frustration and economic depression.

With the outpouring of explanations and rationalizations, two principal courses of action were apparent. The courthouse raid became a catalyst for a new, intensive look at the northern counties with an eye towards reform and repair. On the other hand it gave those pressing the other priority at issue—order and punishment—an opportunity to raise a hue and cry over such suspicious "meddling" in volatile social issues as Father Robert Garcia's office had demonstrated throughout the critical week after the raid.

Locally, the attack cut to the quick the polite but ever touchy relations between Anglo and Spanish. Some were delighted to see the status quo embarrassed by Tijerina's threat to the Spanish middle class. These *Tio Tomases* (Uncle Toms) were felt by some to be worse oppressors of their own people when they obtained public office than the usual Anglo officials. Newspapers north of U.S. Route 66 were swamped with impassioned letters revealing the emotions which had been pent up. Many agreed with Sheikh Khalid Al Quasimi, who was visiting Taos during the excitement to gather new ideas of agricultural development for his Middle East kingdom of Rashlkhamia. "I was surprised to hear of such a thing in the U.S." exclaimed the potentate, who felt the raid was "the result of too much freedom." The crew-cut Anglo cattlemen straight out of the north's "Marlboro Country" echoed the sheikh's comments.

158

They lined up foursquare against the insidious prospect of "revolution" in their range lands.

Meanwhile the Alianza membership was beginning its celebrating. As an Alianza leader boasted, "Al Sanchez has given us more publicity than we could have bought with $10,000,000. . . . The best thing that could happen to us would be if Al Sanchez would jail 200 more members."

Ballads called *corridos* were being composed with stubby pencils in rural shacks. To be droned at Alianza meetings without guitar accompaniment, these strings of quatrains placed the raid and its participants in instant folk legend. Then, as with the Calypso tradition, opposing *corridos* would come along and depict disenchantment with the Alianza.

Authorized Alianza strategy was not forthcoming as long as Tijerina, who had opened this Pandora's box of reactions, proposals, controversies, and land investigations, was still in prison. In his absence Corky Gonzales partly filled the leadership vacuum. But Gonzales seemed wary of trying to assume Tijerina's position. With a small Denver group he had come to Albuquerque, sleeping on the couches and benches of the Alianza headquarters, assisting in the Tijerina Defense Fund which had just been organized, letting a little of his urban militant thinking rub off on the rural land granters. For a Santa Fe rally in support of Tijerina, Gonzales coined the slogan, "We'd rather die in Tierra Amarilla than in Vietnam."

At the same time Tijerina was growing fat and colorless in his solitary cell. He read with deepening pleasure the newspapers smuggled to him, conversed with his Spanish-American guards, who were exceptionally friendly. They showed a kind of admiration which quite a few quiet-living, law-abiding Spanish-American townspeople in the north were showing only in private conversation. A cultural respect for raw *machismo* (code of masculinity) and the revelation that prejudice had indeed disturbed their self-respect produced an underground wave of racial sympathy for Tijerina. He had "put it to them."

159

TIJERINA and the COURTHOUSE RAID

When he had first walked through the disinfectant-smelling hallways of the modern prison, inmates had yelled "Viva Tijerina!" His fellow Alianzans already in prison had developed a cordial relationship with the guards; somehow they were in the noncriminal category of political prisoners.

Once, in a prison courtyard, Reies glimpsed a prisoner he recognized, his brother Margarito. Margarito had come from Indiana to see his brothers in the summer of 1964. On New Year's Day, 1966, he was charged with the stabbing and robbery of an elderly Anglo couple who ran a general store in Rutheron near Tierra Amarilla. Margarito was currently serving a ten- to fifty-year term, and District Attorney Sanchez was trying to have him committed for life on a "habitual criminal" charge.

After a few weeks of what Reies typically termed his "forty days," a few carloads of girl admirers had to be turned away on visitors' day. But life "inside" was mostly uneventful, a time for Tijerina to revive physical and spiritual energy.

"Outside," the state's four congressmen were breaking their nervously noncommittal silence. During the uncertain days of Tijerina's outlawhood the venerable Senator Clinton Anderson, his colleague Joseph M. Montoya, and Representatives Thomas Morris and Johnny Walker had lain low, carefully watching the New Mexico public attitude. An early observer once noted, "In New Mexico racial antagonism is the sword of Damocles ever hanging by a horsehair over the head of the politician." The courthouse invasion had severed that hair, and the state's leading political figures were well aware of the delicate ground they were on.

Senators Anderson and Montoya were reported to be disconcerted by the image of Governor Cargo which had emerged. Playing his central position very cagily, Cargo had preserved his "ethnic" support while remaining free from most Anglo criticism—but not all. A float in the upcoming satirical parade during Santa Fe's Fiesta would represent a sentence being mockingly passed in conservative quarters: "Governor Cargo leads the Tijerina Brass."

Senator Montoya, on the other hand, had been forced to straddle a sharper fence than ever before. He tiptoed through his first public statements. "My great concern," he said, "is that the rest of the state has not been told that this matter in northern New Mexico was led not by natives, but by outsiders." The senator hastily explained that he was not "blaming the news media, but the implications that are being drawn should be rebutted, because the people of the north are law-abiding, religious people. They have always treated the Anglo with great cordiality and hospitality." Montoya was also cautious not to identify Tijerina by name, although soon the political climate would permit him to vent his personal feelings about the "outsider."

Senator Anderson, following the Department of Agriculture's conservationist line which he had been instrumental in formulating years before, was totally unsympathetic to any rationalization of the violence. None of the congressmen had missed the irate response of their home state political cronies who were insulted by the spectacle of a motley crew of unshaven farmers and grazers making mincemeat of a county seat.

On the morning of Tijerina's capture the Washington congressmen sped a joint telegram to statewide media announcing that "We are asking the Justice Department and the OEO to investigate fully the OEO programs in New Mexico and try to determine if the rioting and insurrection in Rio Arriba County is in any way connected with the OEO programs." Following this directive, the state's attorney general began his six-month investigation of "alleged complicity" between the OEO and the Alianza.

Governor Cargo was unimpressed by the congressional telegram. He recalled that Washington-based observer Anthony Tinajero had been on the scene since the raid.

"All they have to do is talk to him. He's back in Washington. Most of what was done was at his direction, not Father Garcia's. I'm sure Father Garcia is not blameless but . . . ."

Cargo disclosed that he had restrained District Attorney Sanchez from arresting Father Garcia for "aiding or harboring felons," during their testy round of confrontations Thursday afternoon.

Sanchez denied this, however, saying that he had simply telephoned Father Garcia and, when the OEO director flatly refused to reveal his "contact," had read aloud the statute. "I merely reminded him of the law," the district attorney said. Now, he added, he would not file any charges against Father Garcia since he had obtained the information he was after from Cargo.

Although not a working day, that Saturday of Tijerina's incarceration was busy with speech-making. Congressman Morris was in Santa Fe intimating that antipoverty funds were "financing a revolution." He demanded an accounting of Knowlton's "midnight plane rides."

Both Governor Cargo and District Attorney Sanchez were slated to address the same audience that morning, a Spanish-American veterans group called the G.I. Forum. It was the Forum that had in earlier days requested Sanchez, then a private attorney, to look into the petition of northern land claimants. Once again the conflict between the two men's treatment of the crisis was manifest. Sanchez directed his remarks towards his audience's racial insecurity. He articulated their worry that "already the public may have a wrong image of our people." He identified Tijerina as the raid's sole mover, a man who had "duped and misled . . . our people."

Cargo completely disagreed with this narrow focus. "Nothing could be further from the truth," he argued, concentrating on the underlying poverty issues. Again he denied "coddling" the Alianza, but insisted "there's nothing wrong with listening." All in all, it was a repetitious exchange.

Just before the raid Cargo had praised Sheriff Benny Naranjo's "quiet diplomacy" in connection with the Coyote meeting, contrasting it with Sanchez's heavy-handed moves. Now, however, the raid had become a political football. Naranjo, the arch-Democrat of Rio Arriba County, exchanged partisan criticism with the governor over who was more sincerely concerned with seeing the land-ownership questions brought under full-scale examination.

But before the governor flew to hearings in Washington the next week he was exposed to a more severe test of local reaction. Six influential Anglo ranchers and resort managers angrily came south from Rio Arriba County to ask Cargo's support in reviving their region's image.

This delegation epitomized the chamois- and fleece-clad custodians of the north's sportsman's paradise where after a long day in the saddle men relax in their shellacked knotty pine dens drinking bourbon neat beneath trophy heads. They glory in independence, cowtown rusticness, and scorn of the citified world they seem to be trying to impress. Some of these visitors lived in the neighborhood of two-room adobe homes whose occupants speak a different language, go to a different church, have different folk heroes and community mores, believe in an entirely different concept of land use and ownership, and eat chili-spiced beans, stewed meat, flour tortillas, and mugs of black coffee with grounds washing in the bottom instead of whiskey, sirloin, french fries, or apple pie.

Now their main commodity, wilderness, was teeming with fish and game. But their main customers, tourists, were still avoiding the danger zone. Streams and lakesides were void of anglers. Lodges were vacant. Cargo promised a publicity-loaded fishing trip to personally demonstrate the area's safety. He also vowed to fight for an emergency $10,000 allocation to promote tourism. Then the meeting got sticky.

The governor was asked his own feelings about the status of titles to land in northern New Mexico.

"You paid taxes on it," Cargo admitted. "You hold it by adverse possession. You hold it, but the land was stolen originally." The governor tried to be more exact. "Legally you own it because you have title that you can get title insurance on. But I do think when the land was acquired initially it was acquired in a most peculiar manner."

Bill Mundy, who had just lost the third barn in his harassed career as a northern rancher, was a member of the group. Now he complained to Cargo that he had lost a $600,000 land sale recently because of the agitation. Tijerina's movement was "a national problem," he informed the governor. Why had Cargo been out of the state that critical Monday, he wanted to know.

"Now listen," answered Cargo, his face reddening. "If you think I planned this thing Monday you're crazier than hell." He said that if he'd known the Monday arraignments were going to be held he would have been sure extra police were on duty in Tierra Amarilla. Before long Mundy's insinuations caused Cargo to ask, "You think the Communist Party is behind it all, is that right?"

Mundy felt that was about correct. The governor challenged the rancher to say openly if he was accusing him of being a Communist.

"I don't know you that well," the crusty cattleman fired back. "When I believe you are one, I'll call you one."

Another northerner was anxious that it be "emphasized over and over again that there are no documents to support these claims," referring to the Alianzans' land arguments. Here Cargo replied guardedly because a legislative proposal on this question was shaping up in his mind.

A year before the New Mexico legislature had created an interim committee to study land titles. An appropriation of $15,000 had been authorized but the group had met only once and spent only $258. The governor was shortly to create his own land-title committee to unravel the incredible tangle of legalities which was the north's landownership.

Cargo was placed on the defensive by other factors as well. Again he had to acknowledge that his wife might have contributed to the Alianza, but he now maintained he had "had no knowledge" that she belonged. When she had idly mentioned donating to a land-grant group, Cargo said, he had put his foot down.

"On my Scout's honor," he pleaded with entertained newsmen, "my wife is seven months pregnant and she did not anticipate the Tierra Amarilla raid."

Cargo also revealed that from his own pocket he was putting up a $500 reward for information leading to the capture of Deputy Sheriff Jaramillo's wild young abductor, Baltazar Martinez. Agent

164

Mason Working of the Albuquerque FBI office said the bureau was hunting both Martinez and Cristobal Tijerina intensely throughout the five southwestern states. Warrants were also issued for the arrest of Reies Tijerina's fourteen-year-old son Danny on the same twenty-eight charges that were filed against the twenty adults already in custody or being sought—twenty-four of kidnapping, three of assault with intent to commit a violent felony (to kill), and one of assault on a jail. In the north, Juan Valdez and Moises Morales were the other names not checked off in the well-memorized list the police kept in their heads.

In Washington, D.C., New York Congressman Joseph Resnick lost no time in construing the raid as a manifestation of that species of rural ailment which his House Agricultural Subcommittee on Rural Development was trying to document. Exactly a week after Tierra Amarilla's afternoon of guns he allotted as much time as necessary to accumulate testimony interpreting the raid and its roots.

The lead-off witness was Alex Mercure, New Mexico director of HELP, the one truly innovative and effective poverty-fighting agency in the state. Mercure warned that there existed a high probability of further violence across the breadth of northern New Mexico, southern Colorado, and parts of Texas. Under conditions where one-fourth of the state's one million people were poverty-stricken, he said—where many families suffered severe malnutrition and felt themselves continually alienated from the dominant culture—the likelihood of more guerrilla-style trouble was high.

To illustrate, Mercure pictured for the listening congressmen the northern New Mexico community of Penasco. Established 200 years ago, around it now live about 4,000 citizens who are almost entirely of Spanish-American descent and culture. Two-thirds of their homes are substandard. Two-thirds have no indoor plumbing. An average of two people live in each room. In the winter, when the thermometer sometimes cannot register the thirty-below-zero tem-

165

perature, half the labor force is without work. The menfolk have few modern skills and an excess of language and literacy deficiencies.

In the Monday hearing Congressman Robert Mathias of California commented that in his state some programs for the poor "actually taught them to dissent." Then he asked Mercure, "You don't go as far as to teach them how to organize a picket line, do you?"

"Not yet," the HELP director replied.

Further disclosures about the quality of life in what Resnick termed "the Watts of rural America" came from Father Robert Garcia. The priest, showing the strain of conservative attacks at home, appealed "to the state and federal governments to help these people follow up on their symbolic attempt to help themselves." Then Garcia heated New Mexico tempers anew by suggesting to the subcommittee that "perhaps these people did not really intend to shoot anybody." Unintentionally, Chief Black had suggested this when a preliminary survey of the TA courthouse just after the attack failed to turn up enough used slugs.

"The only thing I can figure," Black had been quoted as saying, "is that some persons may have been shooting blanks, or shooting out of windows." His men had gouged only four spent bullets from the plaster walls and three from the shattered police cars. "Witnesses we have interrogated indicated many shots were fired," Black continued hopefully. "We may find more slugs before it's all over." Reporter Calloway later remembered a man firing point-blank at a glass door while the pane remained intact. He also puzzled over "hundreds of gunshots" he had heard.

When Father Garcia picked up this point Chief Black suddenly altered his figures. Now he reported about thirty slugs recovered from the cars and roughly ten from the courthouse. While this still did not account for the hundreds of used cartridge casings said to have been lying around, the state's attorney general later upped his estimate to "in excess of fifty bullet holes . . . found in building and cars." But he made no further attempt to deny the possible use of blanks. Enraged at the dispute, State Policeman Saiz assured reporters from his hospital bed that no blank had crashed through his arm and lung.

Next, Professor Clark Knowlton provided the Resnick subcommittee with some historical background on northern discontent. The star witness, however, was Governor Cargo. At first unwilling to be absent from New Mexico again during an unsettled period, Cargo was persuaded that it would be in his interest to fly to Washington for an appearance on Wednesday.

The governor was in good form at the long hearing, handing out criticism in all directions. Historically, he felt, his predecessors in state government had let the north down.

"If you could pave roads with broken promises," he said, "we could have blacktopped all of northern New Mexico years ago."

Today, he maintained, the war on poverty was spending too much money and time researching its deprived areas instead of reconstructing them. In Rio Arriba, he charged, the OEO provided two programs, "one of Head Start and one of frustration." Rural poverty warriors "spend more time counting outhouses than counting people." As for the Forest Service, Cargo ridiculed their iron-clad set of grazing restrictions. On one rule, that herdsmen cannot use horses in federal forests, he commented, "It's pretty difficult to herd sheep and cows on foot."

On another regulation, that sheepherders have to demolish their cabins in forests designated as wilderness areas, he said, "I believe in wilderness areas, but this is ridiculous. If I'm a sheepherder, I'd like to go in style and live in a shack."

Following these charges both Sargent Shriver and Orville Freeman, then respectively national director of OEO and Secretary of Agriculture, were understandably anxious to have words with the governor.

At last Resnick gave the Forest Service a chance to state its case. But Regional Forester W. D. Hurst no sooner finished emphasizing the service's willingness to cooperate in improving its community relations than Resnick was handed a report from Governor Cargo complaining that Hurst's own office was denying him access to land-use records.

The Forest Service's testimony kept undercutting itself with examples of the very communication difficulties earlier witnesses had been decrying. A former official, Gilbert Duran, first maintained that no recreational grazing permits—for saddle horses, that is—had been issued on lands where meat livestock grazing was also forbidden. But he conceded to Resnick that such selectivity in favor of rented ponies had occurred in the Pecos Wilderness Area. Similarly, he first denied that village shepherds were forced to tend their animals afoot, but under later questioning he acknowledged that this had been done in about 1,000 cases.

Finally Resnick accused the Forest Service of acting as a "foreign barrier" to the impoverished northern Spanish-Americans. On the basis of the testimony he had heard about civil rights abuses immediately after the courthouse raid, his committee dispatched a telegram to Attorney General Ramsey Clark calling for an immediate investigation "to determine to what extent the civil rights of innocent people were violated and to punish those responsible."

Back in New Mexico the local Civil Liberties Union was already pursuing this investigation on its own. After open hearings to obtain depositions about what had taken place at Canjilon, the "detained" Alianza members, with ACLU financing and lawyers, shortly filed a $39,000 damage suit against Chief Black, General Jolly, and District Attorney Sanchez. They charged that state police and guardsmen had illegally herded forty to fifty members of the Alianza into a barbed-wire stockade and held them incommunicado from 4:30 p.m. on Monday, June 5, to 5:30 p.m. the following day.

Sanchez turned his wrath on the news media for propagating the image of dung-covered cattle pens filled with prisoners.

"There may be some arrests if I file libel charges against some of these people who have printed lies in newspapers that the people were kept in cowpens. The reports are completely false."

REVERBERATIONS FROM THE RAID

Chief Black said merely that the ACLU charges filed on behalf of thirteen Alianzans were untrue. The Canjilon prisoners had simply been held in "protective custody." General Jolly refused to say anything. (The suit against Jolly, Sanchez, and Black eventually proved unsuccessful when it came to trial in 1969. However, the jury returned a verdict against four state policemen. They had violated the civil rights of an Alianzan whom they arrested when he banned them from his house. They then searched it without a warrant.)

The raid continued to polarize popular sentiment, sometimes with painful results. Two Alianzans who had been held in the outdoor detention camp filed complaints with the Equal Employment Commission accusing their former boss of firing them for belonging to the militant land-grant movement.

"They weren't fired for taking part in that organization," countered Clark M. Carr, president of Albuquerque's Carco Air Service. "But any man that tells me they condone the shooting of police officers and the takeover of our government has no place in my organization."

A sixteen-year-old girl, the daughter of one Abelecio Moya who was charged in the raid, was then being held on a warrant signed by Sanchez. It was learned that Sanchez had waited three weeks to arrest her on all the twenty-eight charges connected with the raid and then took his time scheduling a hearing for her. The district attorney explained, "We try and do justice and we try and be sure on something like this. The wheels of justice may be a little slow." When the girl was later released, all charges against her were dropped.

Meanwhile one of the Alianza members chosen for imprisonment from the Canjilon crowd was keeping an abbreviated diary on New Mexico State Prison stationery. The recipient of a Korean War medal, José Madril of Velarde began his notes: ". . . never have I seen a happier bunch of prisoners in my life as those with me in the New Mexico State Prison. The guards are very nice. They understand our being here, they know we are fighting for justice."

TIJERINA and the COURTHOUSE RAID

Madril described the pre-arraignment hearing two days after the raid.

"The [Santa Fe] courthouse was full and all around that block in that part of town they were yelling 'Viva los Tijerinas!' But nothing could be done that day to set bond for us. May God bless all our people on our side, for we are the happy prisoners of justice. The hours are indeed long without our loved ones. . . ."

Then three Alianzans still at large were captured by the police under different circumstances. At midmorning June 13 Moises Morales, slender and relaxed and sporting a black crepe shirt, opened the doors of the Espanola state police office to surrender. Two days later Juan Valdez, a twenty-nine-year-old Canjilon resident like Morales, drove to Santa Fe with his wife and child and asked Albert Gonzales, the Alianza lawyer, to notify the police that he would give himself up. Valdez told Robert Romero, a state policeman trusted by many northerners, that he had heard of Tijerina's plea that his supporters give themselves up.

Tijerina had dictated and signed the single-page statement during a visit from Attorney Gonzales the day before. In it he charged that "what happended at Tierra Amarilla was sparked by the wrongful and Gestapo-like conduct of Alfonso Sanchez in depriving the people of their constitutional right to assembly." Tijerina insisted that "at no time did I or the people have any intentions of using violence or firearms against any individual of the U.S. The meeting at Coyote was inspired by the hope for the rights and privileges of the Pueblo of San Joaquin; and Sanchez, by terrorizing the people, caused their frustrations to explode." Finally, "To avoid any other violence and possible bloodshed, because I personally detest violence and I would say to those who are still being hunted, my brother Cristobal Tijerina, Baltazar Martinez and Juan Valdez, 'Turn yourselves in.' "

The third suspect was picked up on the sidewalk in front of the Alianza headquarters about this time. Alfonso Chavez had been one of the five men charged in connection with the Echo Amphitheater episode the previous fall. He had also been among the

REVERBERATIONS FROM THE RAID

Coyote prisoners arraigned in Tierra Amarilla just before the raid. Madril's notes recall the arrival of these three comrades.

"Juan Valdez and Moises Morales and Alfonso Chavez came into Cell Block No. 5 and brought good news about how people that are working for us outside. . . . This is God's work through us to bring justice to our people in the state of New Mexico. . . . 2 p.m. on the news today we heard that Mr. Alfonso Sanchez District Attorney is going to ask for the death penalty for us. . . . For the sake of my three daughters and wife I will stay in prison rather than see them live in this humiliation and injustice for the way to demonstrate that you love God is to love your family and your fellow man, this does not mean Mr. Death Penalty D.A. and others like him or should I say Mr. Rat. . . ."

The same epithet introduced a typed threat that Sanchez received on June 14 from "The Black Hand Gang." Postmarked Santa Fe, the note darkly warned that Sanchez was "dealing with the underworld know [sic] and there is no power in the world that can stop us when we want to get rid of someone." The mysterious writers explained they were "not members of 'The Federation' that you arrested but simply a much larger group . . . much concerned with the way those poor people were arrested and corralled like animals." Investigators never came up with the typewriter that produced the letter, but the anxiety it caused in Sanchez's office may have explained the district attorney's inability during this period to study the initial facts of the courthouse attack and draw up ironclad charges from them.

Still in prison, Tijerina began receiving weekly visits from his wife. The penitentiary grapevine gave him fairly accurate reports of the raid's effects. Some prison guards made hushed inquiries as to where they could contribute to the newly-established Tijerina Legal Defense Fund. A sign now swung outside Anselmo Tijerina's house in Hernandez, proclaiming it the fund's main office. Then, about three weeks after the raid, the formal arraignment for the Tierra Amarilla defendants was held at last in Santa Fe.

By now District Attorney Sanchez had amended his original

document of complaint five times. The New Mexico Supreme Court had gone through a few judges, disqualifying them for various reasons, before deciding on genial, portly Joe Angel of Las Vegas. The short district court judge drove south on the day of the arraignments with his tall blond court recorder and found himself in the midst of carnival-like throngs outside the building. The gossipy gaiety of a Saturday shopping noonday permeated the crowd, which contained many northern friends and relatives of the Alianzans. Beneath the adobe portals everyone awaited the hastily borrowed yellow school bus bringing the defendants from prison. State police masked in sunglasses held short-barreled shotguns rakishly against their hips while their white-gloved partners kept the curious traffic creeping along. Heads craned beyond the sidewalk to scan the cleared street, saw nothing, and turned around to chat with neighbors. Children chased each other through adult legs as motorcycle policemen roared around the block.

On the second floor the wooden courthouse doors creaked with the weight of the anxious audience until the pushers were motioned back to give an employee room to open the stubborn doors. After much unsuccessful twisting of the key, the doors swung wide. Women and children hurtled in but were pressed back, told to enter singly and submit to search. A policeman patted his palms up and down coat sides and pants legs. Before the door was finally shut because the wooden aisles were filled to capacity, cries of "Viva Tijerina!" were flung from those left outside.

The seats were jammed with men in work overalls, heavy muddy boots, and grizzled chins, and women in house dresses with perhaps an extra bow in their hair, holding down twisting children. Then a door beyond the guardrail separating the audience from the proscenium opened and sixteen men and a girl walked single file along the polished wooden railing to the jury box. Soon, within the hot and stuffy courtroom, Judge Angel would hear the first cohesive story of those minutes when, in the words of a popular new 45-rpm record about the raid, "The Corrido of Rio Arriba," "We thought the world was ending."

REVERBERATIONS FROM THE RAID

Two rows back in the visitors' pews a little girl stood on her mother's lap and strained out her arms as the defendants were led to their seats in the only area where they all could fit, the jury box. "Daddy!" she yelled, with an edge on her voice that made the audience shake commiserating heads at one another. A man passing smiled gratefully at her and ventured a little wave.

Signs of greeting passed between relatives and friends. Moises Morales wore his black silky shirt, which shifted tones as it swung from his lanky frame. Curly-haired Ramon Tijerina blinked nervously behind tinted wire-rimmed glasses. Reies Tijerina, in unflattering, beltless, oversize khakis, and his son Reies Jr. grinned broadly. Tijerina waved as if to a whistlestop delegation of admirers. Judge Angel opened business with an excusable overstatement:

"The eyes of the world are on this courtroom today."

First he readily assented to an uncontested defense request that the "King Tiger" alias be immediately stricken from the complaint paper—it was sensational and prejudicial besides being a mistranslation. Through the next four and a half hours, Sanchez grew increasingly irritated. Angel had to call for order in the court twice when the district attorney hesitated or lost an objection and the room rippled with laughter. The six defense counsels, after unsuccessfully trying to throw out the charges, shot to their feet like a chorus at Sanchez's every other sentence.

The high room with its carved *vigas* (roof beams) became stifling. When a fan was plugged in to stir up the thick hot air a sirenlike wail rose in pitch until an officer yanked out the cord. Women fanned themselves with newspapers as if in church. Rose Tijerina slumped and was given water. When her mother tried to rush through the guardrail to her, a state police detective sharply escorted her back to her seat.

In order to deny the defendants bail and justify his charges of first-degree kidnapping, Sanchez called his own witnesses. Dan Rivera, reticent and soft-spoken, sat uneasily in the witness chair and pointed out Valdez, Leyba, and Tijerina as actually at the

173

courthouse during the raid, but he avoided looking at them. He said it was Valdez who had met him on the second floor of the courthouse with the scornful words in Spanish, "Here is the unfortunate." The heavy-set undersheriff described how Valdez had beaten him about the head until blood ran. He also remembered Baltazar Martinez darting around.

But it was another state witness who brought the tension to its peak. Limping frailly to the wooden chair, Jailer Eulogio Salazar spoke in Spanish through an interpreter, as if to a priest performing the last rites. His left cheek was bloated and a reddish line meandered down it where he had been shot.

Sanchez began the questioning.

"Now, I notice that your mouth or the area around your mouth, to the right of your face, there is something wrong with it. Who caused that? Who did that?"

After some minutes of legal bickering, Judge Angel permitted Salazar to answer.

"Reies Tijerina," he said.

Every spectator in the hushed courtroom, eyes on the frail figure in the chair, gave an involuntary gasp.

"Would you point that man out to the court," Sanchez asked.

"That one right here." Salazar shakily lifted his arm in Reies Tijerina's direction. Under patient, tender querying by the district attorney, Salazar, in his barely audible voice, recalled:

"I was there with the sheriff, in his office, and we heard a shot in the hall. I went out the door and then I saw Reies coming. And he hit Benny and he brought his gun out and I went there toward the window, and I raised the window."

Salazar stopped, as if summoning up the strength to move the muscles of his mouth. Nothing could be read from Tijerina's studied lack of expression. Sanchez had pleaded with the court that cross-examination be limited and delicate since it was plain that the witness, with a history of heart trouble, was barely on the mend. The jailer continued.

"He said, 'Don't go out because I will shoot you. I will kill you.'

I came back, but I tried to jump out. . . . At the time I jumped out this window I was shot here in the jaw. I turned the corner of the courthouse and he jumped after me there and followed me around the cars and told me to come back. They told me to come back. . . ."

Six months later the next legal investigation of the raid came about in a thorough preliminary hearing containing similar on-the-spot revelations. But Salazar would not be there to repeat his identification of Tijerina as the man who, he said, had nearly killed him. He would be three weeks in a frozen Tierra Amarilla grave, the victim of a brutal bludgeoning that brought terror back to the little town.

14

REPAIRING
THE
NORTH

Two weeks after the courthouse raid, the four members of New Mexico's congressional delegation issued a joint criticism of the unflattering portrait of their state that was being disseminated. The "unfair assessments" of the economic and human opportunities in their home area, they said in a news release, "deserve to be ignored, because they do not tangibly aid those in need. We do not choose to dignify, by rebuttal, the allegations made recently concerning the role of the New Mexico congressional delegation in developing the economy of rural Northern New Mexico."

Then they ticked off "tangible gains." Heading the achievements was the creation of the Four Corners Regional Development Commission, a mammoth redevelopment project patterned after the Appalachia Regional Commission. The state's junior senator, Joseph Montoya, was a major promoter of this consolidated effort to upgrade deprived areas in four southwestern states, and had personally introduced it into Congress. As chairman of a Senate sub-

176

committee he was planning a series of hearings on restoring economic health to the northern counties later in the summer.

But now, while reminding the public of this constructive plan for wholesale economic revitalization, Montoya joined his three colleagues in citing other allocations of funds for the north. Almost none touched on the deep-seated grievances which the Resnick subcommittee had highlighted, nor the basic issues which Alianzans had tried to convey to Governor Cargo before the raid.

Prior to their collective justification, the two senators and two representatives had joined in the initial hue and cry for apprehension of the culprits. Having thus protected themselves politically, they privately began pondering how to sponsor more visible constructive work in the north. At the time, they all seemed to realize, it would be best to route this repair work around the Office of Economic Opportunity.

The uproar over OEO's "wheeling and dealing" during the peak of the excitement had leveled off but not yet died. Cargo had sustained his two minds about the program, ignoring the right-wing accusations but still alternating between endorsement of the poverty program's principles and dissatisfaction with its conduct. After testifying in Washington he recounted his meeting with OEO Director Sargent Shriver.

"The guy was most sympathetic," the governor said. "I told him about the crying need to market handicraft items produced in remote sections of northern New Mexico. He said it might be a good idea for the OEO to send someone down there from Washington to plan it."

Cargo had heard this before. "I told him we don't need any more planners. We need projects. We don't need handouts, either. Money advanced could be paid back in full." Then, to illustrate, the governor used an example from a community Shriver had just heard about, the town of Penasco which HELP Director Alex Mercure had described so pitifully.

"I went to Penasco five weeks ago," Cargo said. "The first thing I asked was what was their biggest need. They told me a community corral. It would cost $9,000, enabling the sale of sheep in lots, raising the sheep sale price by 30 to 35 per cent." The governor asked Shriver, "Instead of paying a guy $13,000 a year to be a planner, why doesn't OEO get Penasco a community corral?"

But when he returned from Washington, Governor Cargo promised a much larger OEO grant package as a result of the disclosure of New Mexico's urgent needs. Still, Father Garcia's state OEO organization remained anathema to many officials and to long-time critics of the poverty war who felt its actions in June epitomized the dangers inherent in social workers dealing with political situations. At their urging—and with the quietly effective approval of the state's congressmen—Attorney General Boston Witt now firmed up an argument to present in a private session with the state's Legislative Finance Committee. He would request special funding for his unusually intensive investigation of subversive links between Garcia's office and the Alianza.

The OEO office itself had tried to lie low when it began to bear the brunt of political attack. Quietly it was attempting to capitalize on the Resnick hearings and the sudden concern with the north. Burning midnight electricity on the fourth floor of the capitol, its staff was preparing for Shriver a huge $5,000,000 crash program to give emergency legal aid, economic development, health services, educational benefits, neighborhood centers, and bus transportation to villagers in Rio Arriba, Mora, and Taos counties. The electricity could have been saved. No money was forthcoming from Washington.

On the other hand, HELP, oriented toward the migrant workers who kept northern New Mexico as their hereditary base camp, emerged unscathed and even strengthened from the post-raid rain of accusations. Alex Mercure, its politically wise director, had been impressive during his testimony in Washington. The Ford Foundation, kept abreast of the events in New Mexico through regular letter-bulletins from Don Devereux, took special interest in Mercure's program. Devereux himself had been hired as HELP program advisor and Ford liaison man. The foundation began clearance of a special grant for HELP's pilot effort in the field of rural agricultural cooperation. In early 1968 their monies would provide additional HELP staff as well as $250,000 in outright investment funds.

The state's venerable Senator Anderson had included his name on the telegram calling for the investigation of OEO's suspicious dealings. Now the senior senator also placed his substantial prestige behind respectable steps to rehabilitate the north. A week after the raid, however, he had replied unsympathetically to a suggestion from a Denver militant that he introduce a bill for partial reparation to descendants of land grantees.

"If these people really believed in legal ownership," Anderson wrote Dan Valdez, head of the New Hispano movement, "they would have been in the courts long ago."

Only New Mexico Congressman Tom Morris took up the Alianza's challenge on its own terms. His office began considering how to introduce legislation that would establish a land-grant investigation panel. This was the most daring reparative measure to be born, and to die, in Washington. An associated problem, which most New Mexicans recognized with hopeless sighs, was the instability of many land titles in the north.

The title question struck to the historic root of Anglo and Spanish-American frictions. The traditional Spanish-American approach to land involved minimal documentation, no established habits of direct land taxation, and no real conception of land as a commodity for private investment and speculation. Written title had originally been needed under the Anglo definition of property ownership. And, as Professor Clark Knowlton observed from Texas, "There's not a title north of U.S. 66 that is worth much"— in the Anglo understanding of the term. There were instead grant documents which had once awarded land to individuals and to communities.

As soon as Governor Cargo released his plan for legislation to research "marketable titles," local newspapers began running in-depth reports on the question of the uncertain northern deeds. Poor

179

courthouse records, incomplete abstracts, primitive surveying markers ("that rock by the fork near the stream"—a stream that had changed channels, a rock that had been carried off, a road that was now under a Forest Service reseeding project), insufficient staffing, cultural confusion over "ownership," and suspected destruction or disappearance of legal documents and archives—these were some of the historical obstacles that gave Cargo's plan little chance of success. But the notion provided a constructive ring to Cargo's comments as he made tours of the shaken northern counties and prepared for his 1968 gubernatorial campaign.

The governor's first venture into Rio Arriba County took him back to Canones, the mountain-shrouded hamlet he had tried to make symbolic of the area's plight. He had campaigned there a year before primarily on the promise of new hardtop roads, the community's paramount need. Now he passed over the sole entrance into town, still a dirt road, with four uniformed state police and four plainclothes officers as bodyguards. Once again he met muddy washouts, deep potholes, and unhappy parents. He renewed his promise to the community's 150 residents that he would personally take their complaints to the state Highway Commission. Beside him Father Robert Garcia looked on. The governor spoke in the one-room schoolhouse condemned as unfit the year before, but not scheduled for abandonment until the coming autumn.

A month after they had returned to California, the Socio-Economic Studies team originally imported by Cargo's office had completed their reconnaissance contract by sending the governor their special report on the north. Citing such patently obvious realities as depressed economy, substandard living conditions, absence of legal resources for handling local grievances, and deep-seated hostility to the federal machinery, the report offered broad recommendations for improving the situation. Under its suggestion for the creation of channels to "surface" complaints, in particular against the Forest Service, the report urged the establishment of a legal aid service and the immediate appointment of a neutral, permanent commission to elicit and process local charges. Among

180

its long-range proposals the report called for a federal task force to review all government methods of relating to the grass-roots villager. Finally it suggested looking once more into the possibility of a private or public commission to dig into the land-grant question.

The skimpy summary was released without comment by Cargo's office. Local reaction was hardly enthusiastic. The document was treated as the end result of a futile, last-ditch maneuver by the governor. One state house veteran echoed the general feeling:

"Hell, I could have written a report like that without getting up from my desk."

Cargo shortly dissociated himself from the entire episode.

"I don't see how," he said with a straight face, "someone can come in from out of state for seven days and do an in-depth study of northern New Mexico. I had nothing to do with it."

Part of this general disavowal resulted from a hardened attitude toward the plethora of past reports which were now being shaken of their accumulated dust. Part also derived from the ultrasensitive scrutiny the area had been receiving since the raid, which made the SES observations seem superficial in comparison. Actually, while the report gave few pointers for implementing its proposals within the political and social realities of the north, its general recommendations were an adequate summary of those being promoted by HELP and the Ford Foundation.

Perhaps one reason Cargo was so touchy about the report was that less than a week earlier another of his attempts to deal with the Alianza had backfired. Baltazar Martinez had joined his fellow Alianzans in prison, but Cargo's personal check for the reward had gone into the pocketbook of the young man's mother, who had arranged the son's surrender. And that would not be the last of the story.

After the seventeen Alianza defendants had filled the jury box in Judge Joe Angel's court in Santa Fe that hot afternoon of the arraignments, four were refused bond because the startling testimony had suggested that they might have committed first-degree crimes during the courthouse attack. Tijerina himself, Tobias Leyba—the host at the Canjilon "picnic"—Juan Valdez, and Baltazar Apodaca, the elderly abductor of Larry Calloway, were all sent back behind prison bars once again.

This meant thirteen new bonds to be sought by the Alianza brotherhood—property or cash in amounts that could be raised and certified only with difficulty. The Alianza headquarters was already bustling during the weeks after the raid. As a result of its new prominence, journalists flocked to the office in the one-time freezing plant, one-time print shop which had been the Alianza's home since 1963.

In the temporary absence of their imprisoned *jefe* who lived in the building's aluminum-painted second-floor apartment, popping downstairs nervously each morning, the Tijerinistas continued to play host to Corky Gonzales and a handful of his Denver followers. Gonzales had become closely acquainted with Anselmo Tijerina, who seemed to be avoiding any titular position of leadership. But Anselmo was picking up ideas from his new colleague. About a month after Gonzales's telegram to President Johnson, the eldest Tijerina brother himself found occasion to write the White House a letter. This epistle complained about the recent whirlwind tour of northern New Mexico by Under Secretary of Agriculture John Schnittker.

Reportedly as a result of the raid's publicity and the Resnick hearing, the Department of Agriculture had dispatched Schnittker for a two-day survey of village needs in the area. A commodities specialist with little experience in grazing matters, Schnittker was hardly qualified to review relations between subsistence grazer and forest ranger. During his rapid tour of the Rio Arriba and Taos countryside he was insulated from confrontations with villagers or even poverty officials. But the folk composer of Taos County, Cleofes Vigil, had managed to break through the under secretary's escort. "You give more land to the rabbits," Vigil said defiantly, "than you give to us poor people."

In his letter Anselmo Tijerina said Schnittker's responses to "the problems of the poor people in regards to grazing, water, hunting, fishing and wood hauling rights were vague and a jumble of double talk most government officials seem to be very adept and professional at." Anselmo ended with his wish that the President personally look into the matter of land grants and "the rights of the poor people in the usage of forest service land."

Gonzales's *chicano* newspaper in Denver, *El Gallo* (*The Rooster*), now appeared with a front-page banner blaring "Viva Tijerina," and devoted its bulk to stories about the Alianza and the raid. In California as well as Colorado, talk of Tierra Amarilla had spread rapidly through urban Spanish-American barrios and along the migrant camps of the fertile San Joaquin Valley, the embattled site of Cesar Chavez's fervent unionizing. Although a strict advocate of Gandhian nonviolence, the introspective, sad-eyed Chavez sent a letter of sympathy to the Alianza, emphasizing the struggle of all Spanish-speaking downtrodden while avoiding precise endorsement of the Alianza's recent activity.

Burt Corona, chairman of California's Mexican-American Political Association, had appeared before the Resnick subcommittee and lauded the Alianza as "a brave band of people." He affirmed proudly, "We believe and we state that their cause is our cause."

A high-level meeting of California Spanish-American figureheads was held at the Center for the Study of Democratic Institutions in Santa Barbara to brief them on the New Mexico situation and discuss how most effectively to demonstrate support.

Beyond the Spanish-American cultural family, too, news of the raid and its aftermath was being perused intently. White radicals and black militants, old-guard leftists and new left activists, discerned in superficial reports of the raid a stirring example of the romanticized confrontation between land baron and peasant in the genre of Robin Hood. Some tied it to more contemporary social protest. The August issue of the SNCC publication, *The Movement*, contained a special supplement on the Alianza, written by an Albuquerque W. E. B. Du Bois Club founder. Author James

TIJERINA and the COURTHOUSE RAID

Kennedy brought all data to bear on his thesis that the Tierra Amarilla incident was part of the larger minority revolution against "imperialism."

From the opposite shore of the political ocean came the first— to date—of three lengthy pieces in the official John Birch Society organ, *American Opinion.* Calling his article "Reies Tijerina: The Communist Plan to Grab the Southwest," writer Alan Stang placed individuals at the scene of crimes as if he had been a witness, and convicted them with supreme self-righteousness. Stang was granted unusual access to the state's law enforcement files, and employed every scrap to prove the Alianza a guerrilla organization akin to the Vietcong, the Algerian FLN, or the Canadian separatists.

Between these extremes fell the romantic rendition of the TA episode in the fall issue of *Colorado Magazine.* Rousingly entitled "Under Two Flags," the story was re-enacted in television-western terms with comic-strip accuracy and negligible insight. The Alianza headquarters promptly purchased 100 copies.

From his prison quarters Tijerina himself was experiencing greater awareness of the larger militant brotherhood. He points to an incident in the penitentiary as convincing him that the Alianza should sign a "peace treaty," at first opportunity, with the new black vanguard. "When I was in prison, between about fifty men, ten Spanish against Negroes and whites. Both jumped on the Spanish-Americans. When they told me about this fight and how the warden had punished the Spanish-Americans in solitary confinement only to prove that he was not prejudiced against Negroes . . . I advised the Spanish-Americans about our struggle and the struggle of the black man and I got them to reconcile and work together." This notion, encouraged by his readings about the Black Power movement, was the seed for the highly colorful October 1967 Alianza convention which the land-grant leader was to begin designing very soon.

While Tijerina remained locked up, District Attorney Sanchez

184

had decided to woo public sentiment by unrolling the mysterious rolled-up documents confiscated from Alianza car trunks the night before the Coyote meeting. Drawn and labeled with different-colored ballpoint pens on translucent paper, these were, Sanchez maintained, to be superimposed on ordinary road maps. Three of the five charts represented "phases" of some operation in the general area of the Abiquiu Dam, near Coyote. They showed such site designations as "position of women and children," "heavy defense stays in position," "prison," and "line of defense." One large map, entitled "Face no. 1," covered a much larger terrain and its labels read "supply rout [*sic*]," "takeover" at Deadman's Peak, and "can be blocked" at two locations on U.S. Highway 84. A final chart, apparently copied from a military handbook, showed a hierarchical chain of command headed by "The President or Commander in Chief" and descending through various army groupings to "platoon." Although for none of this material were there explanatory legends, Sanchez assumed they proved an armed Alianza takeover was being planned to create "a new Cuba in the north."

Other law enforcement agencies were pursuing their investigations more quietly. Federal authorities had intensified their efforts to bring the Echo Amphitheater incident finally to court. Very soon a trial for the five Alianza members charged was scheduled for November.

State police, under the direction of Officer Robert Gilliland, were taking depositions from witnesses and lining up testimony for Sanchez's bulging brief about the raid itself. Officer Gilliland personally made over sixty visits to Tierra Amarilla to interview courthouse employees. The creaky stairs and hallway floors of the building itself—their paint long ago worn to splintery wood—were measured for floor plans which would be used as courtroom exhibits. The peeling, stained plaster walls inside were gone over for bullet holes and new evidence. The entire structure was measured for a cardboard scale model by a Santa Fe architect, complete with authentic outside coloring of brownish pink and smudgy sky blue. The model's roof was removable, to enable prosecution pointer sticks—whenever the raid should come to trial—to retrace the movements of invaders and victims.

Other officers were still trying to turn up the two principal fugitives remaining at large, whose likenesses were now pinned to all police station bulletin boards: Cristobal Tijerina and Baltazar Martinez.

Sanchez had a special reason for wanting Martinez. He had become terribly disturbed about the weapons the young man had supposedly stolen from the state police cars he had shot up on June 5. Sanchez feared this cache, which was said to contain hand grenades and machine guns as well as 15,000 missing rounds of ammunition, had joined the other cache of arms and dynamite he said Governor Cargo knew about before the raid. Since he read the Alianza charts as foreshadowing a takeover of other northern sites like Ghost Ranch, El Rito, and Tierra Amarilla, he was appealing for federal aid in locating the weaponry. Martinez, he believed, could lead them to it. And then came the Martinez surrender.

Governor Cargo's personal outlay of $500 reward for Baltazar Martinez had been outstanding in early July when the young fugitive's mother approached State Police Officer Fred Gallegos near Canjilon. She was terrified that the police would murder her son, she said, but if Gallegos, whom she knew, could arrange a safeguarded surrender she would see that Baltazar gave himself up.

Accordingly Gallegos was assigned to spend his Fourth of July holiday "fishing" by a stream in a grove near the Martinez cottage. While two fellow officers covered the home from the outside, Gallegos knocked and entered. Aurelia Martinez brought her son out of a room. After some discussion handcuffs clicked and an hour later the three emerged. Martinez said he had been existing in the wilds between El Rito and Canjilon, with visits to his mother's refrigerator. During this time he had spied on the helicopters and state police hunting for him. Then the "most dangerous" of the defendants, wearing the enigmatic smile he preserved throughout the next year's court proceedings, adjusted his red beret and ascot and was photographed beside his mother in her Sunday best.

With Martinez peacefully joining the defendants in prison, Governor Cargo was taken aback to have a caller the next week. Shyly stepping into his office, her eyes downcast, Mrs. Martinez whispered through an interpreter her request for the reward money the arresting officer had turned down. She told Cargo she would use the cash for hospital bills. Mrs. Martinez was wearing a pink blouse, a flower-patterned skirt, and seemed very fragile. The governor grew compassionate.

"I feel so sorry for her, " he said. "She's had so much trouble."

In return, Mrs. Martinez told Cargo she would see to it that "when he gets out of this mess he won't be dangerous any more. He promises he won't use arms or violence. I want him well taken care of. May God bless you the rest of your life."

The ensuing lament by Spanish-American motherhood at this betrayal of a son by his mother was somewhat premature. A week later, when young Martinez had already been bailed out, Cargo received the canceled check in his mail.

"She signed it over to him," he grimly acknowledged.

Cargo also volunteered that Martinez had just taken out a marriage license in the same TA courthouse he was accused of blasting apart. The young man must have seen, as he approached the two front doors, the fragments of police car window glass still glinting in the weeds. The wedding, at which Martinez was to marry the sister of codefendant Juan Valdez, would take place the coming weekend in Tierra Amarilla. There was no indication of whether the governor received an invitation.

When Martinez gave himself up, Chief Black commented, "I kind of knew he had been in those mountains all along." Then the chief said that Martinez had disclosed to him the location of the cache of guns and dynamite he was rumored to have had with him. "I'll send somebody up there today to pick them up," Black said. "He had two sawed-off shotguns that he stole from police cars after the raid and the deputy's .38. That and some dynamite."

187

TIJERINA and the COURTHOUSE RAID

A year later, one of Black's deputy chiefs said that the cache of arms was never found.

It was federal authorities, on the other hand, who suffered some embarrassment during the involved surrender of the last major fugitive, Cristobal Tijerina.

Felix Martinez, the busy Alianza lieutenant who had secured most of the bonds for raid defendants, had been in continual communication with the youngest Tijerina brother's hideout. When he felt the moment propitious, he agreed with Judge Joe Angel on surrender arrangements. Cristobal would be secretly conveyed through police-patrolled highways to intercept the judge, on his district court route, along Highway 66 in Santa Rosa. There Martinez would already have certified bonding documents on hand and, hopefully, Cristobal would be bailed out on the spot from Sanchez's state charges. They would tackle the pending federal warrants for Cristobal when this first hurdle was past.

I was informed that the pickup was imminent around the end of July. Toward midafternoon of August 1 Martinez, together with Attorney Albert Gonzales and Gonzales's wife to lead him, idled by the *New Mexican* newspaper office to collect me for the trip to Cristobal's hiding place. With a television newsman loaded down by tape recorder and cameras we drove for two hours in the direction of Las Vegas, New Mexico, before Martinez stopped the car. He drew from his pocket two Halloween masks, eyeholes covered over with electrical tape, and fitted them on us.

Shortly afterwards the car stopped again. There were Spanish greetings and farewells. A new rider had climbed into the back seat. We were moving again.

Cristobal Tijerina appeared changed, I observed when I was permitted to use my eyes. In an attempt at disguise he had forced a part into his springy black hair and had trimmed his mustache into a different style from when I had photographed him in the Santa Fe jail the Monday morning of the raid. While on the road to Santa Rosa he cooperated in a lengthy interview which described his own early years apart from the roaming Tijerina family and his late arrival to join his brother's cause.

Born in Texas in October 1933, Cristobal had been Herlinda Tijerina's last child. When she died about nine months after his birth the baby had been given by his father, Antonio, who was already struggling to feed six mouths, to a man named Nazario Vasquez. "Up to the time Cristobal was married," recalled his brother Reies, "he was reared by this fullblood Indian who is almost a hundred years old now . . . a Texas Indian. He was tall, very straight and very good-looking, like those people, you know."

After that the brothers saw each other no more than six times. "I remember one time," Cristobal told me, "when I was about nine or ten years old, that I saw Reies and my father in church." Then in June 1956 Reies went to his youngest brother in a little village thirty-six miles from Poth, Texas. Cristobal was then married and driving refrigerated trucks.

"He brought out a Bible," Cris said, "and got me interested in the things God demands from a person. I read it only once, that convinced me we should work together. He converted me, or I converted myself to his ideas." After that visit the brothers communicated by letter. Cristobal was working in the fields with his family in early 1961 when he felt moved to join his brother's growing cause.

"I couldn't bring my family. I came to help Reies in whatever I could. There was not much to do at first: talk to people and find out if there was any truth to these land claims." When the Alianza was officially founded two years later, Cristobal became its secretary-general. With the technical dissolution of the Alianza he remained an officer in the "Confederation of Free City States" and a "proctor" of the San Joaquin land grant community.

Cristobal said he was surrendering because, "Well, I guess that's the only out for me, or anybody else that wants to comply with the law." When asked what he'd been doing since he dropped from sight he replied:

TIJERINA and the COURTHOUSE RAID

"I couldn't keep up with all the things that have been going on, and how I've been spending my time, I can say that, hiding." He had not given himself up before, he maintained, because "I did not want to be persecuted for something I didn't do. Seems like now I have a good chance with the judge. Our lawyers would do everything they can, set a bond for me and let me work for the people that I have worked for in the last three years."

About then we were nearing Santa Rosa to meet the judge. Our talk was abruptly cut off by Martinez's calm statement that a state police car was tailing us. We pulled over to the highway shoulder and an officer leaned his head through the window, apparently at a loss for words. Cristobal's head lolled on my shoulder as if in heavy sleep. The policeman scanned us nervously, then told Martinez he had best not drive so slow in the future. Whatever was behind the policeman's hunch that had given us this close call, Cristobal had not been recognized.

At the conspicuous Santa Rosa courthouse in the center of town, Martinez and Tijerina headed for Judge Angel's private chambers, arousing great curiosity in the sleepy, scorching plaza. The "surrender" and approval of bonding papers were conducted with dispatch.

"I'm glad you took this step, Mr. Tijerina," said Judge Angel, the three approved property sureties in his hand.

"I'm glad also," responded the last of the defendants in the Tierra Amarilla raid case.

Martinez had a flair for press-agentry, and other newsmen were waiting outside. Immediately upon his exit they scooped up Tijerina and hustled him off to an Albuquerque television station where he appeared for a short interview a few hours later. When the FBI learned of their fugitive's appearance in Santa Rosa they were reportedly sullen. When they saw him blithely answering questions on a statewide television broadcast they were deeply affronted. A few minutes after the telecast they contacted the station, demanding to know where their man was now secreted.

Throughout the night pressure was applied. Early the next morn-

190

ing Attorney Gonzales was "strongly urged" by the FBI to see that his newest client gave himself up. The successful "surrender" and casual disappearance of the last important Alianzan raised official hackles all day. Later that night Cristobal Tijerina, now with a burning fever, turned himself in.

By the night of his brother's surrender, Reies Tijerina was two weeks past his restive but restful prison stay. Pending reexamination of the crucial clause, "if the evidence is strong and the presumption great" that the defendants did in fact commit capital offenses, Judge Joe Angel, ever struggling to be reasonable, had finally allowed the last four raiders to be granted bond.

Reies walked through the remote-control sliding doors of the last prison fence with his two new attorneys, Lorenzo Tapia and Charles Driscoll, the erstwhile "friends of the court" during the first arraignment. Attorney Gonzales was also in tow. Tijerina's prison khakis now spread a little around his middle. His face had a slightly yellowish cast. He strolled across the prison parking lot, squinting at the unaccustomed light and holding his paper bag of personal items. He gazed around himself.

"It is good to see the mountains," he said.

Two of us had already been able to obtain interviews with the land-grant leader while he was locked up. With Attorney Gonzales's help we had separately conducted lengthy biographical conversations under the unwitting observation of prison guards. These were the first details anyone had of Tijerina's origin and development. Now, about to enter the new political arena into which the raid had carried his organization, Tijerina was asked to enlarge on those details and on his mission.

He had been doing much thinking in his cell. His "new breed," as he now described the Spanish-American, was "developing into manhood and are no longer children to be played with," he told a reporter the day following his release from jail, at a news conference where he swelled with stored energy. His adoring, smiling young wife sat close to him, his followers crowded around proudly.

191

TIJERINA and the COURTHOUSE RAID

Although he had been entreated by lawyers to try to keep from discussing the particulars of the raid, its general impact "around the whole world" filled his head and his words. He had been invited to speak to numerous out-of-state militant groups, *chicano* as well as black. He had received communiqués of support from H. Rap Brown and Cesar Chavez. He was planning a series of in-state rallies, whistle-stop affairs throughout the north, for raising legal defense funds as well as for spreading the cry of "Tierra Amarilla."

15

GROWTH
OF A
LEADER

From the new nationwide interest aroused by the Tierra Amarilla raid sprang a particular curiosity about the intriguing background of Reies Tijerina himself. Now that he was accessible again, after his release from prison, a composite picture of his shadowy past could be put together. As with most elements in the Tijerina and Alianza saga, it was a tale of poverty and discrimination to the dramatic and bizarre extreme. It made his focal intensities a little more comprehensible. It traced his mode of thought and style of oratory to specific experiences. If it did not make the man less mysterious, it made his mystery less mythical.

Born on a mound of cotton sacks in a field near Fall City, Texas, on September 21, 1926, Tijerina received his first insult from the Anglo world that very day. The infant who was later to champion the "new breed" offspring of Spanish and Indian union—who coined the phrase "Brown Power"—was listed as "white" on his Karnes County birth certificate.

The surname Tijerina would appear to translate as "little scissors" rather than the evocative "tiger," but Tijerina characteristically gives it a more legendary origin. "It comes from the Tejas [Texas] Indian people," he says. Then he tells a folktale of a distant ancestor, a young colonial Spaniard who rebelled against his parents to marry an Indian princess, adding the Spanish suffix "ina" to the name which changed over the years from Tejerina to Tijerina.

He tells of a landholding paternal great-grandfather who was robbed of his ranch and murdered by Anglos. He says his mother's people once owned land that is now part of the King Ranch. He vividly recalls the major formative figure in his life, his father's father Santiago. But he speaks little of his meek father, Antonio, who still lives near San Antonio.

His mother, Herlinda, was strong, big-boned, and accustomed to hefting bulging cotton sacks on her back. She had no midwife for her ten children, three of whom died as babies. Antonio Tijerina had already outlived two wives. He did not remarry when Reies's mother died at 28.

Their early existence was supported by sharecropping, a way of life which became self-defeating as the young couple with their large brood were always driven away just before harvest time. Tijerina remembers three such instances when his father, "full of fright and terror," buckled under the pressure from armed ranchers to clear out. His childhood was a series of temporary shacks outside tiny farm communities: "Whiteface, Wilson, Levelland, Forestville, Poth, the names run like stripes through my mind."

But before his mother died she had passed to Reies the outlet for his high-strung psychic energy: her faith.

"My mother was very religious," he remembers, "and she read the Bible a lot. She prayed before meals and in the evening. One time they tried to hang my father—they had a rope around his neck because they wanted his crop. She took me in her arms and cried and prayed. . . . Whenever I cried my mother, to quiet me, she would take me in her arms and say, 'Come now, tell your mother what you saw in heaven.' Wasn't that strange, 'Tell your mother what you saw in heaven.' "

Herlinda Tijerina was asking her four-year-old son to recollect the first of his visions. When Tijerina tries to explain his spiritual resources, he always mentions this "death."

"I came to the table to eat one day and there was only half a cup of tea for me. It was tea made from the bark of a pecan tree . . . I went back to bed. It was like I died. I stayed in bed for twenty-four hours. All the people surrounding thought I was dead, you see, and even they were building my coffin. When I woke up I was cold and hungry. I found a piece of tortilla and started eating it. Then I told them I had been walking with Christ and I had seen the flowers and green pastures. So any time my mother wanted me to stop crying she would ask me what I had seen in heaven."

The boy apparently had frequent occasion for terror. Once a landowner's sons assaulted Antonio and slashed his thigh muscle.

"Finally he survived," says Tijerina, "but he always dragged his foot. . . . He couldn't work very good and relied on my mother. I even remember seeing her carry him on her back to the field when they cleared the land. Yes, she lifted him and carried him to fields, and then home when he was through."

About the year of young Reies's heavenly vision he began having a more prosaic, recurring nightmare. "We were working the Stevens Ranch, five miles from Poth, Texas. I think we were picking cotton. I used to dream that this car would come driving toward our house by itself, without any driver. It would drive up without any driver and then I would shake. I would shake from fright because I was afraid he would think we had stolen it and shoot one of us. I would wake up, and trembling."

These were the Depression years, and for the Tijerinas it was "a life made of bitter hard struggling to survive." Once, on the outskirts of Forestville, Reies remembers his mother contriving a scrap metal bow and arrow and killing a jackrabbit for food. The four boys—Anselmo, Reies, Ramon, and Margarito— each did their part in scavenging for the day's table. The girls, Maria and Josefina, helped their mother keep order in their temporary one-room houses.

"Margarito would dig, how do you call them"—Tijerina fought for the word—"rats, not the kind *del pueblo,* no, *ratas del campo,* of the fields. We'd dig them out of their holes and eat them, and, you know, they're good." The barefoot boys were keen foragers in trash cans and garbage dumps, collecting rags, old rubber, iron salvage, bones, whatever they could exchange for pennies.

And they worked the sun's full hours alongside their parents. Reies began stooping in the Texas fields at the age of seven. During these days he became dearly attached to his grandfather Santiago.

"Oh, he was a lion!" he enjoys remembering. "He's the one I take after. He had barefisted fights with the Texas Rangers. You know, when he died he had rope burns on his neck. Once, when they strung him up for something someone else had done, that Mexican border judge said, 'Wait a minute, I'm not sure that's the same one.' So they cut him down. . . . You know, that old man didn't like me when I was just a kid. But when he was dying in 1947, lasted two days, he called for me. He didn't want to be with anyone else but me. When he had seen me fight injustice he had admired me."

Reies was about six years old when his mother suddenly died. "She was my conscience that stayed with me. That was all I had in my heart, [that was] what she had left me."

With her gone, the hopelessness of attempting a semblance of family life was clear. During the spring, summer, and fall the Tijerinas joined thousands of their Spanish-speaking brethren in the migrant worker stream.

"Then for five years we went to Michigan, in those two-ton trucks, you know, the migrant laborers. I remember fighting in the fields because the rancher didn't clean the fields good enough, just full of weeds and grass. Father used to scold me. When I was talking to those big ranchers he would tremble. But I started talking back to them when I was about fourteen or fifteen. I felt driven by this inner force to defend my rights, to tell them they weren't paying us enough or doing right by us."

Until then Tijerina had accumulated a smattering of cut-short sojourns in roughly twenty rural schoolhouses near labor camps, equaling about six months of grade school. But his untutored gifts were obvious.

"Right from my childhood I was distinguished in the art of persuasion. They called me *abogado sin libros*, 'lawyer without books.'"

During the winters the family scraped out a living around San Antonio.

"Anselmo took on himself to feed the family when he was working with the WPA when he was sixteen. Father had to be relieved because he was infested with ailments. Anselmo was a father more or less. From his paycheck of $20, for fifteen days of pick and shovel work, he was allowed a nickel. I remember once, my father didn't want him to smoke, but he bought a pack of cigarets."

Cristobal had already, at nine months, been placed in the care of the aged Indian, Nazario Vasquez. He would not rejoin his brothers until 1961.

"Margarito, we called him Mario, was the humblest of all. He couldn't talk until he was seven. Everything others would do, he would be whipped. Before the ranchers ran us out, Mario was using one of the tough plows, those middle-busters with four horses, and he plowed those 200 acres all alone. He would go to the nopales cactus and collect the pigeon eggs and after working he would cook his own meals. But after seventeen he left our house and went on his own, to El Paso and Michigan. He only learned reading and writing when he was in jail. That happened when he was picking tomatoes in Indiana."

Of his brothers, Reies grew to feel most intimate with Ramon.

"He learned reading and writing at nineteen. He is the best-

197

looking of all of us and was chased by beautiful girls. Then he married, both he and his wife had graduated from that same Bible school where I went, in Ysleta, Texas. He's a good-living man, straight in his family life. . . . He more or less followed me, when I changed from this religious life to the political."

Reies had already been baptized into the Catholic Church, and his head buzzed with his mother's talk of God and faith. By his mid-teens he was ripe for his own entrance into the religious world, and a profession which fed his hungry talents.

"Around this time, when a Baptist preacher named Samuel Gallindo came to our company house, he handed me a New Testament. I didn't leave that room until I read it all. Then I got my brothers around the table and read it to them a second time. I noticed the word 'justice' used as many times as words like 'love.' So I read about Abraham, David, Ishmael, and the prophets. I found many words in there to reach my heart."

Finally, at eighteen, Tijerina's intense religiosity caused him to enroll at the Assembly of God Bible Institute in Ysleta, Texas. This was his first mature commitment. He does not regret the years of suffering which had prepared him for it.

"Once a Doctor Robert Castillo, that I went to because my vocal glands were bothering me, asked if I would agree to a psychiatrist talking to me. Castillo said that my throat hurts because I think so hard, because of tension when I meditate. One thing the psychiatrist noted was that he admired that I was happy even though my childhood was surrounded by misery and hardship. But I had no hatred, no enmity, and I told the doctor, 'That was all the life I knew. We were happy in poverty. Earthly possessions didn't bother me, but I was always attracted, always preoccupied, by that fascinating power that is justice.' "

In Bible college Tijerina soon stood out for his inspirational fire. For the young man the experience meant self-discovery at last.

"And I read in the Bible there that mercy and truth met, and justice and peace hugged. So then it was the religious life for the satisfaction and yearning of my heart for justice. And my idols, or something like that, was beginning with Moses on."

The institute's superintendent, Brother Kenzy Savage, remembers the intense, hazel-eyed young pupil as "fanatical, more peculiar, in his thoughts. I guess . . . he was not orthodox . . . when he went to school he was a very sincere student. I don't know, when he left school he began to get those rather far-out ideas about how people ought to conduct themselves." Savage explained by classifying the evolving militant as a "reformer."

Tijerina himself now has mixed memories of his three years of "formal" religious training.

"They wouldn't let me graduate because I had gone out with a girl. In 1950 I was going through there and that same man wanted me to graduate, but I refused on the grounds that my past could not be erased by my later actions."

A few months after leaving Ysleta, Tijerina married a fellow student, Mary Escobar (who was not the reason for his ouster), and hit the evangelist circuit hard. Brother Savage remembers that Tijerina joined him in some "pastoring" in the Santa Fe area.

"He was a very good speaker, with a lot of spunk and spirit. I appreciated his ministry at the time."

To Tijerina, however, the calling had deeper value than oratorical satisfaction.

"In my ten years of traveling then, up and down the country preaching, I had my first son and gave him the nickname of David. He was one year old when I would walk. Many times I have in my mind recorded when I walked. My wife would feel bad, but I tried to convince her. In 1947 we walked from Illinois to Texas, with her and that little boy, Reies Jr. Usually I refused rides because I wanted to feel related to the Bible and friends to those men that had defended justice to the world. If I didn't live that life I didn't have the right to preach the words of those holy men. But the leaders of the church planned to kick me out. They didn't like my life, when I told people to stop paying their tithes."

Savage cites an "unorthodox attitude" as the reason for the

revocation of Tijerina's ministerial credentials in 1950. The complete severance from the Pentecostals meant no lessening of the young man's zeal, however. "When I was dismissed I became a nondenominational minister," he says, and he continued to roam on that mission.

Depending on charity for meals and shelter, the Tijerinas wandered through the southwestern states to Louisiana, Michigan, and New York. Reies talked in dingy evangelist halls from Fresno to Brooklyn. A collection of sermons and Biblical commentaries were later privately published in Spanish. Taking his title from St. Luke, datelining each message with the tiny town of their creation, Tijerina called his 119-page book *Hallera Fe en la Tierra? (Will There Be Faith on Earth?)*.

In the midst of his solitary crusade his domestic life became difficult. Growing weary of her husband's driven, self-denying spirituality, his wife Mary became an unwilling companion.

"When I read that Socrates' wife threw a bucket of hot water on him because he wouldn't take money, I would rejoice. Because my wife was always angry that I gave everything away, one time to Mexican nationals, you know, who hoe the beets."

To christen his career, Tijerina says, he gave away three suits, his car, and all his furniture. During the continuing years of sleeping under bridges and on friendly floors, walking through steaming western noons—his training period—he accumulated other possessions from gifts and collection plates, but these too he gave up.

"Three times I felt the need to dispense of all my possessions . . . give away free to poor people to feel at ease with my heart's desire."

"This was a time," he explains, "when my beliefs were greater than my experiences, so I had to put myself through those things, to create a different will."

By the early 1950's, Tijerina's energies began to take a new ideological direction. Chance roadside encounters with strangers who discerned political ability beneath his envangelical gifts persuaded

Tijerina to pursue his goal of *justicia* through more down-to-earth means.

"How I changed from religious to political? One of the things, I remember it very clearly . . . I was walking with my wife and child out of a big church in Dallas where I had delivered a sermon that morning. The minister of the large congregation didn't even offer me a hot meal. My wife only had the dress she was wearing. We just carried a little bag for the baby's things. So we walked out of this church and this man, Anglo, picked me up and took us home and said, 'Wife, get this man a steak.' And he said to my face, 'I don't like preachers, they take advantage of the people. What I think you should do is quit talking religion. What the Spanish-American people need is a Spanish-American politician, you may be that . . . you should study law and history and help your people. . . . I learned then that deeds of love are found in men who don't teach. And I learned that there's no mercy in churches, no justice in religious people."

But impatience with the lack of engagement to be found in evangelizing was probably as much a reason for Tijerina's next move as disillusion with religion. From a traveler passing the Word to imperfect human communities, Tijerina now came to conceive of himself as a utopian colonizer, forging into a "just" society the spiritual principles he had preached. By now he had acquired a modest following. Choosing "the wildest spot in the desert," a plot between Casa Grande and Eloy, Arizona, he pooled the funds of seventeen Spanish-American cottonpicker families to buy about 160 arid acres of the former multimillion-dollar Peralta land grant at $9 an acre. Just north of the Papago Indian Reservation, the settlement was optimistically called Valle de Paz (Valley of Peace), and its families knew each other as "Heralds of Peace."

Tijerina asserts that his communizing band had Arizona state permission to construct their church, general store, and earth-roofed dugout homes. Wages were earned by the adults commuting to cotton fields every day. But life was hardly peaceful. After one of their girls was raped while waiting for a school bus, Tijerina says the community received permission from Phoenix to build their own schoolhouse and hire their own teacher. This grated on some Anglo citizens of nearby Casa Grande and Toltec.

"All of a sudden," says Tijerina, "to our astonishment, the surrounding teachers objected." Also, Tijerina's own legal defense of some of the Valle de Paz youths arrested for misdemeanors apparently irritated the local sheriff.

At the same time, says Tijerina, the price of neighboring land skyrocketed to $1,500 an acre as Rockefeller dollars poured into the "Arizona City" housing project. Whatever the actual reasons, the band of believers began suffering harassment.

"They sent high school kids to our houses while the men and women were picking cotton," Tijerina claims. "They took two years to burn all our buildings down. . . . Then a high-flying airplane flew down into our property. . . . Because of that accident one pregnant girl lost her child and an old woman went crazy."

According to Tijerina, the FBI refused to investigate the crash, pleas to Washington went unanswered, and the local sheriff's office ignored the house-burnings. Finally everything was leveled to ashes. It took the theft of some automobile parts to bring the arm of the law into the dregs of the settlement.

By March 19, 1957, Tijerina and a few followers were living in a "gypsy camp near Pete's corner," reported a lawman in Pinal County, Arizona. That was the day Reies became one of the defendants charged with grand theft, for an incident in which six feed-trailer wheels were reportedly stolen. Although the case was thrown out for lack of evidence, the next month a second grand theft charge was thrown at Tijerina for stolen hardware discovered in the Valle de Paz well. He insists the tools were planted. But while officers were investigating this they discovered that Margarito Tijerina, a prodigal who had returned to the family fold after a troublesome life in the midwest, was a parole violator from Indiana. While he was being held for return and imprisonment, a jailbreak involving a smuggled hacksaw was attempted in the Pinal County jail in early July. Reies was accused of being at the wheel of the getaway car

after the alleged scheme to free his brother failed, and he was released on $1,000 bond.

During a noon recess at his hearing on this charge, Tijerina
calmly strode out of the doors of the Pinal County courthouse. He
kept on walking, and began his successful attempt to run out the
Arizona statute of limitations. Of this chapter-closing he says
simply, "We moved out of Arizona."

The next four years, before Tijerina turned up to stay in New
Mexico, are hazy. "That is for *my* book, those years when I was in
flight," he says to questioners. But one time he gave me a glimpse
into them.

"From 1957 to 1960 I was a fugitive. I escaped from the law
seventeen times. I escaped when the FBI was after me, all around
me, with guns. Once I was in the only room they didn't search,
right behind the door, but they didn't look in. I am an alert man.
Once we were surrounded by five FBI cars in Plainview, Texas.
Texas Rangers also. They had surrounded my house; my wife with
six children was inside. They told her, 'If you don't tell us where
your husband is, we'll arrest all of you.' I went into the bathroom
where Rosina [his oldest daughter] was taking a bath and told her
to show her shoulder if they came in, and I stood behind the shower
curtain. You wouldn't believe the stories."

For a period of three months Tijerina and armed followers hid
on a Texas ranch. During this span Tijerina began wandering
once again. On one trek with his family he found himself near El
Monte, California, and in spiritual turmoil.

"I kept on having a struggle with my conscience, you know,
my soul. I was not satisfied. I was always finding that the Bible
rebuked me. I found things, not outright things, but that I was a
hypocrite, that I was not doing what I could do. So in order to
overcome that struggle and doubt and fear I told her [his wife]
that I was going to seek a better life, a better opening, and I
wouldn't leave that place until God would show me my duty."

In the manner of a Plains Indian striving for a life-guiding
vision, Tijerina proceeded to find a cave hidden amidst underbrush

into which he had to "crawl like a snake." Without food or water, he made his ritual bed of cotton stuffing from a car seat. There he made a discovery:

"There were not so many religions that I studied in school, there was just two strong powers, and the religion was just like gasoline. If you use Texaco or Mobil, it's all the same, it makes your motor, you know, burn, and I had very strong illuminations, and so far so good, I had found that religion now, I knew that there was no difference between Protestant and Catholic, because these and those of the different religions were all the same, they all wanted new automobiles, they all coveted the same things."

The second great power revealed to him, that of justice, had already summoned him in a previous, more prophetic dream. Around the year of Valle de Paz's founding, Tijerina was the guest of a poor family in Visalia, California, south of Fresno. One night he wandered into the countryside and unintentionally fell asleep. The next morning "the sun woke me and that white, how do you say, dew, had covered me all over. It shaked all my life, from there I turned to New Mexico. I saw frozen horses, they started melting and coming to life in a very old kingdom with old walls. Then I saw three angels of law and they asked to help me. They said they had come from a long ways, had traveled the earth and come for me. . . . Those tall pines I saw meant New Mexico. When I started doing research into the land grants I found they are not dead, they are just frozen. They are living, latent political bodies."

Before Tijerina and seven carloads of followers finally drove to New Mexico in 1960 he had already made friends there through his ministerial meanderings. He had also, during his fugitive period after 1957, dropped south into old Mexico. It was during this interlude of mental questioning and outwitting lawmen that he came to focus on the land-grant question. From September 1958 to September 1959 he spent nearly the entire year in Mexico, researching in libraries. He attempted to pass on land-grant data to the Secretary of Exterior Relations in Mexico City, with unenthusiastic response. In August 1959 Tijerina accompanied the president of the International Front of Human Rights, Dr. Benjamin Lauriano Luna, when he met Dr. Milton Eisenhower in Mexico City. A New Mexico newspaper commented that this caused, at 1,000 miles distance, a revival of the century-old dispute over the ancient southwestern lands. From March to May 1960 Tijerina and his brother Cristobal were in Mexico, and an April 11 news item in *Excelsior* described them as "residents of the land grant of Tierra Amarilla," visiting Mexico for aid in retrieving land-grant holdings.

When Tijerina came to New Mexico in 1960 he followed up his old preaching contacts for his new crusade.

"We went to seven families," he says. "I asked them to give us all the stories and documents and maps they had, but they didn't have a copy of the Treaty of Guadalupe Hidalgo. So after a few months I went to Mexico and there I found an old book, eaten by termites, with all the maps, the treaty and the protocol. Later I found the whole legal history, and then I went around to the old people, eighty and a hundred years old, and even though they didn't know each other and lived hundreds of miles apart, their stories matched."

With a little effort Tijerina could have obtained a copy of the treaty between Mexico and the United States in any New Mexico public library. But his concern about the all-important protocol, adopted after the treaty was redrafted, was his point here. It is that added and often overlooked portion which he insists reserves the old land grants to the first grantee's descendants in perpetuity.

As Tijerina began absorbing the rhythms and histories of the northern valley communities, he moved circumspectly. This was in part because of his vulnerable legal status; it was also necessary in order to prospect. His intuition told him that in these forgotten islands lay something approximating a "pure" Spanish-American heritage. His organizational efforts in the north began with caution. Shortly, in the "tall pines" and humble settlements he became assured that he had found his calling and the Athens of the Indo-Hispano world.

16

GROWTH
OF AN
ORGANIZATION

When Tijerina came out of internment in the New Mexico State Prison on July 24, 1967, he was raring to exploit the notoriety of the courthouse raid. A condition attached to his release limited his out-of-county trips to business related to legal defense. A short distance south of Las Vegas, New Mexico, he launched a flurry of harangues legitimized as "fund-raising" rallies.

In the community square of Tecolote, Tijerina stood at the same spot where over a hundred years before an American general had ordered the community's *alcalde* (mayor) to swear allegiance to the American flag.

"We have just started to write a new history of New Mexico," Tijerina declared. "The time is right for us to get rid of fear."

His organization, he said, aimed to set up "pueblos," which he defined as governmental bodies over rural areas with the central unit similar to a city council. These "free city states," he added, would be established within the framework of the United States Government.

While Tijerina talked, an Alianza bodyguard stood just feet

behind him with a pistol under his shirt. Plainclothes officers from the San Miguel County sheriff's office mingled with the 150 Tecolote villagers, many of them "heirs" to the old Tecolote land grant. Before leaving, an Alianza secretary tallied up $222 in small-bill donations. Tijerina had alerted the lawmen to his visit beforehand. "We don't know what the news media will call it," he said, "maybe a *showdown,* but there will be no trouble from us." Restoration of "justice," a federally financed bilingual education for all New Mexico schoolchildren, renewed pressure on the land-grant front— Tijerina used the raid's renown to revitalize his old points. During the Tecolote meeting, George Jaramillo of Anton Chico sang out the song he had composed to honor the courthouse episode. In one verse Jaramillo spoke of Tijerina's capture:

"In the year of '67, because it had to happen that way, taken as a prisoner, the brave Tijerina."

Three weeks later Tijerina began a serious reorganizational meeting of hard-core Alianza members in Albuquerque. The two-day conclave was open to visitors the first day but closed to outsiders the second. In the first full-scale conference since before the aborted Coyote gathering, the organization's name was changed back to Alianza, but now Alianza de los Pueblos Libres (Alliance of Free City States). The less scintillating "Confederation" had never stuck. Professor Clark Knowlton made an appearance, but prime time was allotted to Tijerina's request for approval of escalated moves to dramatize the Alianza's demands.

During the previous week U.S. Senator Joseph Montoya had held his promised series of rural development hearings with much fanfare in Santa Fe, Espanola, and Las Vegas. Tijerina said that, in contrast to Montoya's "open" hearings, the poor people could freely represent themselves during *his* conference. He announced that an "international motorcade" of 500 cars to drive to Mexico City was in the works. Mexico would once more be asked to take the Alianza's claims to the United Nations. Additional conferences would decide whether or not to retain the services of the flamboyant San Francisco attorney Melvin Belli, who had written

TIJERINA and the COURTHOUSE RAID

Tijerina a letter of interest. But the meeting was not entirely placid.

As had become custom, Jerry Noll, lawyer *manqué* and king-jester of the movement, was given an opportunity to reaffirm his royalist view of things. The "King of the Indies" told the villagers packed into the Alianza meeting hall that the United States Government must be ousted from New Mexico. He suggested that if it was necessary to conspire with foreign powers to accomplish this feat, so be it. Around the unplastered concrete block walls of the ill-lit, low-roofed hall the garish symbolic oil paintings of an Alianza artist, the Duke of Aragon, created a weird cultist aura. Flags and banners hung about evoked the mood of a convention of exiled Middle European veterans from some past conflict involving flintlocks and land barons. The audience turned from the "king" as a disturbance broke out behind them.

"We are not traitors to the United States," erupted a man who was standing in the rear and close to tears. "We are not traitors, we are not traitors."

In a flash Tijerina had swept over the microphone, galvanizing the disturbed and murmuring crowd by interjecting, "I go along with the United States when it goes along with George Washington." He said he would not disown the United States, but "I cannot support a whore and a prostitute." At this the original protester silently walked out of the meeting hall. As usual, Tijerina's serious and subtle comparison between a man's tested love for a faithless woman—mother or wife—and his tie to his betraying country was lost in translation, and in the press. The papers gleefully reported Tijerina blaspheming the U.S. as a prostitute.

Ten days later Tijerina boarded a plane for Chicago and the bombastic National Convention for New Politics. By now he had been classified by the national radical hierarchy as an American original. The Chicago experience was to budge the Alianza toward the new arena and the twentieth century.

Tijerina's initial organizing in northern New Mexico in the late 1950's had been an entirely unpublicized procedure. During roughly five years spent getting the feel of the region and pursuing his own concept of land-grant scholarship, he was loosely associated with a strange band known as *los Barbudos* (the Bearded Ones). He is reported by one Alianzan as first staying in the tiny community of Gobernador for close to a year, ostensibly preaching. After that he was said to be working out of Ensenada, where he began "advising and organizing."

One episode that certainly spurred his emerging *causa* took place on Thanksgiving, 1961, in San Luis in southern Colorado near the New Mexico border. Anglo ranch hands bloodily worked over three "trespassing" Spanish-American cattlemen. Then the victims were forced to hike five miles before being heaved into a pickup truck and "dumped out on the courthouse steps like sacks of flour." With Felix Martinez as a guide, Reies and Cristobal Tijerina were shortly there to inspect, and to respond to the wave of new bitterness. "That was the first time there was unity," he remembers. Ever since then Tijerina has stressed the self-protective value of consolidation among Spanish-American communities.

Northern New Mexico's politically acquired predilection for mutually antagonistic factions was an obstacle in his path, however. Tijerina was never entirely able to gather all the land-grant protesters who had preceded him into a coordinated pressure front. He was labeled a "Communist wetback" by an Atrisco land-grant figure. His introductory appearance at a gathering of Tierra Amarilla grant heirs—at their invitation—turned into a bloody brawl. This incident seems to have been some sort of organizational turning point. In one retelling Tijerina, his head dripping from an attack with a wooden club, dramatically unified the group with a Mark Antony-style plea that his blood christen the new alliance. In the police version, the fight started with an outright assault on another man by Tijerina's brother Anselmo, who maintained he was defending Reies. Anselmo was convicted of assault but broke out of the Tierra Amarilla courthouse jail. For this he was sent to the New Mexico State Prison for a term of one to five years, of which he served eighteen months.

TIJERINA and the COURTHOUSE RAID

By this time Reies had fully concluded that "since my people were in need of justice more than in need of religion, I decided to give up so-called religious doctrines and dedicate myself entirely to their more immediate needs. There are too many preachers. People are tired of empty religious ceremonies. They [today's clergy] are no longer like the hard-feeling, warm-teaching religious leaders of old."

As he knocked on the doors of northern New Mexicans, Tijerina brought an appealing package. Usually only a few people would hear him at first, offering their visitor beans, coffee, and flour tortillas. Then they would pass news of this exciting talker to friends; another introduction would be made. From a sofa Tijerina would expound his emphatic message, based on amateurish historical delving, Biblical prophecy, and sprinkled with just the right amount of nostalgic tidbits to recharge his hope-starved listeners. Sometimes his words were only for an elderly woman in a one-room shack, but he would talk for an entire afternoon and his gesticulating hands moved no less furiously.

This was a time of small meetings organized by about eight stalwarts. Felix Martinez remembers that Tijerina had two helpers in Albuquerque, one each in Bernalillo, Canjilon, and Espanola, and the rest working out of Tierra Amarilla. During one home call Tijerina perused an old land abstract and marked up its margin, saying, "You people are blind to let them do this to you. I don't know how you even live."

Particularly Tijerina sought out individuals who had been involved in land-grant disputes before, who could relate tales of what had been lost and describe their fruitless efforts to get lands back. In this manner he met Eduardo Chavez, who later became the Alianza's secretary-treasurer. Through Chavez he connected with figures active in the Atrisco land grant's problems. He became acquainted with the Martinez family of Tierra Amarilla, officers of the Abiquiu Corporation, and he came to know others who had belonged to the Colonia Mexicana. In Chama he listened to

210

GROWTH OF AN ORGANIZATION

Higinio Martínez, a notary public, tell the dark record of the Tierra Amarilla grant.

Circumstances frequently worked to his advantage. Near El Rito about thirty families joined his cause en masse after being informed by the U.S. Forest Service that fencing their grazing allotments was their responsibility. The lack of state government response to the cry of northern communities for gravel on washed-out roads caused others to harken to his message.

Some time in 1960 he settled in Albuquerque. For a period he worked as janitor at a Presbyterian church in the predominately Spanish-American quarter of Martineztown while his wife also worked. He is remembered as doing more reading than sweeping. Until late 1962 his grapevine organizing was conducted underground, but in the first months of 1963 the Alianza was born.

Formal meetings were first held for the purpose of firming up structural guidelines for the new organization. On February 2, 1963, in Davis Hall, Alameda, just outside of Albuquerque, Tijerina and thirty-seven faithful voted to incorporate as the Alianza Federal de Mercedes. The necessary papers were registered by the state on October 8 of that year. They state the Alianza's purpose: "To organize and acquaint the Heirs of all the Spanish Land Grants covered by the Guadalupe Treaty. . . . Thus providing unity of purpose and securing for the Heirs of Spanish Land Grants the highest advantages as provided by the aforesaid Treaty and Constitutions."

With the money from the ultimate sale of the Valle de Paz lands, a 10,000-square-foot concrete block building in an industrial strip within Albuquerque city limits had been purchased. On the front plate glass windows of the former cold storage plant, former newspaper print shop, appeared silver lettering made from cigaret wrapper foil. "Justice is our Cry" proclaimed one sign in Spanish; another, "The Land is our Heritage."

From this public relations center Tijerina began informing the amused and the curious that he based his claim for the return of

211

roughly 100,000,000 acres on a 1573 decree by King Philip II of Spain giving lands to New World colonizers and on Pope Alexander VI's 1493 bull, *Noverunt Universi*, which he interpreted as granting Spain divine right to confer these landholdings. The Abiquiu Corporation, the Alianza's defunct predecessor, had refused to place its land arguments before any tribunal except the International Court of Justice at The Hague, in Holland. Tijerina simply insisted that the 1848 Treaty of Guadalupe Hidalgo, if justly enforced, would restore their lands to the Alianza members.

Tijerina's organizational brainchild was a synthesis of the man's own psychology and his followers' folkways. During its early meetings a flavor emerged that combined a Spanish-American family reunion, a Saturday night evangelistic tent meeting, a *cantina* on Friday night, and a cautious deliberation among embittered villagers.

Tijerina would arouse a pitch of enthusiasm through a masterly, exhausting exhibition of folk rhetoric, savage mimicry, lapses into his backlog of fundamentalist fables, and an actor's shifting of emotional levels. As well as providing the major addresses, his patter would string together the remarks of guest speakers. The session's formalities would usually close with a ritualistic pass-the-hat performance, Tijerina clutching a fist of bills, asking first for twenties, then tens, finally fives. This backwoods method of soliciting funds would be continued through the Poor People's Campaign in 1968, as much for its tradition in the entire spectacle as for its practical value.

In his talks, Tijerina compared the Alianza to a mother dog ("the she dog, after she has had some pups, will not run from anybody, and we in New Mexico will not run"), to a cricket (it bites a lion—New Mexico's officialdom—in the ear and the beast bleeds to death scratching itself), and frequently spoke of himself as a David matched against a bureaucratic Goliath.

At breaks in the regular Saturday night meetings, as well as at nightfall during the three-day "national conventions," a jukebox would blare Mexican *mariachi* ballads. After the raid a favorite was

"Corrido of Rio Arriba," which told of the courthouse incident, when "A group of our race very discontented/Took their revenge upon state officials." Soft drinks and chili with beans and flour tortillas would be sold. There would be some tipping of stronger stuff in the parking area outside, but this was frowned upon. The night would end with the hall cleared of folding chairs and full of dancing couples.

Tijerina's religious temperament and Old Testament training did not lose its hold on his legal arguments and visions of the Spanish-American millenium. Frequently changing his favorite name for his own people—"Hispano," "Spanish-American," "Mexican-American," "Indo-Spanish," "la Raza" (the Race)—he finally hit on "the New Breed," and was even able to specify the day this hybrid was recognized:

" . . . I feel I'm representing a new breed born October 19, 1514, by law of Title I of Book 6 of the Law of the Indies, by decree of Ferdinand V and reaffirmed by Philip II, which legalized the matrimony of Spaniard and the native Pueblo Indians. Out of which decree our 400 years, equal to the years given to Abraham the patriarch that his descendants would be under the servitude of Egypt, after which God would deliver them and grant them perpetually the land of Palestine. Alike [to the Israelites] this new breed has served 400 years of servitude, actually 430 years, of humiliation, injustice, being pushed by everybody, and all because our father, a Spaniard, was hated for the Spanish Inquisition and the Spanish Armada and was thrown out of the American continent, and our mother, the Indian, was held on a reservation, leaving the new breed, a forgotten people and orphans without the heat of their parents."

By 1963 Tijerina was no longer living with his wife, Mary Escobar, but was inhabiting a windowless closet-size freezer compartment in the basement of the Alianza hall. Now he finally divorced Mary and married into a New Mexico family. Patsy Romero was a teenager when Reies met her.

"She has been to school all her life but she cannot read or

write," he later told a *New Republic* correspondent. "You know what that means? You know what that means? She is retarded. I picked a woman who was only kind. I thought they were making fun of her in school—and I decided to marry her and put her above all women. It's the will of God. Modern wisdom is foolishness."

Patsy was also a bona fide land-grantee descendant. To questions about his motives Reies has answered, "I know, to you Anglos, my marrying an heir would be charged as self-interest, but you see, my people think differently. They believe that if I have a genuine self-interest in the cause, I am far more likely to do the job for them."

He had six children by his first marriage: Reies Jr. (also called David), Rosemary, Danny, Rachel, Noah, and Iradeala. ("I named one of my daughters Ira de Allah, the Wrath of God, as a living testimony that I believe in the angry God.") By Patsy he would have two, Iris Isabel and Carlos (as of this writing). Soon Tijerina and his young bride set up housekeeping in a three-room apartment on the second floor of the Alianza building.

In the summer of 1963 Reies Tijerina took his first trip to lay the Alianza's claims before Washington officials. On his way back he stopped over in Chicago and attended the American Emancipation Centennial. Earlier in the summer he had met its director, Dr. Alton A. Davis, at a conference where he also renewed acquaintance with friends from a Mexican organization, the International Front of Human Rights. At this meeting the former President of Mexico, Miguel Aleman, was photographed shaking hands with Tijerina's daughter Rosa, her eyes demurely downcast.

Shortly before the state actually registered his organization, Tijerina held the Alianza's first annual convention. At the Rio Grande High School gymnasium representatives of some fifty grants conferred on September 1, 1963. During the all-day meeting Tijerina, wearing a brush mustache and heavy glasses, described the disheartening results of his personal appearance before Attorney

214

General Robert Kennedy. If they were going to get anywhere, he was now convinced, the heirs would have to "pool their efforts and employ the best attorneys and bring political pressure in Washington" to obtain redress of wrongs. Guest speaker at the convention was white-haired Dr. Alton A. Davis, from the Emancipation Centennial.

By the time of the next year's convention Tijerina had made another trip east, where he received the lukewarm endorsement of three Spanish-Americans—Congressmen Henry Gonzales of Texas, Edward Roybal of California, and Joseph M. Montoya of New Mexico—for a congressional investigation of the heirs' rights under the Guadalupe Hidalgo Treaty. Tijerina had also started a daily radio show, a morning spot on radio station KARA called "The Voice of Justice," advertised as "ten minutes of historical and legal truth—all questions answered." By the time of the 1964 convention Tijerina had also suffered an undignified cloak-and-dagger expulsion from Mexico.

Since the beginning of that year the land-grant leader had been planning a huge automobile caravan to depart from Albuquerque and arrive in Mexico City during its September 16 Independence Day festivities. Tijerina states that "We had advised Lopez Mateos [the President of Mexico] of our trip, handed him our memorandum, and talked with his personal secretary. . . . Everything was arranged with their Gobernacion [which controls travel and immigration] and one of their senators was already chosen as a liaison." The motorcade's mission, he says, was to dramatize again the Alianza's request that Mexico raise the question of land grants under the Treaty of Guadalupe Hidalgo.

But then, according to Tijerina, the Alianza was asked to reconsider by a U.S. Government spokesman, "because they said it would embarrass the U.S." Ignoring the advice, in late spring he ventured south of the border to map out the route. "We weren't going to stay at hotels, but in the *campos* [fields], so I was going to make a mileage schedule of five to seven stops."

TIJERINA and the COURTHOUSE RAID

With his visitor's thirty-day permit Tijerina stopped over in Chihuahua, the capital city of the Mexican state of the same name. There he participated in a gathering in the town's plaza which Judicial Police promptly dissolved. He was held in the Chihuahua State Prison for "violating his visitor's permission by participating in a meeting in which the liberty of some 'reds' were being discussed," according to the state's district attorney. New Mexico Governor Jack Campbell, unaware of Tijerina's imprisonment, now promised a police escort for the Alianza's motorcade as far as the Texas border.

Released and urged to go home, Tijerina nevertheless kept driving south to Mexico City. Secretary of Gobernacion Diaz Ordaz —who would shortly assume the Mexican presidency—thereupon ordered Tijerina's deportation. The Mexican Government sent to all its border consulates circulars which informed (in translation): ". . . He passes himself as president of an organization known as Alianza Federal de los Mercedes which has been working during the past months to form a caravan of North Americans to go to Mexico by car . . . in order to ask Mexico for help in its claims to ancient land grants. Consulates are therefore ordered to deny them documentation for entry into Mexico on any kind of immigration status."

At the termination of his entry permit Tijerina was arrested by agents of the Direccion Federal de Seguridad who had kept him under surveillance throughout his stay in the capital. On August 8 he was expelled for "violation of the general law of the people." Records show that he was discovered shirtless, working on his 1957 car, when picked up in Mexico City. The vehicle was impounded. Tijerina gives an expanded version:

"With my daughter Rosina, fifteen years old, I was staying at this house when four men came to the house, in the night, put me in a car. . . . They took me to an airplane straight, bound for San Antonio. I think it was a Mexican flight. I didn't even have a shirt on. I was in my undershirt and the hostess gave me a brand new shirt. Those men gave my papers to the pilot and told him not to

216

let me off. Then I borrowed money from Ramon, who lived there, and took the bus to Albuquerque."

The second annual convention, in 1964, was a two-day affair at the end of August, held in Santa Fe's Seth Hall. A farsighted journalist, Nigel S. Hey, editor of the Albuquerque *News Chieftain* and the *North Valley News*, had already perceived the Alianza's potential significance. His weekly neighborhood sheets had provided the principal state coverage since the movement began. Space in the *News Chieftain* had been given to the Alianza for a weekly Spanish column. Before the second annual convention Hey wrote a well-balanced summary of the Alianza's aims and a short history of the organization.

Also in 1964, Tijerina attempted to establish friendly contact with several Pueblo Indian tribes. Because of their common documentary basis for their land claims—the Spanish and Mexican archives—Tijerina saw to it that the Alianza expressed its support for the Taos Pueblo's fight to regain control of their sacred Blue Lake area. He would also journey to the Hopi mesas and visit the Apache reservations.

For the Alianza's third annual gathering on September 4-5, 1965, Knowlton was advertised in a handbill as principal speaker. The same notice informed the attending Alianzans entering Albuquerque's huge Civic Auditorium that Senator Joseph Montoya had been personally invited. Montoya's lack of follow-through on his willingness "within the legal framework to resolve title conflicts" was duly censured by Tijerina. He also challenged the Rio Grande Conservancy District as an example of the eroded relations between conservation-minded authorities and the irrigation farmer. He claimed the district had been established "illegally" in 1937 because the land-grant heirs' consent had not been given, "and now they charge us for water we don't even use."

In 1964 the Alianza counted its membership at 6,000. A year later it boasted 14,000 followers. During the 1965 convention a motion to assess each member family $100 was passed, the money to provide a legal action fund. It was reported that a New Mexico attorney and a Texas lawyer were studying ways to open up the subject of vacant lands cut from land grants by the state and the federal government.

By the time the next yearly convention was held in Albuquerque Civic Auditorium, on September 3-4, 1966, the Alianza and its adversaries were in a new ball game. From April 11 through May 11 Tijerina had enjoyed a document-hunting jaunt in Spain. At the Archives of the Indies in Seville he perused ancient Spanish documents for two weeks; he also spent two weeks in Madrid. He had made a point of visiting Don Quixote's home of La Mancha, "a beautiful old place," and had discussed the United States in Spain's prestigious newspaper *ABC*. The U.S. State Department felt the article, published May 7, harmed the U.S. image, and a copy entered a Washington file. Tijerina was quoted as declaring that "Americans want nothing to do with anything Spanish and hope to keep them in a second-class category of citizenship . . . worse than that of Negroes . . . for at least Negro problems are talked of . . . while the Spanish-Americans are regarded only as potential soldiers to be sent to fight in other countries."

Less than two months after his return the Alianza held its widely reported Fourth of July sixty-two-mile protest march from Albuquerque to Santa Fe, camping on the edge of town until Governor Campbell finally talked face to face with Tijerina.

At the 1966 convention the Alianza estimated its membership at 20,000 and broadened its topics to include the high rate of Spanish-surnamed casualties in Vietnam, language discrimination in the schools, the possibilities and defects of poverty programs. An invitation had been sent to Dr. Martin Luther King, but he replied that he had a prior commitment. Then Stokely Carmichael was asked to speak, but at the last minute he too had to cancel. Finally a young Negro staff member of the local poverty program expressed the black sympathy for the Alianza's cause. Again Professor Knowlton was featured. A new star in the Alianza's hierarchy, Jerry Noll, described as a "historian of international law," made a statement.

The OEO civil rights adviser, Tony Tinajero, was also in attendance. Yet another visitor was aspiring gubernatorial candidate David Cargo, who vowed receptivity if elected to office.

The new tone was tough. Nothing had come of Governor Campbell's promise during the July encounter to forward the Alianza's claims to the White House. President Johnson was "too busy with Vietnam," said Tijerina. Now discussions of "reclaiming" cities and grant territories were heard. Tijerina had visited Texas earlier in the year to participate in a Spanish-American demonstration in El Paso. He had also made his pilgrimage to the Hopi mesas, whence came reports of a surprisingly amicable get-together between the land-grant leader and tribal elders. The new mood would manifest itself just a month later in the days of the Echo Amphitheater invasion.

In early fall, 1967, the Alianza headquarters was receiving many inquiries from out-of-state militant groups. The first full-dress conclave attended by Tijerina was the rambunctious National Conference for New Politics, held during the first days of September at the Palmer House in Chicago. Along with Dr. Martin Luther King, Floyd McKissick, James Forman, Julian Bond, Dick Gregory, Dr. Benjamin Spock, and other spokesmen for minority rights, he filled a reserved seat on the platform. He was pleased to find the delegates unopposed to his resolution that the United States strictly enforce the Treaty of Guadalupe Hidalgo.

Tijerina came home via Texas so he could join a fifty-mile protest march ending in Austin. At a rally on the state capitol steps he brushed aside local accusations of being a "Latin Stokely Carmichael" and supported the demonstration's demand for a $1.25 minimum wage for farm workers. When he returned from the journey he held vivid impressions of his new colleagues. He discussed Dr. King:

"Well, I took it that he was very anxious to have an official

219

alliance with the Spanish-American throughout the southwest. They look upon the Spanish-American for a future balancing of power and a future support for their cause."

To Tijerina, King was "sort of a philosopher, a slow-spoken man, who weighs his words very much before making his statement." He was obviously intrigued by the Negro leader. "I noticed he writes his speech. He seems to be worried between the two factions among these Negro people, between the left and the right. He has hard pressure on both sides."

Tijerina tried to explain that "the reason why I met with all the leaders—I don't care about their cause and their ideas but I wanted an alliance for moral support and a mutual push for the pursuit of justice. That's why I met with Elijah Mohammed. The primary things is to avoid future frictions between the Negro and the Spanish-American." He was struck that Dick Gregory "talked a lot and is a quick thinker."

Now Tijerina revealed that the Alianza's fifth annual convention would be held October 21-22. He had again invited Martin Luther King to speak. "We only want him," Tijerina explained to his regular Saturday night Alianza crowd in the Albuquerque meeting hall, "to come so that the people can see him . . . and I want, at the speech, for there to be more raza [Spanish-Americans] than Negroes."

Tijerina announced during this meeting that a "coalition" with the Black Muslims would soon be formed, as well as alignments with other black organizations. Throughout this rush of new experiences he seemed unable to transmit his precise intentions into something the press could not misinterpret. Of the blacks expected at his convention he said, "Of course we are only going to admit the Negroes when Martin Luther King speaks. Following that speech, they have to get out because the convention belongs to our raza." If one realized he meant it when he explained that his prime objective was to protect the Alianza from future friction with black militants, Tijerina's idea of "peace treaties" made his own sort of odd sense.

220

Perhaps Tijerina also worried that his unique cause and his rural following would be usurped once they lost numerical strength and single attention amidst the vocal, sophisticated, well-known ranks of the black radicals. He probably did not want to bring an avalanche of home state fears down on his organization by visions of black separatists arm in arm with Alianzans descending en masse upon the Anglo community. Nor did he wish to jeopardize the hard-won success of the courthouse raid and his new stature among black as well as white radical leadership. Naturally such subtleties were missing in the news reports of his intent to "unite" with the Black Muslims.

The October 1967 convention was soon an item of wide antici-pation. But while it drew near Tijerina kept up his "fund-raising" speech-making. At St. John's College in Santa Fe he made an un-fortunate reference to the racial origin of one of the masterminds of the so-called Santa Fe Ring, the clique of New Mexico business-men who in the late nineteenth century amassed gigantic land-grant holdings. "I understand Thomas B. Catron, leader of the Santa Fe Ring, was a Jew," he said. His garbled point, which did not get through to his listeners, was that if the long span of Jewish culture could produce such legal and financial abilities, then his equally ancient "New Breed" could show forth as effectively. But the re-mark, which was quite untrue, shocked his otherwise sympathetic audience.

In another appearance at Chama, New Mexico, Tijerina was forced to talk in the open air after the American Legion hall was padlocked to prevent his entrance. Under cloudy skies he ad-dressed standing listeners while plainclothes officers were on their guard. Cristobal Tijerina had accompanied his brother and also had his eyes open. An Anglo man who acted drunk shouted loudly for the land-grant leader to speak in English. Cristobal had noticed him, a Chama storekeeper, sidle close to his brother. The head of the state police narcotics division approached the man, who was later reported by police to be "apparently" carrying a gun, and told him to drive off.

TIJERINA and the COURTHOUSE RAID

Finally, on a Friday afternoon, October 20, the Alianza's colorful, bizarre "fifth national convention" opened. Tijerina played host to a most incongruous but resplendent array of visitors. From California came Maulana Ron Karenga, head of the Los Angeles Afro-American organization "US." (His red calling card, passed around to the gawking press, read "Wherever we are, US is.") Clad in a brilliantly colored tunic like his eleven-member delegation, Karenga was rendered somewhat sinister by his smooth-shaven head and black-rimmed glossy sunglasses. His similarly shaven bodyguards also wore shades and copied Karenga's droopy Manchurian mustache, carved talisman on a thong around the neck, and sandals. Karenga's dazzling pearly smile flashed on Saturday as he strode very fast to the podium of the Albuquerque Civic Auditorium, flanked by decidedly unsmiling US guards.

From the Student Nonviolent Coordinating Committee (SNCC) came its program director, Ralph Featherstone, in an African print *dashike*, followed by SNCC members also regally attired in Afro-American garments. Corky Gonzales, the Denver militant, brought cheers from the audience when he said, "We are going to get up and start a revolution. It was sparked by the Tierra Amarilla raid. The change for the Spanish-American has to come with a revolution for social reform."

Also from California came Burt Corona, head of the Mexican-American Political Association (MAPA), looking like a *chicano* version of a 1940's shirtsleeve labor organizer. Corona's center-of-left platform was useful in translating radical rhetoric into progressive planning. Other black groups represented were the emerging Black Panthers, the Black Congress, the Black Youth Congress, Black Students Union, Congress of Racial Equality (CORE), and the Black Anti-Draft Unit. Spokesmen for other *chicano* organizations included Chicago's Mexican-American Youth Organization.

The "first Americans" were present in the persons of two Hopi leaders. Tomas Banyacya, a tribal spokesman of Hotevilla, was poised and eye-catching in his brilliant forehead bandana, shining shoulder-length hair, turquoise jewelry and flower-patterned shirt.

222

He slowly guided an ancient, stooped Hopi medicine man by the elbow through the vibrating capes and yokes of the Afro-clad blacks, to a metal folding chair on the stage which faced the floor audience and the encircling balconies above.

The hosts were hard put not to be outdone. Tijerina had urged his Alianzans to wear "traditional" Spanish-American festive clothing, but the best they came up with were a few Mexican *mariachi* outfits, Spanish hoop dresses, roses in hair and ruffles on shirts. Tijerina himself did not seem quite at home in a lacy dress blouse and scarlet waist sash.

The convention's overriding tone was self-congratulatory, excited by the racial spectrum on the podium which seemed to promise across-the-board racial unity. It was highly salutatory toward the Alianza. For the first time, and very likely the last, the urban had made a pilgrimage to pay tribute to their rural origins. In the case of some out-of-state *chicano* guests who had been born in New Mexico, it was literally their origin. In the case of the black visitors, it was the romantic origin of guerrilla warfare within the continental United States. (When Tijerina appeared on California black rally platforms, his introducers would admonish the audience, "While we're talking revolution, this cat's making it.")

The dislocated had come to homage the residue of cultural homeland left to them. The young had arrived to praise an act of the old which had awed them: the courthouse raid.

There were a few problems. Alianzans crowded angrily around police officers who were apparently taking down license numbers in the spacious auditorium parking lot. Tijerina and his brother Cristobal talked to the lawmen and they withdrew. In a defiant reaction to a district court order instructing him to refrain from discussing the raid, Tijerina said, "If Judge Bratton asks me I'll tell him I told the witnesses what to say and what to do. I may get arrested. This is fine. It is all right with me because we don't judge Bratton the judge in this case." The result was a contempt-of-court citation.

Although the speaker's platform was festooned with the customary home-embroidered coats of arms identifying various land grants, the free city state of San Joaquin del Rio de Chama was conspicuously never invoked. At least for this weekend, Tierra Amarilla no longer symbolized the disputed land grant but rather the violent incident which had made such a diversified cultural gathering possible. A popular sticker passed out during the convention read: " 'Che' is alive and hiding in Tierra Amarilla."

A folk-fair air had been created by the variety of costumes and the wild variance between rhetoric, subject matter, and life philosophies being piped from the podium over a faulty public address system. The wizened Hopi holy man with wispy white hair delivered his endless benediction in his native tongue, a monotone prayer as ancient as the legends recited in it. Ralph Featherstone began his get-the-honkey harangue with an upraised fist and a loud "Poder Negro [Black Power], Poder Negro, Poder Negro." Self-consciously the shy Spanish-American ranchers and farmers of the Alianza stood up from their block of seats directly in front of the stage. The men doffed battered straw cowboy hats and held up calloused hands, drew them into fists, and replied as requested, "Poder Negro, Poder Negro, Poder Negro." Ron Karenga had spoken in singsong Spanish, heavily Dixie accented, flailing the "white devil" for all he was worth. The brogue of Alianza sympathizer Father Clarence Duffy delivered irrelevant liberal hopes. Finally, Jerry Noll stood elevated on a wooden box so his shiny pate was visible over the lectern. It was literally Noll's crowning moment.

"Thank you, Mr. Tijerina." Noll drew bewildered smiles from the newcomers as he began in a lispy, high-pitched voice. "If I had known beforehand that I was going to be given such a grand introduction I would have had six silver trumpets blown to add a touch of pageantry. . . . I have long awaited this opportunity to formally address you in my official capacity as King Emperor of the Indies, and make this official declaration from the throne. . . ." The rest of Don Barne Quinto Cesar's thirteen-page prepared revelation testified to his complex royal lineage and told the

224

United States that it must repair to its original thirteen colonies and leave the rest of his kingdom alone.

But the convention was not simply colorfully incongruous. Underneath the entire affair lay a tone of hardness. Whatever the wording of the secret "pact" signed during closed-door sessions Sunday back at the Alianza headquarters, it boded at least minimal contact between *chicano* and black militants. From the speakers came intimations that on the West Coast black and Spanish-American radicals were exchanging tactical information and consolidating goals. The winds of social discontent would ride over the stagnant, the staid, and the nostalgic. Whether it liked it or not, the Alianza was being told, it had become a current in those winds.

Beneath the well-wishing and the extreme warmth which sprang up immediately—to the surprise of some urban *chicanos*—between the Alianza fellowship and the black delegates lay the unrelenting tenor of the times. To an audience that included practically no teenage Alianza members, Burt Corona appealed earnestly for politically aware youth. The black delegates brought the same urgent advice expanded into a warning: Unless you adopted appropriate strategy, looked ahead to the political organization of your youth around ethnic solidarity, pragmatically assessed your gains and priorities, you would wither.

The guests were tender with these rustic hosts who had played out their own romantic fantasies of domestic guerrillahood. You made an honorable shot with one eye, they were acknowledging, but you will have to shoot again with both eyes open.

The message did not escape Tijerina, nor his brother Cristobal. But before they were able to broaden the Alianza's scope structurally, other urgent matters were to intervene. The Echo Amphitheater trial was on the next month's court docket in Las Cruces, New Mexico. Its outcome was to break the Alianza's momentum. But another reversal would occur just after the New Year to bring storm clouds once more to the battered north.

17

RETURN TO VIOLENCE

The showy October 1967 convention and the courthouse raid had been about sapped of publicity value and potential for attracting new comrades to the Alianza's side. In keeping with his pattern, Reies Tijerina needed another Event in the offing to build up new fire in his followers and create an atmosphere of public anticipation. But that would not be forthcoming until spring and the Poor People's Campaign. In the meantime, the winter was rough on the Tijerina movement. The first in a string of setbacks took place shortly after the California-bound charter bus—after being emptied and replaced because of a bomb scare—took the black convention delegates home.

A year after the Echo Amphitheater takeover, a trial for Tijerina and four others had finally been scheduled for November in the southern New Mexico town of Las Cruces. The charges stemming from the "invasion" of a national camping site ranged from assaulting federal officers (when the forest rangers were tried at the kangaroo court) to shooting a deer.

226

Federal Judge Howard Bratton was already acquainted with the legal background to the land-grant struggle. He ruled the Las Cruces trial with an iron hand. Defense counsel had been denied a change of location for the trial; they felt that the conservative stronghold of Las Cruces would greatly handicap their clients. It was soon obvious that there was no love lost between Judge Bratton and Defense Attorney Charles Driscoll. As the trial progressed, it was also clear that the meek jury did not warm to the New Yorker's eruptive and occasionally belligerent treatment of prosecution witnesses.

Driscoll and his co-attorney Lorenzo Tapia tried to transform the proceedings into an exposé of historical injustice and sociological disruption in northern New Mexico. In a grandstand play they subpoenaed Governor David Cargo.

"Government to them," Cargo was ready to admit, referring to the villagers, "is made up of people who only abuse them, never help them." Believing the land-grant question to be "an ancillary issue," Cargo said rights to scarce water, a decent education, and passable roads were the real wants.

The federal prosecutor, U.S. Attorney John Quinn, stuck to the facts of the takeover. Forest Ranger Walter Taylor recalled being hauled up before Jerry Noll, acting as a "San Joaquin land-grant magistrate." Expediently "sentenced," Taylor had been hustled away, but not before he had heard Tijerina address his followers from a park bench. For the jury Taylor translated a television tape of the leader's oratory:

"Fidel Castro has what he has because of his guts. . . . Castro put the gringos off his island and we can do the same."

Tijerina was given his day in court. He broke into tears at the finale of a three-and-a-quarter-hour recital of his harsh childhood and youth and the history of his land crusade.

"In this land of enchantment," he said, playing on the state's slogan, "the people are enchanted—they are sleeping. It takes time for a poor man to build up to something."

He was closely queried about whether his organization actually planned to file in court any claims to specific grant lands. This question had been heard increasingly over the past months. To legalistic minds willing to give the Alianza the benefit of the doubt, the answer would either mark Tijerina's intentions as naively honorable or brand them as suspiciously dishonorable. As usual, Tijerina replied carefully.

"Now that the claim is known all over the world," he said, "I think a judge would think twice before he would refuse to consider these claims. The pattern was established—we must have enough power to break that pattern." He added that Attorney David Rein of Washington was being retained to prepare a brief to submit to the United Nations.

On the day the jury closed its doors to deliberate, a typical Tijerina outburst brought down a contempt citation on his head. According to the prosecuting attorney, Tijerina had been heard accusing Judge Bratton of "using the law to drink blood and humiliate our race."

The five defendants were convicted of assaulting the two forest rangers and molesting federal property. But before Judge Bratton delivered the sentence he listened to statements by the land-grant leader and his Alianza colleague Noll. With the Treaty of Guadalupe Hidalgo, Tijerina said, "there begins the biggest conspiracy of the United States against another nation." Because a "political matter" was really at issue, he contended, Judge Bratton had no jurisdiction.

Noll's argument was even less defensive. "I am immune to prosecution in foreign courts," he began imperiously. The Echo Amphitheater incident, he said, "occurred in one of my territories. . . . I deny that this alleged court and alleged judge have a right to pass sentence." Sentence was passed, however, and Noll received the longest term, three years in prison. Reies was given two years with five years' probation. His brother Cristobal was given a split sentence of two years in prison for assaulting Ranger Taylor and was ordered to serve six months with five years' probation. Finally, Esequiel Dominguez and Alfonso Chavez were given the "very minimum sentence" of sixty days with five years' probation.

The reversal made Tijerina seethe. He openly broke with his two defense counsels. Relations had already grown testy over their fee (close to $20,000) and their strategy of defense. "If it's tried again," Tijerina promised, "I'm going to direct it." Then he scorned the entire affair:

"We were dragged to Las Cruces where the people thought of me as King Tiger and thought I should be hanged."

In the anxious lull between conviction and sentencing Tijerina was gratified to have a visit from another well-known Spanish-American leader. The revered migrant labor organizer Cesar Chavez met him for the first time during a round of talks to liberal groups. At a regular Saturday night Alianza meeting, Chavez announced that if he were a New Mexico resident he would surely be an Alianza member. Avoiding outright praise of the courthouse raid, Chavez said he hoped all the state's Spanish-Americans would join the Alianza. True to his pacifist ideology, he emphasized soulfully the road of sacrifice which the Alianzans would have to travel in order to win their crusade.

Also before the sentence was handed down on December 15, 1967, another official blow was aimed, obliquely, at the Alianza. The long-awaited results of the investigation undertaken by the attorney general into suspected clandestine relations between the Alianza and the state's Office of Economic Opportunity were made public.

The Echo Amphitheater trial outcome had been a disheartening psychological defeat. But through appeals it could be prevented from keeping Tijerina out of circulation for months, possibly years. On the other hand, Attorney General Boston E. Witt's five-pound document proved to be no threat at all.

Ever since legislative outcry after the raid gave Attorney General Witt's office the green light on digging into Father Robert Garcia's OEO office, the investigation had been conducted with the kind of ominous-sounding "leaks" that investigators cherish.

TIJERINA and the COURTHOUSE RAID

In mid-September a newsman had come across two state Department of Finance travel vouchers which revealed that two operatives from Witt's office were on a "confidential mission in Mexico." Don Devereux, the Ford Foundation liaison man who had been active in the negotiation efforts before the raid, was interrogated at a private house in Santa Fe for hours one Sunday.

But the attorney general gravely declined to respond to follow-up questioning. His "no comment" extended to another report that he was seen talking with Bobby Mayfield, chairman of the state's Legislative Finance Committee, before entering an unusual closed session of the committee, presumably to ask for part of the $8,000 to pay for his secret probe. The hush-hush atmosphere prevailed for nearly six months. Then the "preliminary" report—a thirty-six-page summary padded with fifty xeroxed "exhibits"—was made available to newsmen.

In the first stages of its work, the document said, the attorney general's office "constantly came into possession of evidence of a rather close relationship" between the Alianza and various OEO programs. Then it began receiving complaints about "the conduct of some OEO personnel as well as the goal of some programs." With the purpose of "informing" the state legislature, the document swung back and forth between these two targets, hardly ever supporting its arguments with solid facts. When it lacked evidence of direct OEO-Alianza cooperation it hastily shifted to some obscure OEO problem, giving the impression that a creeping plot was being unveiled.

Where the summary got down to cases, hard evidence continued to be elusive. The attorney general seemed to equate insinuation with indictment. He was clearly pleased at having dug up some unpublished details about our visit to Tijerina in the hills, yet never explained why he had so meticulously investigated that trip. True, Professor Knowlton and Social Worker Joe Benitez had taken the secret journey to the mountain hideout. But Witt drew no explicit conspiracy theory out of this mission. He merely complained that in his opinion the $157.50 price of Knowlton's trip

230

from Texas constituted an "illegal expenditure" of public funds.

In regard to the OEO director, Father Robert Garcia, the report began that while his "expressed concern for the poor is a laudable one, his rather intimate involvement with Reies Lopez Tijerina and the Alianza Federal de Mercedes can hardly be called laudable conduct." Some pages later, this "involvement" had become "allegiance," and Witt cited as evidence the outspoken young priest's statements to the U.S. House subcomittee about the courthouse raid and the alleged civil rights violations at Canjilon. This testimony, interpreted Witt, "can be fairly characterized as defending or attempting to justify the violence by the Alianza Federal de Mercedes on June 5 rather than expressing a public official's normal concern for alleged criminal conduct."

So went the rest of the summary, climaxing with a note that, because of pending litigation, the rest of the plot could not be unfolded at this point. The "exhibits" were a large array of private letters, newspaper clippings, dossiers, and OEO financial statements and project reports. It was not clear how they fitted into the implied order of wholesale complicity between OEO and the Alianza. To most news analyzers they seemed pseudo-evidence. But the summary's last sentence—"A final report will be submitted at a later date"—provided a ray of hope that the expensive "Witt's hunt" would ultimately deliver the goods.

For the remainder of December Tijerina tried to break out of the depressive pall left by the Echo Amphitheater trial verdict. There were festivities at the Alianza headquarters on Christmas Day and New Year's Eve. But he enjoyed only two days of peace in the beginning of 1968.

A few hours after sunset on January 2, 1968, Casilda Salazar, the wife of the courthouse janitor and jailer, Eulogio Salazar, peered out of her window near Tierra Amarilla. She had been waiting for her husband to return from work to escort her to a friend's wake. It was already after 8 p.m., but now she saw the headlights of his Chevrolet at the outside gate. His bent figure was outlined briefly in their beam. Hurrying to be off, Casilda went to the bedroom to untie her apron and change shoes.

After several minutes Eulogio still had not walked through the door. His daughter saw something peculiar: the vehicle was slowly backing down the road. His wife figured "something had come up" at the courthouse. She went to bed thinking that very likely her husband was spending the night with his brother Tito. She knew there had been a burglary there the night before.

By the next morning she still had no news. About 8 o'clock she telephoned his working partner, Undersheriff Daniel Rivera, who drove over. Pulling up to the gate, Rivera spotted Salazar's white hat in the middle of the lane. Then he noticed a stain in the road that looked like blood and hair. Back in the courthouse, he called Sheriff Naranjo out of bed. State police were hastily radioed in. An all-points alert went out for Salazar's beige car. A broken piece of plastic gun butt was discovered near the fallen cowboy hat.

Two hours later a rancher flagged down a state policeman near Tierra Amarilla. About six miles from Salazar's home on the country road to El Vado Lake there was a vehicle fifty feet down a snow-blanketed slope, with what looked like a body inside. It proved to be the jailer's corpse. Twenty-four wounds were later counted. Salazar's face was beaten beyond recognition.

It was inconceivable that this could be viewed as anything but a legacy of the courthouse raid. Salazar had been one of that incident's principal sufferers and was thus far its key witness, testifying that Reies Tijerina had been in the courthouse during the raid. His pathetic figure had afterwards shuffled through the courthouse halls, the face permanently disfigured by a bullet he had sworn was delivered by Tijerina. Strangely enough, the slaying of Salazar was more terrifying than the furious daylight afternoon of guns. On a bitterly cold winter night a silent killing, tied in some mysterious way to the past, threw northern New Mexico into fright.

The new terror derived from the underlying truths that such a killing automatically told. Salazar had not been a victim of the raid's brand of passion. His murder was the direct, or hired, result of methodic planning and disciplining. This was the kind of act parents kept from their children, the kind they kept from each other. In the gossipy small town of Tierra Amarilla it sank beneath conversation.

From the look of the car, Salazar had put up a struggle. Blood was splattered over the back seat upholstery and floor. There were kicked-in dents in the door paneling and the dome light was shattered. From bloody patches on the road pavement, investigators determined that Salazar's body had been transferred to the front floor before his car was put into neutral and ditched down the steep embankment, bursting through a barbed wire fence.

Two hours after a tow truck cable had drawn the car up onto the road, an Alianza-owned pickup truck bearing Cristobal Tijerina and Felix Martinez was halted north of Tierra Amarilla. Late in the afternoon District Attorney Sanchez's office charged the two men with being "material witnesses and accessories" to the killing. Both Alianzans kept insisting they had attended a McCarthy-for-President rally in Santa Fe the previous evening.

Almost instantly the identical conclusion, with no hard facts to back it up, swept official circles. "Your prime responsibility," an angry Chief Black briefed his men, "is Reies Tijerina. . . . Tijerina is bound to be tied into it somewhere."

"Nothing more or less than a brutal murder, terrorism," asserted Governor Cargo. "I'm not sure if they [the Alianza] had anything to do with it . . . the bonds, right now, are no deterrent."

Apparently Judge Joe Angel in Las Vegas was persuaded by a hurried visit from Alfonso Sanchez that the governor was right: the bailed-out Alianzans posed a threat. That same day he signed an order revoking all bonds for the twenty defendants charged in the courthouse raid case.

"Of course, who else?" responded District Attorney Sanchez when asked outright if the Alianza had murdered Salazar.

Attorney General Witt fell in with the common opinion that other potential witnesses might be in danger. "We think Judge

233

Angel did the best he could under the circumstances of time and pressure."

During the critical twenty-four-hour investigatory period after the body was discovered, police energy was feverishly devoted to putting Alianza members behind bars. The "TA Twenty," as the raid defendants were now known, lost their freedom with a stroke of Judge Angel's pen. Less than a day after the jailer's car had been discovered, the entire group had been transported to the Santa Fe city jail. They were then remanded to the custody of the state penitentiary warden.

Defense attorneys aligned to apply pressure against what they called "this capricious and arbitrary naked exercise of judicial power." While the new wave of arrests appeared to them "without any rational basis," they were also aware that the alarm throughout the north was anything but rational.

The police zeal and official verdict over the slaying proved to be self-defeating. The Alianza roundup was accomplished before Salazar's body was ever examined. In fact the corpse had been sent, unidentified and without a police guard, to the Los Alamos Medical Center's morgue with no instructions for the resident pathologist. Identification and authorization for autopsy did not come until 8:30 that night. This delayed clinical investigation of the cause and time of death until the next working day. Then the coroner said the killing was "one of the most brutal" he had ever seen.

Aside from everyone's certainty that the Alianza was implicated, there was no attempt to pursue alternative theories immediately. Consequently in the important twenty-four-hour period after Salazar was found there was no thorough questioning of all types of cleaning establishments between Albuquerque and the Colorado border, no checking of commercial airline passenger lists between Albuquerque and Denver, no coordination of roadblocks with the Colorado state police, no roadblocks to speak of, no blanket survey of all gas stations and used-car lots and automobile dumps between Albuquerque and the Colorado border, no foot-by-foot search of the roadside for twenty yards in each direction along the supposed route taken by the murder car from Salazar's house to its final resting place.

Before the state's highest court decided to open its habeas corpus hearing for the twenty defendants who had been rejailed, Cristobal Tijerina and Felix Martinez had been absolved of the charges against them. Police decided to check out their alibis after newspaper reports printed testimony from people who had seen the two in Santa Fe the night of the killing. The *New Mexican*'s state capitol correspondent swore he encountered them shortly after 9 p.m. at Santa Fe's First Christian Church when the McCarthy meeting broke up. No one was now being charged in connection with the jailer's death. Twenty persons were still being held.

The New Mexico Supreme Court began to examine the matter a few days later, eventually deciding to reinstate bond for all but Reies Tijerina, Juan Valdez, Baltazar Apodaca, and Tobias Leyba. In the case of these four, the justices felt, "the proof is evident or the presumption great" that they had committed a capital offense. Once more in prison blues, Tijerina was returned for his second long stay in jail.

During one icy cold, brilliantly clear afternoon I visited the Tierra Amarilla courthouse and tried to pump the two-man state police team assigned full-time to the Salazar murder investigation. Neither Freddy Martinez nor Carlos Jaramillo expressed surprise that a second car, abandoned and bloodstained, had been rumored found in Cumbres Pass.

"By George, that's news to me," offered Martinez, cleaning a sawed-off shotgun with bayonet mount. "What did [Captain T. J.] Chavez say to that? He didn't know of any such car. Well, there are so many rumors."

That could not be disputed, and they grew as time went by. The weird tale of a Magnum-wielding private detective and his vicious dog who mysteriously showed up the day after the murder and were shooed off by Sheriff Naranjo was only plumbed a month later. The detective turned out to be an old colleague of Chief

Black's from El Paso who thought he could investigate on his own. After badgering Mrs. Salazar he was ordered out of town by the sheriff. Thereafter he had stayed incognito in a private El Paso hospital room, believing there was a conspiracy in Tierra Amarilla to keep the crime quiet.

Rumors of "professionals" flown in from Denver or Los Angeles vied with suggestions that Salazar was not as harmless as he had appeared, that he was going to change his crucial testimony at the preliminary hearing, that jailers always incurred grudges, and that the extended Salazar family suffered internal feuding.

Now it came out that poverty workers had been warning that "something is going to happen between Christmas and New Year's." Two weeks before the murder Chief Black was remembered to have told Salazar to be extra careful. And the night that Salazar left the courthouse he had confided to Dolores Romero, a typist in the county assessor's office, that he was scared someone "would pick him up sometime."

Since the round of hasty accusations caused by the Salazar murder, Judge Angel had forbidden all persons with any relation to the courthouse raid case to discuss any aspect of it. Now the principal effect of his "gag order"—which enraged state newspapers—was to keep the total lack of progress in the Salazar investigation from public knowledge. As the full-scale preliminary hearing for the Tierra Amarilla raid opened in Judge Angel's Santa Fe court on January 29, 1968, it was surely not an unprejudiced atmosphere in which to obtain first-hand accounts of the courthouse attack.

For eight days the twenty Alianzans again filled the jury box while men and women who happened to be caught in the Tierra Amarilla courthouse on June 5, 1967, relived that afternoon.

The purpose of the hearing was merely to let eyewitnesses describe their treatment and place at the scene as many as possible of those charged. Their accounts offered little to clear up the confusion over the exact sequence of actions and movements of individuals during the raid. Discussion of the earlier weekend's trouble over the Coyote meeting was not allowed, despite Judge Angel's otherwise permissive direction. What interest remained in the long days of testimony came from subtleties of personality rather than dramatic factual revelations.

State Policeman Nick Saiz, still on limited duty because of chest pains and three numb fingers, pointed at Juan Valdez when asked who had shot him.

Already awaiting trial was a $1.5 million damage suit filed by Saiz and Jailer Salazar's widow against Valdez and other Alianzans. Before stepping down from the witness chair, Saiz had identified five defendants at the scene of the raid. Reies Tijerina, he recollected, "had a rifle strapped on his arm." Saiz also had recognized Tijerina's son, Reies Jr., and daughter Rose in the besieged building.

Rio Arriba County Assessor Estanislado Vigil had been in the courthouse basement when the shot that hit Saiz rang out. Heading up the stairs, he encountered Reies Jr. near the doorway.

"He had a gun pointed toward me. . . . I told him I didn't know what his motive was, but I only worked at the courthouse. He said, 'I know that. I want to get you out of there because I don't want you to get hurt.' "

Rio Arriba County Clerk Cipriano Padilla saw the same men fingered by both Officer Saiz and Assessor Vigil. He remembered that young Baltazar Martinez carried a rifle, a dagger, and "five or six sticks of dynamite" stuck into his belt. Padilla had also seen Baltazar Apodaca at the door of the County Commission room while the courthouse employees were being held prisoners inside.

"An old man was standing there guarding the door." An unseen male voice had ordered, "Take prisoners." Young Martinez had shouted back, "Who?" The reply was: "Take Pete Jaramillo and that gringo over there [Larry Calloway]."

Then it was Deputy Sheriff Jaramillo's turn to tell about the ride that he and Calloway had been forced to take up and down the main street in Tierra Amarilla. Before their tour, Jaramillo said, Tijerina had placed a rifle in his ribs.

237

"Where is Alfonso Sanchez?" he remembered Tijerina saying. "Tell me or I'll kill you."

A visitor to the courthouse that afternoon, E. R. Gleasner of Albuquerque, was waiting for Larry Calloway to finish with the telephone when he was caught in the midst of what the prosecution tried to show were three waves of courthouse attackers. Gleasner first testified that Salomon Velazquez had threatened to kill anyone who left the County Commission room. Then he admitted he had made a mistaken identification; it had been young Martinez. Gleasner pictured Tijerina as "dressed like Castro," which meant in his explanation an olive-colored military cap, jump boots, military-type blouse, and khaki pants stuck inside the boots. Tijerina, he said, carried a rifle which "had an extended clip."

Reporter Calloway said that from his hiding place in the telephone booth he saw Jose Madril in green shirt and green pants standing at the top of the stairs. "He had a pistol in his hand . . . he was pointing it down the stairs. At one point I saw Reies Lopez Tijerina—perhaps twenty minutes after I heard the shooting."

The slain jailer's testimony at the earlier bond hearing was admitted as evidence by Judge Angel. That was when Salazar had identified the man who shot him with a pistol as Reies Tijerina.

Typist Dolores Romero remembered Esequiel Dominguez wearing a yellow construction helmet. "The gringos are not the bosses now," Dominguez had told the workers in the county assessor's office, "but we are the bosses."

The memories continued, including statements from several physicians who had assessed the severity of the wounds suffered by Saiz, Undersheriff Rivera, and Jailer Salazar. This was crucial for the state's claim that first-degree kidnapping, involving great bodily harm, had indeed been committed.

On the final afternoon of the hearing Sheriff Benny Naranjo offered the most interesting recollections. Just before the raid, he said, he had seen Moises Morales, Tony and Lee Valdez (brothers of Juan), and Danny Tijerina milling around near a car parked across the street. When the shooting broke out in the hallway,

Eulogio Salazar had run out to see what was going on. He had shortly returned and remained in the office while Naranjo dashed out, pistol in hand. Then, he testified, Reies Tijerina had knocked the pistol from his hand with a rifle butt and hit him to the floor. Tijerina went on into the sheriff's office. While on the floor, Naranjo heard a shot.

"I'm certain there was one," he said, "because I thought it was shot at me." When he reached for his pistol again, someone stepped on his hand. Finally shoved into the County Commission room, Naranjo remembered Juan Valdez putting a gun to his head and cooing, "Little politician." Jose Madril, Naranjo continued, was "running around and yelling [in Spanish] 'Now they are not so brave! Now they are not so brave!' "

Still cooped up, Naranjo saw one raider approach County Commissioner Alvarado Martinez, believing he was District Attorney Sanchez.

"Stand over here to the side," the raider ordered Commissioner Martinez, "so we can shoot you, you son-of-a-bitch." Before he fired, however, he was told that the man was not Sanchez.

The upshot of these vivid but inconclusive flashes from that chaotic afternoon was Judge Angel's decision to reduce the capital crimes to twenty-four counts of false imprisonment, release nine of the twenty defendants on lack of evidence, and allow the remaining eleven to be freed on bond.

The defense reckoned it a minor victory. Not long afterward the New Mexico Supreme Court ordered Judge Angel pulled off the case. Now another district court magistrate, Paul F. Larrazolo of Albuquerque, took up the burden of the snarled legal consequences of June 5, 1967. It looked like a fall trial for the courthouse raid.

18

THE
NEW
ARENA

After this stretch of thirty-six days in the New Mexico State Prison, Tijerina came out somewhat subdued. Halting briefly on the windswept roadside near the prison turnoff, he commented, "We're going to organize harder, work harder, and sacrifice more to expose the federal conspiracy against the Spanish pueblos." But he seemed to be playing a tape of some past pronouncement while he waded through private worries. He verified reports of a West Coast fund-raising tour.

"I think it is scheduled to begin February 19," he said distractedly, "and we have invitations from New York City, Washington, and San Antonio."

With a brother at each elbow—Anselmo and Cristobal—Tijerina hastened to California. He stood on the podium of the Los Angeles Sports Arena on February 18 during the Huey Newton Defense Fund rally and embraced Stokely Carmichael and H. Rap Brown. The brown and black peoples, he said, "agree to take the same position as to the crimes and sins of the government of the United States. . . . I'm getting tired of going in and out of prison,

240

but I will not fight against our colored brothers in Vietnam. . . ."
With that, the hall of 4,000 predominantly black people yelled
approval: "Viva Tijerina!"

While Tijerina was talking to a noon gathering at East Los Angeles College on February 23, the Alianza's exploits received
oblique recognition from a most unlikely source. The White House
released a statement by President Lyndon Johnson which resulted
from the creation the previous June of an Inter-Agency Committee
on Mexican-American Affairs.

The committee's first act had been a three-day Cabinet level
series of hearings on Mexican-American problems, held in October
1967 in El Paso, Texas. Testimony was delivered by some fifty
speakers about the deep grievances in both urban and rural Spanish-speaking communities. The hosts had seen to it that there would
be no unforeseen bombshells: Reies Tijerina, Corky Gonzales, and
Cesar Chavez had not been invited.

Now President Johnson's statement recalled the El Paso hearings. On the basis of evidence accumulated there, the President
said, he had asked "the Congress to authorize a major project
to improve Forest Service grazing lands in the southwest, to serve
the small rancher. . . . I have instructed the Secretary of Agriculture to expand the activities of the county extension service to
meet more fully the needs of the small Mexican-American farmer."

In California Tijerina continued visiting campuses and political
platforms in Santa Barbara, San Bernardino, and Berkeley. Just
before departing for the San Joaquin Valley to attend the fast-
breaking of Labor Organizer Cesar Chavez, Tijerina received a
telegram. It had been sent March 7, 1968, to the Alianza's Albuquerque headquarters and forwarded. It read:

"The time to clearly present the case of poor people nationally
draws near. . . . May I request that you meet with me in a closed
session at the Paschals Motor Inn, Hunter Street, Atlanta, Georgia,
Thursday, March 14. . . ."

It was signed by Martin Luther King Jr. The Poor People's
Campaign had begun.

241

TIJERINA and the COURTHOUSE RAID

When Tijerina touched down in Albuquerque after the Atlanta conference he was ecstatic. Dr. King had told representatives from various black protest groups, Appalachian poor white communities, and Indian reservations that his thinking had taken a strategic leap from civil rights to human rights. To Tijerina this meant "from jobs to land claims."

The all-day session had included Corky Gonzales and Burt Corona. Still desperately weak after his fast in California, Cesar Chavez had been unable to appear. When the meeting was over, Tijerina felt that all had witnessed "the greatest foundation for the interracial pursuit of justice. What I understand from what Martin Luther King said he is now committed to all the poor peoples."

From Atlanta Tijerina had flown in Corona's company to San Francisco to resume his West Coast touring. In Richmond, California, he was proposed as a vice-presidential candidate for the fledgling Peace and Freedom Party, joining presidential candidate Dick Gregory on the ticket. He also prepared to accept a New York invitation from the General Assembly of the Presbyterian Church. At issue was the Ghost Ranch, near Abiquiu, owned by the Presbyterian Church. The Alianza demanded the property because it occupied the old Piedra Lumbre land grant. Then, on April 4, Martin Luther King was assassinated.

Tijerina poured out his feelings over the murder in Berkeley: the wrath of God was finally being visited upon America. Directly he flew to King's funeral in Atlanta, where he talked with Black Panther leader Bobby Seale, civil rights sympathizer Marlon Brando, and militant Stokely Carmichael. The reins of the Poor People's March in Washington were picked up by King's colleague, the Reverend Ralph Abernathy, another officer of the Southern Christian Leadership Conference.

Meanwhile concern had grown in New Mexico as Tijerina's new associations brought him further into the national limelight. The prospect of the Alianza leader involved with such a widely publicized protest for the country's poor made state officials feel he was slipping from their grasp. On April 17, with a disavowal of any extraordinary purpose, the first Rio Arriba County grand jury in five years was quietly sworn in by District Court Judge Samuel Z. Montoya in the Tierra Amarilla courthouse. The judge explained that he had called the men and women on his own, but "at the request of District Attorney Al Sanchez" who was "expected to submit several criminal cases to it." He added disarmingly, "It will consider only routine things."

The previous night in Albuquerque a former Bernalillo County sheriff's deputy had driven up to the curb in front of the Alianza headquarters. Reaching under his front seat, the man had felt for one of two dynamite sticks lying alongside a loaded .22-caliber Magnum revolver. He was heading for the Alianza building when he tripped with the lighted fuse sputtering in his hand.

Three Alianzans ran out after hearing the blast. Outside the shattered front windows they found a hubcap and pieces of a right hand and wrist scattered for a distance of thirty feet.

Minutes later police cars began pursuing a vehicle weaving crazily at high speed through downtown Albuquerque knocking into nearby cars. Driving with his one remaining hand was William R. Fellion, fifty-one, who in 1962 had been arrested by his former boss, Bernalillo County Sheriff Lester Hay, for possession of burglary tools. Extradited to Springerville, Arizona, he had been charged with assault with a deadly weapon.

Fellion was held at a hospital on charges of reckless driving and carrying a deadly weapon. After he had spent fifteen days in the Bernalillo County jail, all charges against him were dropped.

In this atmosphere the Rio Arriba County grand jury was secretly deliberating in Tierra Amarilla. Less than a week later the subject matter of the discussion was made public. Under New Mexico law the grand jury was able to make a second appraisal of all the evidence that Sanchez had already presented during the early February week-long preliminary hearing in Santa Fe. Against the same Alianzans singled out then by Judge Angel, the thirteen jurors now returned charges of kidnapping, false imprisonment,

243

and assault on a jail. Warrants for rearrest were expediently signed.

Two days after being officially announced as leader of the south-western Poor People's contingent, a shocked Tijerina was stopped by state police ten miles south of Albuquerque. He was coming from El Paso, where he had spoken at a branch of the University of Texas. He had been under surveillance since crossing the Texas border. Before being hustled to New Mexico State Prison he de-cried the action as "a criminal conspiracy on the part of the courts to keep me from my Alianza work."

He spent three nights in prison before being released on bond. Immediately he made up for precious lost time as he transformed his Alianza headquarters into the central offices of the Poor Peo-ple's Campaign in the southwest, appointed local staffers, and set out for his meeting with the SCLC steering committee in Wash-ington.

Tom Houck, the SCLC minority group overseer, visited the Albuquerque headquarters in late April to assist in the organizing. It was Houck, apparently, who had first urged Dr. King to invite Tijerina. It was also Houck who backed Tijerina during the per-sonal conflicts which began brewing soon between the Alianza leader and the younger, more militant black strategists.

Tijerina's appointment as southwestern coordinator had already come under heavy attack. An Albuquerque newspaper editorial on April 26, 1968, was headed, "Tijerina: The Wrong Choice." In view of the Alianza's tainted past, it stated, Tijerina's involvement "seems almost certain to lessen the prospects that the march will be a nonviolent one." At the same time, internal disputes kept tempers on edge at the Albuquerque home office during Tijerina's absence.

A discouraging setback for Tijerina was the disenchantment of both his brother Cristobal and his lieutenant Felix Martinez with the land-grant movement's new direction. On-and-off family re-lationships had already become common between Anselmo and his brothers, but they had never seemed to interfere with basic loyalties to the *causa*. Now, in an unrelated incident, Cristobal and

Felix were charged in a jewelry robbery in Grants, New Mexico. But details of the internecine difficulties were carefully kept behind the Alianza's new metal-reinforced doors and bricked-up windows. When asked why they weren't busily soliciting for the Poor People's Campaign, all that Felix and Cristobal would reply was, "Why? We're not poor."

New Mexico's Archbishop James Peter Davis joined the hot local debate over the "questionable" leadership of the southwestern campaign with a statement on May 13:

"I do not support Mr. Tijerina and what he stands for. It is my hope that those who feel as I do will be able to do as I am doing, to look beyond Mr. Tijerina and . . . to approve the march and hope that it will be successful despite his connection with it."

Another Alianza friend who now lost sympathy was Father Clarence Duffy. The grim, red-faced priest's brand of socialist enterprise could not countenance this pleading for government handouts.

Through self-confidence and stamina Tijerina weathered these desertions and a host of other organizational blunders, bitter misunderstandings, and external obstacles, maintaining his place of leadership.

On the night of May 17, the eve of the southwestern contingent's departure for Washington, a celebrative rally was held in Albuquerque. It was over a month since the leaders gathered on the podium had had something to savor. The nation at large had briefly joined hearts and minds with its militant vanguard in mourning Dr. King's assassination. But then the minorities had been abandoned to their sorrow and organizational confusion. The racial color wheel played a predictably large part in everyone's address this evening.

The Reverend Abernathy, in the Poor People's uniform of blue coveralls, motioned Chief Mad Bear, in traditional Iroquois costume, toward the lectern. Vigorously he gripped the Tuscarora leader's hand and turned to the audience.

"My red brother," he announced, in rolling stentorian syllables.

245

TIJERINA and the COURTHOUSE RAID

With his other arm he reached to clasp Tijerina's hand, looking him full in the face. "My yellow brother," he proclaimed. Tijerina whispered to him behind a cupped palm. "My brown brother," corrected Abernathy with an apologetic grin. The empathetic occupants of the seats in Albuquerque's cavernous Civic Auditorium laughed.

The following morning a carefully approved and charted four-and-a-half-mile route through Albuquerque was filled with joyful campaigners and a large sympathetic regional following. Archbishop Davis slipped from a doorway into the amiable placard-swinging crew, but dropped out before the crowd began swirling into the Old Town Plaza. Waiting for their chartered buses, the groups of northern New Mexicans, with their gear for three weeks stowed in twine-tied sleeping rolls and cardboard suitcases, fell on the sparse grass.

A misunderstanding over funds for more than one bus made Tijerina hold up the caravan. After he and SCLC representatives had held tough-worded discussions the money appeared. At last the "sons of San Joaquin" and their friends were bound for the enemy's capital and Resurrection City. But the difficulties in getting the buses out of Albuquerque foreshadowed the campaign's continuing troubles in Washington.

Since May 2, when Mrs. Martin Luther King and the Reverend Abernathy had dedicated a marble memorial plaque on the site of Dr. King's murder in Memphis, the packed cars and busloads of people trickling toward the fifteen-acre tract of Washington's grass-carpeted Mall had been closely covered by the press.

On May 14 hundreds of blacks braved chill and rain for their first night in the prefabricated A-frame plywood shelters which lined Resurrection City.

On May 21 the southwestern contingent, its numbers increased to about 600 by Oklahoma Indians, wearily wound up a two-hour rally in Kansas City and re-embarked for St. Louis. From there they proceeded to Chicago, Indianapolis, Cincinnati, and Baltimore, taking on new recruits in each town. Tijerina had sat in a bus seat as far as Denver, then had flown directly to Washington to arrange lodging for the new arrivals.

Ten weeks later the entire episode could be evaluated. In retrospect Tijerina emerges from the pathetic, disjointed ranks of Resurrection City as the most creative of the leaders of contributing groups. But it was a good bet that Abernathy regretted the day Dr. King had allowed his aide to summon the New Mexico figure to Atlanta.

On a cold, rainy morning soon after arriving Tijerina came out with an astounding declaration, considering that the campaign's only power would have to come from indivisible resolution. His band of 350 Spanish-Americans, he said, had been "abused, humiliated and discriminated against" by the black majority of Resurrection City. Standing in a downpour, Tijerina said that he was also speaking for poor whites and Indians when he charged that "the black militants seem to have taken over out here and nobody else gets a chance to talk." He threatened to boycott the sodden, muddy campsite and conduct separate demonstrations.

While the campaign was still in its organizing stage, Tijerina had formulated plans to run nightly "peace councils" in Washington. These were to educate the diverse groups of people in each other's folkways and to invent strategies for forcing legislative reform. I had watched him talking on the telephone with some aged followers, saying in Spanish that during the May 31 pinnacle Washington march he wanted them to be the tip of his *flecha* (arrow). He was well aware that the blacks lacked solid flanks of elders, the Alianza's strong point. In addition, Tijerina had appreciated at the outset the value of American Indians adding their emphatic colors to such a program. Now, he felt, these promising forethoughts were being ignored.

The Reverend Abernathy had rushed out of the Pitts Motor Hotel in Washington earlier that day to deal with the sagging morale in the dripping lean-tos and the health threat the weather

247

was posing. The land-grant leader's remarks to the press caught him off guard. He hurried for a confidential discussion with Tijerina at the well-to-do Hawthorne School where the southwesterners had been lodged since their arrival. Although the two emerged arm in arm, Tijerina still wanted black militants "screened out" of the 2,400-person poverty village.

Tijerina's group also made their special presence known by a demonstration before the Mexican Embassy, demanding once again that Alianza claims be placed before the United Nations. They pressured Secretary of State Dean Rusk into scheduling an audience, but indignantly turned it down when they learned that the press was to be excluded. Publicity could not be denied them, however, as Spanish-Americans and Indians in full regalia staged the campaign's most blatantly symbolic confrontation before the locked bronze doors of the Supreme Court. During this all-day demonstration Danny Tijerina, Reies's fifteen-year-old son, was arrested in a minor skirmish with police.

There were also suggestions of rifts within the *chicano* brotherhood as Corky Gonzales referred privately to his colleague as "T. V. Rina," while Tijerina would only remark later, "Some people got into squabbles. They were insecure. . . . We take pride in saying that we had very few problems."

On June 24, Resurrection City was closed down by the Washington police as threatened. Many dislodged blacks now knocked at the thriving Hawthorne School for shelter. Tijerina had been enjoying the separated existence. When he first provided succor for the homeless blacks he felt vindicated:

"I felt eventually we were to prove our point of being in the Hawthorne School and keeping our forces scattered for strategic reasons. You don't want to put all your eggs in one basket."

A month later, however, he had a different view of their arrival. Describing it as an "invasion," he charged that they "took over the kitchen and dining hall," assaulted whites and Spanish-Americans, and molested women using the school's bathrooms.

Finally Tijerina accused the SCLC of ignoring Dr. King's original plan to demand the redistribution of southern plantations to black farmers. He claimed that the SCLC had rented costly walkie-talkies and airconditioned Cadillacs but wouldn't let Spanish-Americans use them. During one flare-up Tijerina had wrested a bullhorn from Hosea Williams, demonstrations director, to charge that Williams personally threatened the racial coalition. Despite the hard work of the Reverend Abernathy and the Reverend Andrew Young—"sincere, trustworthy men"—Tijerina felt the campaign had been "betrayed."

Between hassles in Washington and an appearance at an all-Indian convention in Tulsa, Oklahoma, Tijerina had managed to keep abreast of affairs at home. Throughout the Poor People's Campaign Judge Paul Larrazolo had been understanding toward him, excusing him from returning to New Mexico for the string of proceedings before the coming trial. On July 22, however, Tijerina was in attendance as Judge Larrazolo opened court in Santa Fe to hear all motions relating to the case.

During a recess Tijerina patted his pregnant wife's stomach and bragged, "This one will be born in Washington." The idea seemed to delight Patsy Tijerina, who beamed. Defiantly her husband swung out a fist. "We need more Tijerinas," he said. Also in the hall, leaning against a radiator, Tobias Leyba was dispensing to fellow defendants "Alfonso Sanchez for District Attorney" election cards. All thought it hilarious.

Then Reies blurted out that he was giving "strong and serious consideration" to running for office during the upcoming race for New Mexico's governorship. His entry "would be a good way of exposing bad elements in the state, would raise issues to embarrass other candidates and shake up the legislature."

Very soon Judge Larrazolo scheduled a trial for all the defendants, to begin November 12, 1968, in the Bernalillo County courthouse in Albuquerque.

Tijerina returned to Washington for the dying days of the Poor People's Campaign, then came back to New Mexico to run on a low-key slate of candidates for the November elections. The Alianza headquarters was given a facelifting, suddenly appearing —in large lettering on the facade—as the center for Tijerina's People's Constitutional Party.

The summer of colorless electioneering seemed a proper season for reflection. What had actually been the effects of the courthouse raid? What constructive suggestions turned out to be more than temporary appeasement of local ills? Was it too soon to determine whether irreversible social change had resulted from that incredible cloudy afternoon a year before? Were the entire incident, the Tijerinas, and the Alianza itself merely anomalies that would be absorbed and forgotten in the rhythms of New Mexico life?

The day before the first anniversary of the courthouse raid Governor David Francis Cargo had quietly dropped into the hamlet of Canjilon. It was surely more than coincidence that he visited the little village precisely a year after it had been the planning site for the courthouse raiders. Again the governor was making his personal emphasis during a political campaign. He hit on the tried and true vote-getting issue of roads, promising to prod the state Highway Commission into getting all-weather routes to nearby schools.

Still nothing had been fundamentally changed in the condition of the Canones Road, which the governor had made a point of inspecting and criticizing before. The state said it was not a state road; county officials at the Tierra Amarilla courthouse reported it was being maintained "as usual." A condemnation suit for a shorter route was pending, and as soon as that was settled. . . .

In Canjilon, Cargo passed the local HELP center. He had been as strong a supporter of this pilot program as he could be of anything that was risky. Throughout its respectable growth the previous winter the governor had made a point of publicly citing HELP's achievements in cooperative farming, adult education, and revitalized village handwork workshops. In Canjilon Cargo made

250

little mention of the Alianza or its leader. He had embraced Judge Angel's "gag order" as if it had been handed down by a parent. It was a good guess that he would not attend the Alianza convention that fall.

Tijerina had a celebration planned for the anniversary of the raid, a demonstration on the steps of the State Department in Washington. But the assassination of Robert Kennedy on June 4 made that impossible. Already beloved by Spanish-Americans because of his brother's sainted reputation, Senator Kennedy had cemented that bond by his pilgrimage to break bread with Cesar Chavez at the end of his arduous fast. A *chicano* celebration of a violent event like the raid was not in order now.

A bizarre development on the anniversary of the raid was the Santa Fe *New Mexican's* report of District Attorney Sanchez's claim that Alianza members were receiving guerrilla warfare training "in Communist Cuba and on a ranch in the Taos area." Primary elections were scheduled for August, with the final runoffs, state as well as nationwide, in November. Sanchez was in an uphill battle to keep his district attorney's office. His wild disclosure seemed to some observers an alarmist's frantic move to rally support. Whatever its motive, the release caused those who were most anxious to stop Tijerina to hold their heads in their hands. Motions for "mistrial" had been made ever since litigation about the raid began; now the Alianza defense had been handed a new argument gift-wrapped.

One would expect that the shock waves of an event so nationally publicized as the Tierra Amarilla raid would rock a representative forum such as the state legislature. Either a "fall guy" for the unwelcome notoriety would be sought or reform measures would be adopted to make sure similar disturbances would not occur again. By the time the New Mexico legislature began its 1968 session, however, the first reflex reaction had already taken place.

Under the pressure of controversy over the Office of Economic Opportunity's actions just after the raid, Governor Cargo had done some bureaucratic reshuffling: the state Planning Office was placed over Father Robert Garcia's OEO staff. Now vulnerable Community Action and VISTA programs would be tightly controlled. At the same time there had been state house rumors that Father Garcia, already on leave from pastoral duties, was planning to marry. Smarting under his demotion, Garcia went on vacation in January. When he never returned to work he was fired. Within a month he had married and moved to Austin, Texas.

Garcia's friend and Alianza confidant Professor Clark Knowlton also suffered repercussions from those suspenseful days after the raid. For his mission to the land-grant leader in the mountains he came under fire at the University of Texas. It was rumored that Texas Governor John Connally was behind the brief conservative drive to have him dismissed as chairman of the Sociology Department of the University of Texas at El Paso. A letter-writing campaign in Knowlton's favor made the conservatives back down. But after winning the fight to stay, Knowlton shortly resigned to pick up his studies in Spanish-American sociohistory at the University of Utah.

The state's official pursewatchers, the Legislative Finance Committee, had recommended to the legislature that the OEO's state appropriation to be cut to one dollar, but then wrath had apparently cooled after Father Garcia's departure. During the 1968 session the legislators lightly castigated the OEO, but talk of abolishing it altogether ended with its retaining its $15,400 state support. For all the reams of publicity about the "Appalachia of the southwest," however, there was practically no discussion about the plight of northern New Mexico.

In the long run, possibly the only piece of "social" legislation passed during the session was a $1,100,000 appropriation in highway construction funds, issued on a statewide basis to open up isolated communities to economic development. It was felt that this promise of construction of secondary roads would not hurt the governor's upcoming campaign.

No new proposals were heard from the land-title study commission set up the previous year. Indeed Cargo had conspicuously left the topic out of his address to the 1968 session. He had made a great show after the raid of establishing his own land-title commission, but it also remained mute.

In Washington, too, the bold question of just what land belongs to whom was considered too complex or too unimportant to consider seriously. After the raid New Mexico Representative Tom G. Morris had been the architect of a bill calling for a nine-member commission that would have $1,000,000 and two years to research the Spanish and Mexican land grants of the southwest. He had forwarded a preliminary draft to his colleagues. The dean of state politics, Senator Clinton Anderson, noted that land-grant cases had been adjudicated nearly a hundred years ago, which he thought "established pretty permanent title." His fellow senator, Joseph Montoya, was said to be even less sympathetic, but recuperation from an illness kept him out of the public eye.

Montoya's feud with Tijerina had mounted during the winter. The senator had denounced Tijerina as an "enemy of the United States" and a "damned liar" for calling America a prostitute. Montoya said his own inquiries indicated that Tijerina had collected over $50,000 and "never made an accounting of it." He recollected that when Tijerina first came to him for support, "After I quizzed him, I found out it was just a racket on his part."

Early in April the Alianza picketed public hearings Montoya had held in Albuquerque. A Montoya project had been given a shot in the arm as the New Mexico legislators approved their 20 per cent share of the cost for an Espanola vocational school. But this was still considerably less than the $1,000,000 Montoya had hoped for.

In May, Assistant Secretary of Agriculture John A. Baker had visited northern New Mexico, presumably in line with President Johnson's request that the department make a greater effort to help the subsistence farmer and grazer. Baker's visit turned out to be another two-day "whirlwind tour," conversations with local politicians, and minimal contact with the area's poor. Baker stopped briefly at the home of Alfredo Muñiz, a HELP farmer, and perhaps he got a taste of northern life. In a cardboard box lay the

253

body of the two-year-old Muñiz daughter who had just died of pneumonia.

For a time the Forest Service appeared to relax its grazing restrictions. There was also a decided effort to recruit Spanish-speaking rangers and improve personal relations with the Spanish-American communities. But the Forest Service's much-vaunted "multiple use" policy and its lack of true understanding of the small grazer would soon prevail as before. Just after New Year's the agency proposed a substantial increase in fees for grazing private cattle on federal pasturage.

Senator Joseph Montoya had also kept informed of the state's investigation of the Alianza, which he had been instrumental in getting under way. After the release of Attorney General Witt's report about the OEO and the Alianza, the "final report" had been awaited. To this day nothing new of substance has appeared. The third installment of Alan Stang's rightist exposé of the Alianza came out in the March 1969 issue of *American Opinion*. Usually a reliable indication of what was in the attorney general's vaults, Stang's piece contained only simulated evidence and vulgar innuendo.

The Tierra Amarilla raid's reputation had helped encourage revolutionary romanticism among the "emerging young *chicanos*" of urban barrios like East Los Angeles. Their creation, the Zapata-mustached stalwarts of the Brown Berets, had made a midwinter appearance in an Albuquerque chapter. Unlike other minority group militants, the Alianza had been accustomed to drawing its *valientes* from the white-haired side of the generation gap. But now the Brown Berets in turn gave birth to a northern New Mexico youth group, centered in Tierra Amarilla, calling themselves Los Comancheros. During one of the Comanchero street rallies, the Tierra Amarilla courthouse employees found themselves again diving to the building's floor as rumors of an attack spread. A state police intermediary arrived in time to calm the junior Alianza roustabouts and reassure the office workers. With these bands now asking for civilian police review boards, bilingual education, and special courses in Spanish-American history, New Mexico's official-dom was clearly up against a twentieth-century wall.

Even in Tierra Amarilla a new awareness was there to stay. During the commencement exercises at the local high school, just off the road where Eulogio Salazar's car had been ditched, forty-six seniors had graduated. A Spanish-American linguist had addressed the 1968 graduating class.

"I am offering them a cause," he said, without reference to the previous year's momentous events. "A wedge has been driven between the Hispano of New Mexico and his language. . . . A dynamic and aggressive Anglo culture mispronounces his name and has come between the Hispano New Mexican and his language. . . . This is precisely the crisis of the minority groups throughout the land."

Still no one had come up with a single clue to the mystery of the Salazar slaying, despite reward monies totaling over $10,000 and a promise of anonymity to informers. Five months after the murder Sheriff Benny Naranjo had asked for FBI assistance, a move he had previously withheld despite local pleas. Prior to the electioneering summer Naranjo had rashly sworn to abstain from seeking public office again until he had run down the killer of his jailer. As the closing date for filing for the job of Rio Arriba magistrate drew close, there were no likely culprits or even suspects.

Then his father, U.S. Marshal Naranjo, leaked the news that "strong and positive evidence" had been uncovered, the first "break" in six months. Naranjo said that while he was taking annual leave to help his son on the case the new information had turned up and been given to the state police. Marshal Naranjo said he had helped because "Salazar was a former employee of mine and because I wanted to clear the name of the people of Rio Arriba County." Nothing came of Naranjo's personal intervention in the investigation except that his son soon felt free to file for the November election. The Salazar murder remains unsolved.

A year and a half after the raid, however, it seemed likely that one antiquated aspect of the Tierra Amarilla landscape would be changed, indeed obliterated. The old courthouse building itself was a feature easier to eradicate than entrenched political habits or deep-rooted human misery.

Years after Pancho Villa's 1916 attack on Columbus, New Mexico, the Columbus city fathers permitted the erection of a monument commemorating that event. It appeared that there would be no chance of a similar irony in the north, as the state legislature authorized a ½ per cent gross receipts tax to pay off the bond for a proposed new courthouse structure for Rio Arriba County. In Tierra Amarilla a few months later about fifty citizens came to a public hearing to discuss the idea. County Commissioners Abe Gallegos, Abelardo Martinez, and Nick Salazar displayed sketches of the planned $544,980 structure. There was no opposition to placing the idea on the November 5 ballot for countywide approval.

Election day came and went. Richard Nixon became the country's President-elect. Governor Cargo won reelection, with Cristobal Tijerina and Felix Martinez reportedly campaigning for the Republican slate in the north of the state. District Attorney Al Sanchez and Attorney General Boston Witt returned to private practice. All of Tijerina's People's Constitutional Party candidates lost; he himself had been found ineligible to run for public office. The idea of replacing the pink and blue edifice which had been the scene of the extraordinary events of June 5, 1967, was thrown out by the voters. A week later, the first trial for the courthouse raid opened in Albuquerque.

EPILOGUE

The work week was over on Friday the 13th, December 1968, in the Bernalillo County courthouse in downtown Albuquerque. Typists and clerks and lawyers had bundled up and left their offices darkened and locked. Down the deserted hallways janitors pushed brooms and sifted ashtrays—on all five floors but one.

The public area of the third floor, from elevator door to washroom door to the closed courtroom, was jammed with people. But the atmosphere seemed one of meditation. Only by looking closely could the anxiety of waiting be detected. The five-week-long trial for the first criminal charges drawn from the Tierra Amarilla courthouse raid of a year and a half before was almost over. The jury had finally been handed the case at 2:18 p.m. this afternoon. Now it was about four hours later.

The trial had taken its own unpredictable route; it had become its own drama, apart from the complicated events it was resurrecting and judging. When Tijerina had led nine fellow defendants into this courtroom on November 12, it was readily apparent the proceedings would be unique.

Unlike the earlier Alianza hearings and arraignments, the trial did not enjoy the picturesque western setting of the Tierra Amarilla or Santa Fe courthouses. The trip to the third floor in an

257

elevator, the absence of sheriff's deputies in western garb, the lack of curious bystanders outside the office building, all this boded a seriousness unalleviated by local color.

After the disqualification of three other magistrates, the choice of Judge Paul Larrazolo as umpire and conductor of the celebrated trial seemed appropriate. His thin, tall, white-haired patrician form, draped in black, seemed to exude an air of humorless gravity. His father, Octaviano A. Larrazolo, had been a major figure in New Mexico history, and a vociferous pro-*raza* governor. While his Republican Spanish-American contemporaries had tried to downplay the racial element, the liberal governor had stressed improvement in bilingual education, free textbooks, and other measures that were explicitly for Spanish-Americans. During the trial's opening days Judge Larrazolo grew increasingly unhappy over what he saw taking place in the wordy, confusing area between his bench and the twelve rows packed mostly with Alianza relatives and sympathizers.

Behind the prosecution table sat the man many in the audience considered the villain of the entire affair, District Attorney Alfonso Sanchez. The trial represented his swan song as protector of the citizenry of Rio Arriba, Santa Fe, and Los Alamos counties. Beside Sanchez sat his assistant E. E. Chavez, an older man who coughed frequently and permitted himself to call witnesses by their nicknames. Easily the most able of the prosecution trio was Jack L. Love, a former assistant U.S. attorney who had been coolly effective in the Echo Amphitheater trial held in Las Cruces. Wearing his straight blond hair brushed back, standing lanky and unruffled while he did most of the examining, Love looked and spoke like an amiable cowhand who had received honors at law school.

Around the defense table a veritable football squad of defense counsels began buzzing among themselves as soon as the trial opened. Tijerina had already pleaded that he was penniless and had been assigned two court attorneys. One, Gene Franchini, was an Albuquerque lawyer and seemed to be attending reluctantly. The other, Beverly Axelrod, had come to the Alianza's side some months before from California. The recipient of Eldridge Cleaver's prison letters published in the bestseller *Soul on Ice,* Beverly Axelrod had helped launch northern New Mexico's contribution to the rash of *chicano* underground newspapers: a semimonthly called *El Grito del Norte (The Cry of the North).* The third member of Tijerina's personal team was William Higgs, a blond young attorney who had been James Meredith's first lawyer and who had become allied with Tijerina's cause during the meeting in Washington.

Actually Judge Larrazolo's problems had been somewhat simplified already. Out of a possible fifty-four charges which had already been listed on the complaint against the "TA Ten," six days of pretrial hearings had reduced the charges and concluded on the single mass trial. This had come after defense attorneys contended that with over 584 counts altogether against the defendants, more time would be needed to represent their clients adequately.

But as the first week of the trial slogged to a close, it was clear that Larrazolo's court was sinking deeper into a legal bog. There were bickering and disputes among defense counsels as they strove to agree on a precondition to the conduct of the trial, then on second thought reserved their willingness to go along since otherwise it might prejudice their own client.

Facing an endless and expensive morass of such problems, the judge apparently thought better of the merits of a mass trial. Larrazolo began the second week with a surprise decision: the case of Reies Tijerina was "severed" from the others. He was being charged with the gas-chamber offense of kidnapping Undersheriff Dan Rivera, falsely imprisoning Undersheriff Rivera, and assault on a jail. He was to be tried first.

Both sides were taken aback by the prospect of so significant a solo trial so suddenly. With only one day's respite the "new" trial, and the second act in this legal play, began on Wednesday, November 20.

True to his need for the spotlight, Tijerina entered the courtroom that morning with his own surprise. He asked to represent himself. When Larrazolo replied calmly that he could, Tijerina seemed disappointed.

"Don't I have to state any reasons or grounds?" he asked. Larrazolo said that wasn't necessary. Then the judge explained that he would expect Tijerina to do his own examining.

"Then I want five months to get prepared, Your Honor," Tijerina replied.

"No, I'm not giving you five months," Judge Larrazolo responded, almost wearily. "I will give you thirty minutes to decide if you want to represent yourself."

"You know," Tijerina later told a newsman, "that was the biggest test of my life . . . testing myself and my courage. I wanted to break through that barrier of fear and terror that only a lawyer can speak for justice. I decided that even if I lost, I would give my people an example of courage."

When Tijerina walked back into the courtroom he said that he had decided to represent himself. Now the taxing job of selecting a jury began.

Al Sanchez and Reies Tijerina had been opponents during the cat-and-mouse games before the Coyote meeting. The struggle between lawmen and Alianzans had thereafter become highly personalized into the conflict between the ideologies and methods of these two individuals. During the raid itself it was not unlikely that they could have become actual duelists. Now, enjoying equal footing on his enemy's own professional terms, Tijerina was not only finding an outlet for his nervous energy, which at most previous hearings made his hands writhe with frustration. He was also in a *mano a mano* engagement with Sanchez again. Now the *abogado sin libros*, as Tijerina had been called in childhood, was having a last chance at the man who had escaped the Tierra Amarilla raid. The object of the raid and its alleged perpetrator, aged forty and forty-two respectively, were arguing a case from which they were anything but removed and calm legal minds.

Tijerina moved around the red, floral-patterned new carpet be-

260

fore the jury box in the scuffed black work shoes he had worn
since the Poor People's Campaign. His hand-laundered appearance contrasted with Sanchez, whom attorneys describe as "a black
suit man." But Tijerina's conduct of his own case caught everyone
by surprise.

All agreed later that it was a remarkable performance, amateurish but astute, flamboyant but with an astonishing feel for "getting
what he wanted out of the witnesses," as one juror later observed.
The majority of the six Spanish-Americans, five Anglos, and one
Negro, finally seated in the box after several days of exhaustive
questioning, agreed after the trial that as a lawyer Tijerina was "a
pretty good one."

The defendant and counsel for the defense felt himself out during the selective questioning of jurors. In these queries he hinted
at points he would stress in his examination of witnesses.

—"Will these [land-grant claims] affect your judgment of the
case?"

—"You realize that if acquitted, I and the Alianza will have
won a big victory."

—"I'm a controversial figure. Newspapers say I'm a bad man,
a rabble-rouser, do you believe it?"

—"Are you possibly sure you can bring an impartial verdict?
You know this case probably will bring in a general of the army,
the governor, and the state police chief."

Actual testimony took just about two weeks, and there were
numerous dramatic sidelights as it progressed. Tijerina's principal
point was that the courthouse attack had been a justified "citizen's
arrest" which had become fouled up after State Policeman Nick
Saiz went for his gun.

"Do you know," Tijerina queried a state police officer on the
witness stand, "that citizens of the United States could arrest an
officer if they believed they had a grievance against him?"

"No," answered Juan Santistevan, the officer who had fled on
foot when his car was caught in a hail of bullets in front of the
courthouse.

TIJERINA and the COURTHOUSE RAID

"Isn't it possible," pressed Tijerina, "these people, pushed to the brink of desperation, had to teach you a lesson, teach you what you were not taught by your superiors?"

With a bumbling but intuitive logic he wandered through the murky legacy of the state's land grants, by obtaining exactly the testimony he wanted from sympathetic professional social scientists Dr. Frances Swadesh and Dr. Clark Knowlton. Through a skillful array of hardy villager witnesses he brought this background up to date by steering testimony about rough handling before the Coyote meeting through prosecution objections. Then he threw out a new name to everybody, a Joe Salazar who Tijerina said told him when the raid's confusion was at its peak, "Reies, don't blame anybody. Blame me."

Tijerina claimed that the plan to arrest Sanchez was lawful on the grounds that he had violated the civil rights of Alianza members by arresting them because of the meetings at Tierra Amarilla (May 14) and Coyote (June 3) before the raid.

The state maintained that these meetings had violated the 1964 court order ordering land-grant groups to desist from militant activities aimed at getting land grants back.

To defend his contention that the "citizen's arrest" plan had been justified, Tijerina asked for Al Sanchez to take the stand. The district attorney was reluctant, and the next day the young bloods of the Comancheros picketed outside the courthouse with signs accusing Sanchez of cowardice. After being confiscated by the police, the signs appeared in court. With irritation Judge Larrazolo looked at them, and at District Attorney Sanchez who was decrying them. The head of the Comancheros, a robust young man named Pedro Archuleta from near Tierra Amarilla, strode up to the bench to demand their return. They were given back, and a feeling of victory was in the air as court ended that day.

The prosecution, hoisted on its own duty to tie Tijerina to Dan Rivera's head beating, had a tough time of it. Sheriff Naranjo remembered that Tijerina "had a rifle in his hands and was wearing a dark overcoat and wrap-around sun glasses." Some days

262

before E. R. Gleasner had said that Tijerina, who he had earlier testified was dressed "like Castro" in fatigue clothing, hit him on the head. Obviously surprised by the volunteered revelation, Tijerina asked the witness how he was so sure he could identify who had hit him. "By his inclination, voice, and speech," said the Albuquerque businessman. "The man who hit me," Gleasner insisted, "is the same man who spoke to me, and even though I did not see him hit me, no one else could have done it." And when Undersheriff Rivera, the actual victim of the trial's three charges, sat in the witness seat he addressed Tijerina and said, "I don't hold anything against you, sir."

The most curious testimony came from Tijerina himself. Beverly Axelrod led "the man of destiny," as he proclaimed himself, up through his childhood, years of pastoral wandering, and into the Alianza's origin. Then she asked directly about his movements during the raid.

Tijerina said he had learned of the gunfire at the courthouse while he was holed up in Felix Martinez's home in Tierra Amarilla, waiting to hear whether his brother Cristobal had been released after his statement.

"I felt cold and numb immediately," recalled Tijerina. Driven to the courthouse by a friend, he came upon frantic people outside the building. "Some were panicked, some frightened, some excited." He added, "Today I remember the yelling. It was here a busting headache developed in my head. I'm pretty sure it was the pressure." Through his subsequent actions, taking a rifle and exchanging it for a pistol, running around with a handkerchief over his face, Tijerina seemed to be describing himself in a trance.

The final arguments were delivered by Tijerina, Love, and Sanchez. In an urgent *sotto voce* Sanchez said, pointing to Tijerina, "He could have been a great man." Then he implored the jury for a first-degree kidnapping conviction. "I don't care if you recommend life imprisonment," he concluded, "but the court must have complete jurisdiction over this man's life."

In contrast, Tijerina's words crackled. "I stand before you like

David before Goliath," he said, striding around furiously and jabbing his finger into the air. He accused District Attorney Sanchez of using "the whole National Guard to kill a three-month-old child in the womb of her mother," referring to Patsy Tijerina's miscarriage after she was released from jail. But it was Tijerina's court-appointed attorney who stuck to the facts of the charges and whose words probably carried the greatest weight with the jury. Gene Franchini said simply, "The state has charged him with the wrong crimes, the wrong offenses. . . . Who restrained Daniel Rivera? Who confined him? Who took him anywhere? He did everything of his own free will."

Before the jury retired for their deliberations Judge Larrazolo gave them a complex set of legal instructions. The most controversial of these turned out to be the judge's emphasis on the conditions under which a "citizen's arrest" can be attempted.

"The court instructs the jury," he wrote, "that anyone, including a state police officer, who intentionally interferes with a lawful attempt to make a citizen's arrest does so at his own peril, since the arresting citizens are entitled under the law to use whatever force is reasonably necessary to effect said citizen's arrest and to use whatever force is reasonably necessary to defend themselves in the process of making said citizen's arrest."

The jury re-entered the courtroom nearly four hours after leaving it. The foreman stood up. At the first ringing verdict of "Not guilty," Reies Tijerina threw his arms on the table and buried his head in his sleeves. During the second and third identical verdicts he did not move a muscle. It was some minutes before he lifted himself up, his cheeks tear-stained. Across the courtroom, District Attorney Al Sanchez sat stonily while the jury panel filed past him and to the homes they had not seen for five weeks.

At the Alianza headquarters the next night, Saturday, Brown Berets stood guard as Tijerina staged a victory celebration. He was bursting with a plan: a new book disclosing his "science" by which the brown race would bridge the chasm between the black and white peoples. He remembered that he had dreamt some time during the trial of Judge Larrazolo with tears in his eyes, and of his acquittal. He would ask Spain, in a direct telegram to General Franco, to help place the Alianza's claims before the United Nations. He would demand a 25 per cent increase in grants to welfare recipients. He would severely castigate the Board of Education for failing to meet the needs of Spanish-American youngsters. He would. . . .

The state's officialdom was left shaking from the verdict.

It came "as a complete shock," admitted Prosecutor Love. "And I guess I'm still in a state of shock. Never can I remember so completely misreading what the mood of a jury seemed to be."

"This is a complete surprise," said a stunned Sanchez. A few days later he said that the state should have the right of appeal in criminal cases. And, he maintained, the prosecution should not be blind as to the line of the defendant's defense. "It catches you by surprise," he complained, "and shouldn't be that way."

Jim Thompson, Sanchez's successor to the office of First Judicial District Attorney, was "astounded by the verdict." (Thompson now inherited the many remaining charges against Tijerina and his nine fellow defendants. Now it was his responsibility to prosecute in the face of a wave of defense motions to have all the remaining counts dismissed on the grounds of double jeopardy.)

The *New Mexican* newspaper termed the trial a "travesty on our New Mexico system of law enforcement." Describing the "lengthy and costly" proceedings as "a Roman holiday," it reflected that the verdict "will lend encouragement to men like Tijerina to stir racial unrest and hatred."

The catch phrase, "Anybody for shooting up the courthouse?" was heard on the streets, in hotel lobbies, and in bars. Particularly the latitude of the "citizen's arrest" definition alarmed lawmen and legal observers alike. The Alianza leadership's no-holds-barred notion of their new legal weapon caused lawyers across the state to stress the very limited set of circumstances under which a citizen's arrest might be legitimately performed. While a U.S. attorney would later dismiss Tijerina's unrestrained application of the right as "legal nonsense," after the trial several local law firms seriously researched the question. They came up with a clear network of narrow conditions for a lawful citizen's arrest which, they implied, called Judge Larrazolo's jury instruction into question. Tijerina's legal adviser Williams Higgs was jubilant over this aspect of the case, as was the militant press across the country.

"That citizen's arrest instruction was a breakthrough," Higgs said. "Not many people have been aware fully of their right to make a citizen's arrest." Immediately it was placed atop the Alianza's arsenal.

The following spring Tijerina's attempts to place under citizen's arrest Chief Justice Warren Burger, Governor David Cargo, and the head of the Los Alamos Scientific Laboratories would land him back in prison. His bond revoked on the ground that he was a threat to society, Tijerina would once more wait while lawyers from as far away as New York were unsuccessfully imported to try to secure his release.

But in the weeks after the victory, Tijerina was content to relish his psychological vindication. The Anglo courts, which he had so long accused of being in conspiracy to steal the Spanish-American birthright, had strangely enough come through. Although he never voiced it, Tijerina must have been a little curious over this uncharacteristic turn of events. If he was serious in his belief that the Anglo judicial system was nothing but a pack of lies and deceptions, he must have wanted to probe this astounding exception which, for the moment, had saved his life.

In a later series of interviews most of the jurors said simply, and some apologetically, that the evidence and the charges did not mesh. They felt that the state had not charged Tijerina with the crimes that witnesses had testified he had committed. Despite almost insurmountable obstacles it appeared that fair and impartial justice had been achieved in New Mexico. But neither side in the conflict seemed to appreciate how. Neither side seemed humbled by the momentary success of rationality. Justice was not followed by a time of neutral silence in which the state could reflect upon its past strife. "We'll get you yet," screamed a passing motorist as Tijerina exited from the courthouse on the day of the verdict. The fact that a cumbersome but honest trial had failed to reconcile anything or to create an atmosphere of trust for working out differences in a judicial system, boded more of that polarization which had brought about the raid in the first place.

NOTE
ON
SOURCES

This is a résumé of materials used in the preparation of my book, most of them now consolidated in three portable storage files which will eventually be given to the Zimmerman Library of the University of New Mexico.

The bedrock of my documentation consists of coverage in the daily editions of the *Albuquerque Journal*, the *Albuquerque Tribune*, and *The New Mexican* of Santa Fe. In addition William Olson, a University of New Mexico graduate student, preserved for my use every pertinent scrap of United Press International copy received by the university radio station.

My former colleagues on *The New Mexican*, knowing I was embarked on this project, placed all their material in my hands.

Vina Windes, education editor, gave me her photos, notes to various articles concerning the Alianza and Tijerina, and such documents as "Report on the Evaluation of Rio Arriba County Schools by the State Department of Education, November 12, 13, 1964."

John Crenshaw, general assignment reporter, gave me his photos and provided notes on police strategy sessions he had covered before the Coyote meeting. Crenshaw's excellent summary of the Eulogio Salazar murder, featured in the Sunday (January 14, 1968) issue of *The New Mexican*, was the basis for my account of that story.

Carrol W. Cagle, state house correspondent, obtained a copy of the attorney general's preliminary report on alleged complicity between the state Office of Economic Opportunity and the Alianza. This document included a wealth of appendixes, news clippings, and private correspondence which aided my work.

Jim Neal, news editor, had covered the Echo Amphitheater incident before I ever came to the paper, and loaned me his thorough photo coverage of the affair as well as recalling it verbally for me.

Others who wrote about the Alianza helped with their notes, conversation, and copies of their published efforts.

Richard Gardner, also preparing a book on the subject, attended the Alianza's October 1967 convention with me, obtained the complete text of Jerry Noll's speech for me, and allowed me to have access to his files. He also gave me duplicates of all his taped interviews with Tijerina and other Alianza figures.

Michael Jenkinson, who wrote *Tijerina*, a 103-page paperback published by Paisano Press (Albuquerque, 1968), exchanged research material with me.

Nigel S. Hey, a former Albuquerque newspaperman and a painstaking researcher, generously gave me his preparatory notes for a March 1968 article in *Interplay*, "Reies Lopez Tijerina: A Study in Brown Power."

The June 8, 1967 edition of *The Rio Grande Sun*, a weekly published by Robert Trapp in Espanola, New Mexico, was most informative. Various editions of the *Taos News* provided information. Martin Waldron's coverage for the *New York Times* added sidelights and new quotations, and Tom Wicker's occasional commentaries on the editorial page were valuable. Ed Meagher of the *Los Angeles Times* had been covering the story since the Echo Amphitheater incident and sent me his features and analyses. Charles Howe of the *San Francisco Chronicle* shared news tips and drafts just after the raid.

270

Other newsmen whose work assisted me were James C. Tanner, *Wall Street Journal*; David Braaten, *Sunday Star* (Washington, D.C.); Robert H. Weber, *Christian Science Monitor;* and Paul R. Wieck, Washington correspondent for the *Albuquerque Journal.*

Magazine writers produced material that frequently helped to fill gaps in the jigsaw puzzle I was trying to piece together: Calvin Kentfield (*New York Times Magazine,* July 16, 1967); George W. Grayson Jr. (*The New Republic,* July 1967); David Lyle, "The Magic Rider" (unpublished); David Lyle and Don Devereux, "Blown on the Wind" (*New Mexico Review and Legislative Journal,* March 6, 1969); Clark S. Knowlton (*The Nation,* June 1968); John Gregory Dunne and Joan Didion (*The Saturday Evening Post,* April 1968); Tony Hillerman (*True,* January 1968); Larry Calloway (*Argosy,* February 1968); Thorne Bacon (prepared for *Kiwanis Magazine*); Alan Stang (*American Opinion,* October 1967, March 1968, March 1969); Jerry LeBlanc (*Boston Sunday Globe,* April 6, 1969; and *Movement,* August 1967, February and July 1969).

Essential to the first part of the book was the correspondence between Don Devereux and the Ford Foundation. Devereux gave me these letters and later recapitulated for me the events before the raid. The results of Richard Gardner's similar interview with Devereux were also turned over to me.

Shortly after the raid I managed to take notes from a private memorandum prepared for Governor Jack Campbell on the Alianza, and obtained copies of the dossier and confidential investigation of Tijerina and the Alianza then in official hands. This included portions of District Attorney Alfonso Sanchez's files, early clippings of press coverage of the Alianza, 1965 reports by Hal Simmons of North American Newspaper Alliance, and miscellaneous correspondence.

For background material I used Don Devereux's September 1968 paper, "Some Thoughts from New Mexico," which he delivered at a rural development conference at the Center for the Study of Democratic Institutions in Santa Barbara, California. Senator Edmundo R. Delgado kindly gave me a copy of "An Economic, Social, and Educational Survey of Rio Arriba and Taos Counties," by John H. Burma and David E. Williams (mimeo., 1962), Northern New Mexico State College.

I also drew information from *The Spanish Americans of New Mexico: A Distinctive Heritage* by Nancie Gonzalez (Mexican-American Study Project, Division of Research, Graduate School of Business Administration, University of California, Los Angeles, 1967. Advance Report No. 9) ; *The Spanish-Speaking People of the Southwest,* edited by J. Edward Mosely (Council on Spanish-American Work, 1966) ; *Forgotten People* by George I. Sanchez (Albuquerque: Calvin Horn, Inc., 1967) ; *New Mexico, A History of Four Centuries* by Warren A. Beck (University of Oklahoma Press, 1962) ; *Economy of Rio Arriba County* by Margaret Meaders (*New Mexico Business,* April and May 1965 reprint, Bureau of Business Research, University of New Mexico) ; "Community Information, State of New Mexico," a 32-page statistical report by the state of New Mexico, October 6, 1965; and Clark S. Knowlton's series of studies on Spanish-American history and problems collected and reprinted in their entirety in *Effect of Federal Programs on Rural America:* Hearings before the Subcommittee on Rural Development of the Committee on Agriculture, House of Representatives, Ninetieth Congress, First Session. U.S. Government Printing Office, Washington, 1967. (This document contained the complete transcript of Congressman Joseph Y. Resnick's probe into the New Mexico "rebellion.")

Facundo Valdez gave me a copy of his 125-page file of original documents covering the history of the Polvadera Grant. Carrol W. Cagle's three-part series on land-grant history in *The New Mexican* (June 1967), prepared with the assistance of New Mexico State Archivist Myra Ellen Jenkins, was helpful.

For Jailer Eulogio Salazar's testimony on June 22, 1967 in the Santa Fe County courthouse I purchased from Judge Joe Angel's court reporter a complete transcript of that afternoon's proceedings. The New Mexico Civil Liberties Union newsletter, *Torch,* filled the bulk of its July 1967 issue with portions of ACLU depositions concerning alleged civil rights violations during the raid's aftermath. Much of this information was corroborated by the first-hand reports collected by Ruben Dario Salaz in his *Tierra Amarilla Shootout*, a 15,000-word tabloid published privately in Albuquerque, August 11, 1967. I acquired the official National Guard report on the Tierra Amarilla raid, "Civil Disturbance, Rio Arriba County 5-8 June 1967," dated July 12, 1968.

For Tijerina's background I turned mainly to my lengthy interview with Tijerina in the New Mexico State Prison on June 27, 1967. George W. Grayson Jr. had visited Tijerina in prison before me and his question-and-answer session appeared in *Commonwealth* (July 28, 1967). Don McNeill published in the *Village Voice* (August 1, 1968) his exploration of Tijerina's past. V. B. Price and Katy Woolston came out with good investigative work in the *Albuquerque Tribune* just after the raid. Alice Gruver of the *El Paso Times* covered Tijerina's autobiographical testimony during the Las Cruces trial on November 10, 1967. Clark S. Knowlton wrote a profile of Tijerina for *The Texas Observer* (March 28, 1969). Della Rosa of the *Los Angeles Free Press* included biographical information in her running coverage of the Tijerina movement. Vina Windes of *The New Mexican* (June 8, 1967) also pursued Tijerina's elusive past. Subsequent interviews of my own and taped interviews with Tijerina by Richard Gardner, as well as additional research, helped to fill in blank periods in the Tijerina biography.

The Alianza itself was most helpful, loaning three cartons of clippings and notes to Dr. Frances Swadesh and myself. This material was of great value in retracing the Alianza's early years. It contained copies of Albuquerque's *News Chieftain* through the early 1960's and a wide spectrum of articles on Tijerina and the Alianza from the Mexican press.

At the request of *The New Mexican*, Reies Tijerina wrote three articles in Spanish outlining his movement's goals. Never printed, these articles were translated by John MacGregor. They were xeroxed before being returned to Tijerina and I obtained copies. Eduardo Chavez, Alianza secretary-treasurer, kindly showed me a thumbed copy of Tijerina's book *Hallera Fe en la Tierra?*—appropriately beginning with "Clamor de la Tierra" as Chapter I. I also used copies of various

273

chicano periodicals: *Carta Editorial, El Gallo, El Papel, Chicano Student News, La Raza, El Grito del Norte.* They were useful in assessing the Alianza's impact on the larger Spanish-speaking community in the Southwest.

During my final months with *The New Mexican* I prepared an assessment of the Home Education Livelihood Program (HELP) for the Educational Systems Corporation, Washington, D.C. On this assignment, I obtained copies of HELP data on the U.S. Forest Service's activities as well as other community information which was of value in the preparation of this book.

For an academic perspective on Tijerina and the Alianza I consulted E. J. Hobsbawm's *Primitive Rebels, Studies in Archaic Forms of Social Movement in the Nineteenth and Twentieth Centuries* (New York: W. W. Norton and Co., Inc. 1965) ; and Vittorio Lanternari's *The Religions of the Oppressed: A Study of Modern Messianic Cults* (New York: New American Library of World Literature, 1965).

Peter Nabokov

INDEX

INDEX

INDEX

278

INDEX

280

INDEX

INDEX